REGNUM STUDIES IN MISSION

A Missional Reading of the Fourth Gospel

Series Preface

Regnum Studies in Mission are born from the lived experience of Christians and Christian communities in mission, especially but not solely in the fast growing churches among the poor of the world. These churches have more to tell than stories of growth. They are making significant impacts on their cultures in the cause of Christ. They are producing 'cultural products' which express the reality of Christian faith, hope and love in their societies.

Regnum Studies in Mission are the fruit often of rigorous research to the highest international standards and always of authentic Christian engagement in the transformation of people and societies. And these are for the world. The formation of Christian theology, missiology and practice in the twenty-first century will depend to a great extent on the active participation of growing churches contributing biblical and culturally appropriate expressions of Christian practice to inform World Christianity.

Series Editor

Paul Bendor-Samuel Oxford Centre for Mission Studies, Oxford, UK

REGNUM STUDIES IN MISSION

A Missional Reading of the Fourth Gospel

A Gospel-Driven Theology of Discipleship

Sung Chan Kwon

First edition published 2022 by Regnum Books International

Regnum is an imprint of the Oxford Centre for Mission Studies
St. Philip and St. James Church, Woodstock Road
Oxford, OX2 6HR, UK
www.regnumbooks.net

09 08 07 06 05 04 03 8 7 6 5 4 3 2 1

British Library Cataloguing in Publication Data
A catalogue record for this book is available from the British Library

ISBN: 978-1-5064-9728-0
eBook ISBN: 978-1-5064-9729-7

Typeset by Words by Design

Distributed by Fortress Press in the US, Canada, India, and Brazil

Dedication

For God who has been with me all the time. This is also dedicated to my father who is now resting in the bosom of God. Thank you.

Acknowledgments

I would like to express my sincere gratitude to a number of people who have encouraged and supported me on this academic journey.

Firstly, my sincere thanks go to Dr. Peter Phillips, my first supervisor, and Antony Billington, my second supervisor, for their insightful comments and encouragement, but also for thoughtful questions that enabled me to widen and deepen my research from various perspectives. I would also like to thank Dr. Tim Keene, my tutor, for his mentoring during this research. I could not have imagined having a better advisory team for my research.

Thanks are due to Wycliffe Global Alliance and Yum-Kwang Presbyterian Church of Korea for providing prayer and financial support toward my research.

My special thanks go to Mrs. Dawn Kruger who has read and edited my work and also shared her thoughts with me for this research. Without her precious support it would not be possible to complete this research.

To Jahwa, my wife, I rather close my mouth for your love, sacrifice and support during this journey. And to my two sons, Yong-Sung and Yong-Su, I want to thank you for your love.

Contents

Part I
Introduction and Methodology

1. Introduction 1
2. A Missional Hermeneutic for Reading the Fourth Gospel 15

Part II
A Missional Analysis of the Fourth Gospel

3. A Johannine Grand Narrative (1:1–2:12) 49
4. Encountering the Jews and Interacting with Individuals (2:13–12:50) 79
5. Equipping the Discipleship Community (13:1–17:26) 107
6. The Accomplishment of Jesus and the Commissioning of the Discipleship Community (18:1–21:25) 137

Part III
Findings and Conclusion

7. Findings and Implications 163
8. Conclusion 187

Bibliography 193

Abbreviations

AAP	Adopt-A-People
BDAG	Bauer, W., *A Greek-English Lexicon of the New Testament and Other Early Christian Literature*. 3rd ed. Revised and edited by F. W. Danker. Translated by W. F. Arndt, F. W. Gingrich, and F. W. Danker. Chicago and London: University of Chicago Press. 2000
EDNT	Exegetical Dictionary of the New Testament
FTT	Finishing The Task
GBT	Global Bible Translators
GNB	Good News Bible
ISPCK	Indian Society for Promoting Christian Knowledge
LXX	Septuagint, Greek translation of the Hebrew Bible
NA28	Novum Testamentum Graece. 28th ed. Edited by
Barbara Aland,	Kurt Aland, Johannes Karavidopoulos, Carlo M. Martini,
and Bruce	M. Metzger. Stuttgart: Deutsche Bibelgesellschaft. 2012
NGO	Non-Governmental Organization
NIV	New International Version
NKRV	New Korean Revised Version
NT	New Testament
OT	Old Testament
SBL	Society of Biblical Literature
SIL	Summer Institute of Linguistics
SPCK	Society for Promoting Christian Knowledge
UPG	Unreached People Group
WUNT	Wissenschaftliche Untersuchungen zum Neuen Testament

PART I

INTRODUCTION AND METHODOLOGY

1. Introduction

My Missional Journey

When I became a missionary in 1992, I thought that I knew what mission was about. After more than 25 years of experience as a missionary, the more I participate in mission work, the less I know what mission is.

This project, *A Missional Reading of the Fourth Gospel*, is motivated by that struggle. C. S. Lewis (1970, 125) says, 'What you see and hear depends a great deal on where you are standing: it also depends on what sort of person you are'. I see that my understanding of mission was not based on the Bible but based on what I was learning within various mission movements from the 1990s. The changes of my location through the years enabled me to come out of a movement-based mission concept and see different pictures of mission, and it was some questions raised from that journey which led me to read the Fourth Gospel from a missional point of view.

My missional journey could be divided into three phases; each phase raises different issues in mission, and these issues provide the backdrop against my missional reading of the Fourth Gospel.

Three Phases of My Missional Journey

Since I was accepted as a member of a Bible translation agency in Korea in 1992, I have served in different roles in that organization. In 1995, after attending a Summer Institute of Linguistics training in Singapore to be a translator and literacy worker, I went to a South Asian country with my family which was dominated by a non-Christian religion, and acknowledged no official Christian presence. Engaging in any Christian religious activities was strictly forbidden. I was seconded to an international relief NGO in the country as a literacy worker and later became involved in a community development project. I served in it for six years. In 2001, I came back to my home country as I was elected to be the director of my sending organization, Global Bible

Translators.[1] As director, I looked after three domains together with an associate in each domain. Those domains were general administration including finances, member care and mobilization. Since mission movements, including *Adopt-A-People* and *Finishing the Task*, were spreading in Korea during those years, there were many invitations to speak about missions in churches. Several mission education programmes, such as *Perspectives,* were being introduced and run in various cities, so I had many opportunities to teach and to share what I had experienced regarding mission. When I finished my service as director of Global Bible Translators in 2008, I was invited to join the leadership team of Wycliffe International[2] as Director for Research and Development for two years and then was asked to serve as the Director for the Asia-Pacific Area for six years. The organization was in the process of changing from an international agency paradigm to a global mission community paradigm together with various participants around the world. Thus my role as an area director was mainly serving and challenging local participants, including church denominations and local mission agencies, to build their capacity for mission in their own countries and beyond. The capacity-building we focused on helped them start their own journey in mission as opposed to merely helping them do something by themselves. We all needed to understand what that meant. It is from those various experiences that the three phases of my missional journey arose, each of them providing a different lens for me to form my missional understanding.

Task versus Relationship

The first phase of my missional journey is the six-year period when I was in the South Asian country with my family. Before I went to that country, I had already spent ten years in training, including seminary and linguistic training, since I had committed myself to a translation ministry. I knew that I might not be able to do typical mission activities in this country since mission activities were limited, but I expected that at least I could give assistance to a minority people-group in terms of literacy, education and even Bible translation through the skills I had acquired from my training. However, the situation in the country was worse than I had imagined.

Furthermore, many unexpected things happened within a year of my arrival, including a change of regime in the country, the new one being a fundamentalist group of the major religion. I literally had to give up all of my plans. It seemed that all of my training was in vain. During that time, we had to send our eight-year-old son to boarding school in a neighbouring country. I was

---

[1] A Korean affiliated organization of Wycliffe International in 1992, which is now Wycliffe Global Alliance.

[2] The organization name has been changed into Wycliffe Global Alliance since 2011.

not even able to visit the minority people-group I was supposed to serve in a mountainous area. All doors were closed. I was filled with the anguish of my own inner conflict, wondering if I needed to be there at all. All I could do was go to a *bazaar* (market) to sit and drink tea with the shop owners, join the local men and play football with them in a rough field, or look after my local friends' store while they were eating. People called me *Adamkhan,* which was just a common name in the country, like the names *John* or *James* in English.

Since I was not able to do any education work, I became involved in short-term relief work instead. A local friend and I began a team for a newly designed relief programme. We visited refugees in desert areas and distributed chickens for them to raise so they could have eggs for their malnourished children. After a few months, I got permission to visit the minority people-group I had planned to serve and officially started a pilot community development programme among them. Through the programme, I was able to visit many different villages in a valley and a mountain area. Eventually, I was also able to start a literacy programme in many villages.

These experiences helped me to rethink my understanding of mission. Of course, I am neither saying that I lived just as the local people did, nor that I identified completely with them. Rather, the gap between my local friends and myself was huge. However, as much as I was able, I endeavoured to eat lunch with local people every day while I was in their country. The day my family and I departed from the country to return to our home in 2001, the local friend who had worked with me from the beginning accompanied us to the border to say good-bye. After a moment's hesitation, he told me that I was not his guest. I was surprised to hear him say that because it was an inappropriate farewell message.[3] After a pause, he continued, saying, 'You have been my brother'. At that moment, and later as I reflected on the experiences I had in that country, I understood that I was not there to accomplish my own plans but to be a brother or a friend to the people I served.

These experiences and my reflection on them showed me the importance of relationship-focused mission rather than task-centred mission. Indeed, the length of time it took me to learn this lesson reflects the lifelong journey which relationship-centred mission requires. The missional hermeneutic I propose in this study will be more relationship-based than task-oriented for reading the Fourth Gospel. What are the key relationships that are emphasized and developed over time in the Gospel, particularly the relationships into which Jesus puts his time and energy?

---

[3] He is supposed to say 'You were my best guest' according to the culture of the country since the word 'guest' has prestige.

Delegation vs Engagement

The second phase of my missional journey began when I returned to my home country, South Korea, in 2001 and became involved in mission mobilization. As the director of a mission agency, I was invited to speak about mission in many different gatherings of campus-based ministry organizations and also in many local churches.[4] I challenged young people to commit their lives to mission, and I urged local churches to support mission through prayer and finances. Since the international organization to which Global Bible Translators belonged had a goal to recruit a certain number of translators and related workers to finish the global translation task by a certain year, we set a national goal each year and developed strategies accordingly. While I was director of the organization, we registered between fifteen and twenty new members each year. It was a good number of new long-term members for a mission agency at that time. The more I was involved in mission mobilization, the more I found that the mission movement I was a part of was a sodality-centred mission – it sees mission as the task of special forces such as mission agencies rather than encouraging local congregations to engage in the mission of God.[5]

Mission agencies had developed many programmes to help local congregations understand mission, but those programmes were primarily designed to support mission activities being run by the mission agencies. Local churches were viewed simply as resource providers from the mission agencies' point of view. Indeed, mission committees in local churches generally followed the same paradigm: the committee saw the congregation as a resource provider rather than as a participant in the mission of God, and delegated the work of mission to mission agencies, providing for the agencies the resources the committee gathered from the congregation. In this paradigm, there was institutional progress regarding mission activities. However, the paradigm disengaged the local congregation from mission in that it operated as a system of delegation – a congregation delegated mission to the mission committee of the local church, which in turn delegated mission responsibilities to a mission agency. This meant that many believers understood that mission was not something to which they were called. I understood Van Engen's (1991, 20) concern when he lamented, '[a]round the world one of the most neglected areas

---

[4] In this section, the term 'local churches' refers to the churches in Korea, so it is sending churches rather than local churches on mission fields.

[5] The terms 'Modality' and 'Sodality' were introduced by Ralph Winter in the early 1970s. He insists that these are the two structures of God's redemptive mission. Winter (1973, 224) says, 'a modality is a structured fellowship in which there is no distinction of sex or age, while a sodality is a structured fellowship in which membership involves an adult second decision beyond modality membership, and is limited by either age or sex or marital status. In this use of these terms, both the denomination and the local congregation are modalities, while a mission agency or a local men's club are sodalities'.

of missiological research has been ecclesiology'. If God's people lose their missional identity, the mission activities supported by them do not have meaning and eventually, even those activities would dry up.

This period of my own work showed me the importance of local congregations' engagement in the mission of God and the need to work against models of delegation which allowed individuals to opt out of mission, by delegating it to others. As such, in my missional reading of the Fourth Gospel, I will focus on the tension between delegation and participation – between organisational mission and organic engagement in mission. How does this impact Jesus' shaping and equipping his disciples for mission? Does Jesus imply a disciple-only concept of mission, particularly 'the Twelve'? In what ways does the commissioning of the disciples in John 20 present the organic engagement of God's people in the mission of God?

Dependency vs Self-Initiative

The third phase of my missional journey began with my new role at Wycliffe International in 2009. For the first two years, as the Director for Research and Development, I was allowed to spend time in 'inefficient lingering' as I reflected on what mission would or could look like as the Global South becomes more actively involved. When I took the role of area director for Asia-Pacific at Wycliffe Global Alliance in 2011, one of the most frequently used new terms in our organization was 'missiological reflection'. Because of its focus on translation, the organization had two essential identities: one was a linguistic identity and the other was a missional identity. Historically, the organization had contributed to language development around the world, securing the former identity, but there had been less opportunity to develop the latter. The international leadership team hosted many missiological reflection gatherings on various issues such as Bible translation, community, leadership, funding, and organization history. What I noticed through the reflective process was a dependency issue in the Asia-Pacific area. In the countries where translation and related ministries were proceeding well, the participation of the local stakeholders, including denominations and other agencies, increased more than ever before. If, however, projects were examined closely, dependency became quite serious. Financial dependency could be easily found, but a more serious problem was the lack of self-initiative.

I began to rethink the 'three-self' mission theory suggested by both Henry Venn and Rufus Anderson. As Shenk (1981, 168) says, '[b]oth [Venn and Anderson] are credited with formulating the classic "three-self" definition of the indigenous church: self-supporting, self-governing, self-propagating'. I found that the denominations and mission agencies in the so-called 'mission field' performed those three self-generated activities well. Nevertheless, it was hard to say that they really showed 'selfhood' in their ministry. I thought that the selfhood of the church should include something that would sustain those three selves as more than simply performing them. The way of conducting the ministry, including translation and other practices, had been standardized by outsiders. The issues I had to care about most as an area director were determining how the area office could help the local leaders in each country to root themselves in the Word of God rather than simply to accept the interpretation of others, and how to help the local leaders participate in the mission of God with their own gifts and strengths.

To that end, we started an annual gathering for 'missional readings of the Bible' and also hosted various missiological reflections at the area level. The following are a few examples of comments I heard from local leaders in our area. The Archbishop of the Solomon Islands told me that his congregation believed that mission was something outsiders did on their behalf, so there was no need to add more mission in his country unless his congregation's understanding of mission changed. John Ruhulessin, the head of a Presbyterian denomination in Indonesia (2015, [7]) claimed 'a new pattern of church theology' in his presentation at the 80th anniversary of the denomination. He said that the denomination 'is not only an organization or church that is understood through scholarship and high theology. Our congregations have faith through their own theology'. In one of our area meetings, a mission agency director from Bangladesh shared his feeling after deciding not to receive outside funding for their ministries, saying: 'Now, I see you as friends. Before I hesitated saying something that was on my mind, but now I can share what I think freely'. A seminary principal living as a minority in an Islam majority context in a country in South Asia told me that 'what we need to teach our students is not apologetics to argue with them [Muslim neighbours] but how to love our neighbours'.

In this phase of my missional journey, I had many chances to reflect together with local leaders in many different contexts in Asia-Pacific on how each of us could respond to and participate in God's mission. This period of reflection together with local leaders showed me the importance of being self-initiated by all of us rooting in God's Word and participating in the mission of God. The text may not address this issue directly, but I will examine the ways in which the Gospel can be seen as a self-reflection of the Evangelist.

So, my experience working in different aspects of mission organisation gave me the opportunity to explore the following tensions: task vs relationship, delegation vs engagement, dependency vs self-initiative. In each case, I felt that the latter term was important for a new understanding of mission – mission needed to focus on relationship, organic engagement and self-initiative. My experience of mission challenged my concept of mission. *What is the position of relationship in mission? What is the missional identity of the church? How can the local churches in mission fields improve their self-reflection? Where did my understanding of mission come from?*

Those questions became an external motivation for my research. They led me to be interested in the biblical foundation of mission. Additionally, they provided me with a context from which I could read the given text. However, if I try to find mission in the Bible, the implication is that I already know what mission is about. Then, I would probably end up finding some proof-texts for the mission I already know (or think I know) regardless of my intentions. Chris Wright (2006, 21–22) describes the problem as follows:

> *Mission* is the noun, the given reality. It is something *we* do, and we basically know what it is; *biblical* is the adjective, which we use to justify what we already know we should be doing. The reason why we know we should be doing mission, the basis, foundation or grounds on which we justify it, must be found in the Bible. As Christians, we need a biblical basis for everything we do.

What I desire to know is *what the Bible really says when viewed through a missional lens* rather than *what the Bible says about mission*. In other words, the study has to do with interpreting the Bible in light of God's mission rather than interpreting those various mission themes in light of the Bible. Chris Wright calls this the search for the missional basis of the Bible instead of the search for the biblical basis of mission.[6] To do so, it is necessary to stop looking for mission in the Bible and to sincerely search for the central message of which the Bible speaks. I will clarify how those two are different and what it meant by a missional reading of the Bible in the next chapter.

My desire to read the Bible missionally prompted me to focus on reading the Fourth Gospel. As I mentioned, I am not trying to find any specific mission themes in the Gospel. Instead, I will read the Gospel in light of God's mission which includes the participation of his people in it. Thus, the research question of the study will be: '*To what extent does the Fourth Gospel as a whole contribute to the biblical understanding of mission?*' The two sub-questions relating to the main one are 1) 'In what ways does the Fourth Gospel present the triune God's mission?' and 2) 'In what ways does the Fourth Gospel present the participation of God's people in mission?'

Reading the Fourth Gospel with a Missional Perspective

So why choose the Fourth Gospel for a missional reading of the Bible?

Passion for mission without sufficient and continued reflection on biblical mission leads to a task-oriented approach. Once we decide on the goal, we develop many strategies to fulfil the goal, including different mission agencies as part of the strategy. This awareness led me back to Scripture. I found that my biblical foundation for mission was very selective in a proof-text way. Around that time, a new perspective called a 'missional reading of the Bible'

---

[6] The module he was teaching at All Nations College was called 'The Biblical Basis of Mission', which he renamed as 'The Missional Basis of the Bible' (2006, 21–22).

by Chris Wright was introduced to me. He and others, such as Michael Goheen, explore a grand narrative approach to the reading of the Scriptures, insisting that Scripture has a missional direction as a whole. Several books[7] have been published to introduce a grand narrative view which provides a missional sketch of the whole Bible. Additionally, some scholars have suggested a different perspective on this new way of reading called missional hermeneutics, which I will discuss in the following chapter. The next steps for this new development would be reading each book in the Bible missionally bearing in mind the grand narrative. There have been a few contributions[8] to the field of reading books of Scripture from a missional perspective. The current study of a missional reading of the Fourth Gospel is an attempt to take further steps in this direction.

Secondly, the reason to choose the Fourth Gospel particularly is that the book has been largely ignored in the modern Evangelical mission movements compared to the Synoptic Gospels. The most frequent Bible passage I have heard to justify mission is the 'Great Commission' in Matt 28:18–20. A 'Go and do something for the Unreached' type of mission advocacy has been the mainstream position in Evangelical circles since I have been involved in the ministry of mission. The heavy burden that the 'Great Commission' passage carries for mission has often been shared with other 'missionary texts' such as Luke 4:43, Acts 1:8, Rom 10:14, Gen 12:1, and Isa 6:8. The Fourth Gospel has not been an attractive book for providing the basis of the modern mission movement. Bosch (1991) chooses three authors (Matthew, Luke, and Paul) from the New Testament to reflect on mission in the early days of Christian expansion saying, '… perhaps more important, I believe that the three New Testament authors chosen for my survey are, on the whole, representative of first-century missionary thinking and practice' (55). In this respect, the new reading of the Gospel may provide a new perspective on mission. Harris (2004, 223) insists that the Fourth Gospel 'provides us with the most developed theological understanding of mission', whereby the Gospel becomes complementary to the portrayal of mission in the Synoptics.

The next reason for choosing the Gospel is because the complementary aspect may help us to redefine the meaning of 'sending'. One of the 'missionary texts' frequently quoted from the Fourth Gospel is when Jesus says to his disciples, 'As the Father has sent me, I am sending you' (20:21b; cf

[7] *Mission of God* (2006) and *Mission of God's People* (2010) by Chris Wright; *The Drama of Scripture: Finding Our Place in the Biblical Story* (2004) and *A Light to the Nations: The Missional Church and the Biblical Story* (2011) by Michael W. Goheen; *Reading the Bible Missionally* (2016) edited by Michael Goheen.

[8] *Ezekiel* by Chris Wright (2009b), *Philippians* by Dean Flemming (2011), *The book of Job* by Tim Davy (2014). There are many other Master level dissertations on this development.

17:18, NIV).[9] That verse cannot be isolated from the whole narrative of the Gospel. Instead, it should be interpreted in the context of the Gospel. Some may ask what the purpose is for 'sending' the disciples since it does not appear clearly in the commissioning statement. Since Jesus' sending of his disciples is based on the Father's sending of him, it should not be understood as simply 'go and do it'. Instead, the purpose of the sending should be found through the whole narrative where Jesus reveals the way in which the Father sent him and the purpose for which he was sent. This missional reading of the Gospel clarifies the characteristics of 'sending' in the Gospel.

Many scholars have written about mission in the Fourth Gospel.[10] However, I will focus on the work of three authors, plus add a few other articles for reference. The three primary works are *The Johannine Approach to Mission: A Contextual Study of John 4:1–42* by Teresa Okure (1988); *The Missions of Jesus and the Disciples according to the Fourth Gospel* by Andreas J. Köstenberger (1998); and *Abide and Go: Missional Theosis in the Gospel of John* by Michael J. Gorman (2018). The reasons for surveying those particular works are as follows. First, those authors do not study the subject of mission in the Fourth Gospel merely as a part of their research. Instead, they devote their entire book to the subject. Secondly, the authors of the works represent different perspectives in some ways. Importantly, to add to my own East Asian missional reading of the Gospel, Teresa Okure is both a catholic nun and a professor at the Catholic Institute of West Africa in Nigeria. Okure's Global South insights into mission reflect an important holistic view on the subject. Andreas Köstenberger, an evangelical biblical scholar originally from Austria but who has done most of his academic work in the United States, represents a Global North, Anglo-Saxon perspective: an analytical approach to the subject centred on the historical critical tradition. Michael Gorman also represents a Global North perspective, with degrees from Princeton and serving as a professor in a UK research university. However, most of Gorman's work to date has been Pauline studies. His recent book brings Gorman's Pauline understanding of mission alongside contemporary trends in missional hermeneutics, which he shared through his Didsbury Lectures in 2016. Thirdly, the selected texts are relatively recent studies which build on similar approaches to the subject by previous researchers. After looking at these three major texts, I will outline a few other articles on the subject which have been published within the last 20 years: *Mission in John's Gospel and Letters* by Martin Erdmann (1998); *As the Father Has Sent Me, I Send You: Toward a Missional-Incantational Ethos in John 4* by Kobus Kok (2010); and *A Mission*

[9] All Scripture quotations are taken from the *New International Version* (2011) unless otherwise noted, Zondervan, 2012

[10] There are a few scholars who devote their entire books to mission in the Fourth Gospel. Kuhl (1967), Bühner (1977), Precott-Ezickson (1986), Okure (1988), Köstenberger (1998) and Gorman (2018).

of Sending Love: Being, Doing and Telling in John's Gospel by Dean Flemming (2013).

Okure's Work (1988)

Okure claims that 'mission itself is a leitmotif or "foundation theme" of the Gospel' (1). She divides previous major approaches to the subject of mission in the Fourth Gospel in the twentieth century into four categories: 'the missionary character of the Gospel' (9), which argues whether the Gospel is written for non-believers or believers; 'the quest for models' (16), which examines models that most inspired 'the Johannine portrait of Jesus as God's envoy' (16); 'the theological-Christological approach' (23); and 'the Johannine community's interest in mission' (28), which views the subject of mission from a so-called Johannine community's perspective. After the above survey, she concludes that 'a proper treatment of these issues, therefore, calls for a method which will view them in a unified perspective, rather than through one-sided or either-or approaches' (35). For this reason, she proposes a 'contextual method' for her study, which is 'a method which combines rhetorical and literary analysis in the quest for theological meaning viewed from the standpoint of the Evangelist and of his intended audience' (50). She selects the Samaritan episode (4:1–42) for her study because she thinks the episode is 'a miniature of the whole Gospel' (55). She sees the episode as a unified story following the Johannine *semeia* structure with three main parts: 'Jesus and the Samaritan woman (vv 1–26), Jesus and the disciples (vv 27, 31–38) and the Samaritan woman and the Samaritans *vis-à-vis* the mission of Jesus (vv 28–30, 39–42)' as *narratio*, *expositio* and *demonstratio* (182).

This structural approach to the text shows both the advantage and disadvantage of her study. The advantage is to see the given text from an organic and holistic point of view within the Gospel. In this view, those three individual stories mentioned above in the Samaritan episode form a story as a unit, as opposed to being just three different stories. In this regard, her research and my study agree. On the other hand, this approach has the risk of trapping and manipulating a given text in its structure. She (194) enlarges the approach to the entire Gospel dividing it into five sections: *exordium* (1:1–51), *narratio* (2–12), *expositio* (13–17), *probatio* (18–20), and *demonstratio* (21:1–25). Thus, she (195) concludes that 'the Gospel does not try to contain Jesus' all-encompassing mission, summed up in the ἔργον except (4:34; 17:4), within the restricted category of the disciples' mission, best understood as an entering into the labor of others (4:38)'. I see that this conclusion came as a result of examining the entire Gospel through her structural approach rather than reading the entire Gospel as a progressive story. Therefore, her interpretation of *Sitz-*

im-Leben[11] based on her findings might be 'the weakest point' in her work, as Köstenberger points out (1998, 14).

Köstenberger's Work (1998)

Köstenberger's revision of his doctoral thesis examines both the mission of Jesus and the mission of the disciples in the Gospel. He uses a method called 'Semantic Field Approach' for the study. His study differs from Okure's study in a rudimentary way. Okure concentrates on a vertical selection of a portion of the text to find unity in the chosen episode. By contrast, Köstenberger incorporates a horizontal selection of certain domains which he calls 'Semantic Field Approach' (18) throughout the entire Gospel such as mode of movement. By doing this, Köstenberger is able to extend the scope of the study to the entire Gospel rather than leaning on a portion of the Gospel. He chooses two semantic fields in the Gospel. He (27) proposes that 'John's teaching on mission appears to be centered primarily around two semantic fields'. One is activity involving movement from one place to another, such as 'send', 'come', 'go' and so on; the other is the accomplishment of a task, such as 'work', 'sign', 'harvest', and so on.

Köstenberger's approach to the mission of Jesus (ch 3) and his disciples (ch 4) confirms his definition of mission (41, 199): 'Mission is the specific *task* or purpose which a person or group seeks to accomplish, *involving various modes of movement*, be it sending or being sent, coming and going, descending and ascending, gathering by calling others to follow, or following'. However, the legitimacy of this conclusion is somewhat questionable in that it represents the outworking of his specific choice of semantic domains. What if he had chosen a different semantic field, such as *modes of being* including 'remain', 'with', 'oneness', and so on. He would have then arrived at a different definition of mission in the Gospel. Therefore, I view that his approach represents or emphasizes one aspect of Johannine mission as understood through a so-called 'proof-text' lens. Gorman (2018, 36) points out that Köstenberger 'limits, or nearly limits, mission to evangelism'.

Gorman's Work (2018)

Gorman's Didsbury Lectures (2016) are revised and expanded in his latest monograph (2018) entitled 'Abide and Go: Missional Theosis in the Gospel of John'. This book reads the Gospel from the view of missional hermeneutics

[11] She (232) says that 'the basic missionary problems in the Johannine community lay in the tendency on the part of some, at least, of the missionary disciples to set themselves against Jesus by claiming for themselves the glory of the missionary enterprise, thus forgetting that they were sent, which means dependent'.

and from the view of missional theosis in particular. Among many 'streams' of missional hermeneutics, Gorman focuses on the 'text-oriented' approach.[12] Therefore, his primary questions are: 'What does the Gospel of John say about the *missio Dei*, about humanity and the world, and especially – for this is the focus of the book – the participation of Jesus' disciples in the *missio Dei*' (7). He explains *missional* theosis as follows: '… participating in the life of God means participating in the *missional* life of God because the God we know in Christ is missional – the sending Father – who is of course the loving Father' (23).

The strength of this book lies in the author's in-depth study on Jesus' encounter with his disciples in the second half of the Gospel. He views the textual segment (chs. 13–16) not as a 'farewell discourse' but as 'John's mission discourse' (71). Gorman uses 'opening' rather than 'prologue' for the beginning of the Gospel, and sees chapter 21 not as an 'epilogue' but rather in continuous unity with the previous chapter. Since he reads the Gospel from the view of a missional hermeneutic as I will do, what he perceives in the Gospel accords in some ways with what I will argue. Nevertheless, his explanation of the first half of the Gospel is too brief to be helpful except as an introduction to the second half of the Gospel, to which he gave focused attention. I think this comes out of applying the frame of missional theosis to the Gospel rather than allowing the theme to come out of a missional reading of the Gospel.

Three Other Articles

Erdmann's (1998) article, *Mission in John's Gospel and Letters*, reflects the same issues, findings and problems that are found in Köstenberger's book. He also sees the Gospel as an evangelistic book for unbelievers. Even though he deals with many mission issues in the article, his understanding of mission is based on 'sending' and other modes of movement, similar to Köstenberger's view.

Secondly, Kok's (2010) article, *As the Father Has Sent Me, I Send You: Toward a Missional-Incantational Ethos in John 4*, focuses on the story of the Samaritan woman in John 4 as Okure did. He asserts that Jesus broke socio-religious barriers in the story, and that such action flowed from 'Jesus' missional-incantational ethos' (192). He adds that 'Jesus' mission has become our mission and therefore it has to become part of our ethical conduct, derived and motivated from the basis of our understanding of God, ourselves and others and our calling with regards to the *Missio Dei*' (193). He supports the

---

[12] Gorman (2018, 6) explains that the approach 'focused on the missional purposes, theology, and especially spirituality of one biblical book'. This approach relates to one of four streams in missional hermeneutics identified by George Hunsberger (See 2.2.3 of this thesis), the second stream 'the missional purpose of the writings' in particular.

continuation aspect of Jesus' mission by the disciples and focuses on the characteristics rather than movement.

Thirdly, Fleming's (2013) article, *A Mission of Sending Love: Being, Doing and Telling in John's Gospel*, assumes that 'John's target audience is most likely a group of second (or subsequent) generation of Jewish and Gentile Christians, people who were not eyewitness to Jesus' "signs"' (113). In the article, he focuses more on the character of mission, stressing the relationship between 'being', 'doing' and 'telling' the Good News. He insists that 'for John mission is more about "being" than "doing"' (128). His view is close to Gorman's missional theosis.

In Conclusion

As I mentioned above, each approach has its own value and benefit as well as weakness for studying mission in the Gospel. Even though each of the authors takes a different approach on the subject, there are common perspectives among them. All of them develop a mission theme within the text and apply it to the entire Gospel. Okure and Kok develop it in the Samaritan episode, while Köstenberger and Erdmann find it in mode of movement in the Gospel. Gorman (and Fleming, as well) brings an already-established theme, which is 'a missional theosis', and finds it in the Gospel. A possible danger of such an approach is that a reader may read the text within the imported theme and thus miss the whole and integral picture of the Gospel.

In this regard, the contribution of my work will be to show the whole and integral picture of the Gospel. My purpose is neither to find mission in the Gospel nor to read the Gospel from a specific mission theme. Instead, I will read the Gospel within the larger canonical context, the grand story of God's mission in particular. The reading does not exclude the missional character that the Gospel portrays but, more importantly, reveals the whole story of God's mission including Creation, Israel, and New Discipleship Community.

2. A Missional Hermeneutic for Reading the Fourth Gospel

Introduction

In this chapter, I discuss an approach for studying the Fourth Gospel called 'a missional hermeneutic'. Of course, it should not be *the* missional hermeneutic but *a* missional hermeneutic. I do not insist that the reading proposed in this study is the only missional reading of the Gospel, rather it would be the one filtered and reflected on through the author's own mission experience and from the author's own point of view: a missional reading of Scripture as a valid hermeneutic

The Emergence of a Missional Hermeneutic

There have been debates among scholars and historians about whether the early Protestant Reformers were concerned about mission. This current piece of work is not sufficient to judge the extent to which the Reformers' understanding of mission influenced mission activities of churches in the post-Reformation era. Regardless of how much it did or did not influence church activities, however, it is hard to find any evidence that churches in that era had engaged in mission. Pietists and the Moravians formed the first outward mission movements of Protestant mission. Their contribution toward the modern mission movement is significant. Nevertheless, Bosch (1978, 438) points out that 'in the case of the earliest Protestant missionaries, the Pietists and the Moravians, very little of a real biblical foundation for their missionary enterprises was in evidence'.

William Carey was one of the early missionaries of the modern era who attempted to build a biblical basis for mission. In his day, there was an opinion that 'because the apostles were extraordinary officers and have no proper successors, and because many things which were right for them to do would be utterly unwarrantable for us, therefore it may not be immediately binding on us to execute the commission' (Carey, 1972, 8). Carey used the Great Commission (Matt 28:18–20) to demonstrate that the command was as valid to him and all Christians as it had been to the apostles. Verkuyl (1978, 24) points out two important contributions of Carey as follows:

> One of Carey's most important contributions is his extensive refutation in section one of the *Enquiry* of the thesis defended by the Reformers "that the missionary commission (Matt. 28:16–20) was sufficiently put into execution by what the apostles and others have done…" A second important contribution of Carey is his basing the call to do mission work, not in the lost condition of sinners or in pity for them, but in obedience to the Lord's command.

Even though Carey's insistence was a proper response for the people who denied the missional responsibility of Christians for the world in that day, it is hard to say that this view represents a sufficient biblical basis for mission overall. Of course, Carey was not trying to explain the whole biblical basis for mission but only to respond to a specific issue, which was a general misunderstanding in his time. Therefore, taking the Commission as a primary biblical basis for mission without an understanding of the context Carey faced may lead us into a narrow view of mission. Bosch (1984, 17–18) points out the problem as follows:

> Subsequent generations of Anglo-Saxon missionaries and missionary spokesmen have, however, tended to miss the point that Carey had invoked the Great Commission in the context of *polemics*. To them, the Great Commission constituted the major biblical *foundation* for mission. This is true, even today, of many conservative evangelicals, particularly in the United States where they tend to respond to all questions about the justification of mission with a single answer: "The risen Lord has commanded it!" Their scriptural reference, time and again, is *Matthew* 28:19.

Carey and others chose to defend and support the mission of the church against the argument that there is no evidence of mission in Scripture. Chris Wright (2006, 24) uses the term 'biblical apologetic for mission' for that approach. On the one hand, this apologetic has its context and value within that context. On the other hand, it poses the danger of narrowing an understanding of mission because it is dependent only on isolated texts to prove the biblical basis for mission. Bosch uses Carey's case as an example to point out the problem. He says there are two underlying assumptions in Carey's case: that 'the validity of the missionary mandate can be founded on isolated texts' and 'everybody would agree with Carey's definition of what mission is' (1978, 439). He continues that the first assumption had been challenged by 19th-century criticism regarding the authenticity of the text as Jesus' own words, which caused missionary circles to labour to prove its authenticity. The second assumption also has been challenged by the shift of the definition of mission itself. Carey's definition of mission crosses geographical boundaries to 'convert heathens', but it could be redefined as Bosch (1978, 441) suggests,

'Mission is, in fact, the totality of the task *God* has *sent* his *Church* to do in the *world*'.[1]

This kind of so-called 'proof-text' or 'missionary text' approach, which is 'to pull a series of proof-texts out of the Old and New Testaments and then to consider the task accomplished' (Verkuyl, 1978, 90), has been a common one and has created a vision of mission that is narrow and thus distorted. Even though the 'proof-text' or 'missionary text' approach has its value and contribution in a specific context, as we see in Carey's case, it is not able to lead us into a portrayal of mission in the Bible as a whole. Furthermore, presumptions about mission would interfere in the process of selecting which texts are seen as foundational, which would eventually lead the users of the approach to a certain biased or narrow concept of mission.

Several scholars have attempted to overcome this problem by reading Scripture in the broader context rather than leaning on those few missional texts. Since mission has been challenged not only for its method but also for its validity in the 20th century, it has become essential to determine whether or not Scripture really talks about mission as a commission from God. J. Blauw (1962, 16–17) insists that a 'theology of mission' should 'be based not only on the narrow strip of some "missionary texts", but on the whole witness of both the Old Testament and New Testament'. He chooses the first eleven chapters of the Bible as a 'point of departure' for Old Testament theology and uses 'universality' as 'the basis for the missionary message of the Old Testament' (17). He points out that the election of Israel also should be seen in this inclusive perspective, saying, '[t]he election of Israel is a matter of divine initiative which has as its goal the recognition of God by all nations over the whole world' (24). This understanding of Israel naturally connected the cosmic scope of the missional message of the Old Testament, which eventually linked to Christ. We may not say that approaching the Bible with the wider perspective helps us to find more 'missions' we already know about in the Old Testament, but it helps us to understand the whole picture of the mission God has initiated.

Verkuyl (1978, 89–90) points out the importance of hermeneutics in examining the biblical foundation for mission, saying, 'whenever one inquires how the Bible develops its foundation for mission, the matter of how he goes about his search is not unimportant'. He also points out four motifs in the Old Testament, which are universal, rescue and saving, missionary and antagonistic. He insists that these four motifs 'form the indispensable basis for the New Testament call to the church to engage in worldwide mission work'

---

[1] International Congress on World Evangelization at Lausanne (1974) known as Lausanne Congress declared that '[w]orld evangelization requires the whole Church to take the whole gospel to the whole world' in Article 6 of the Lausanne Covenant (http://www.lausanne.org/en/documents/lausanne-covenant.html).

(91). Even though he did not use the term 'missional hermeneutic', his analysis of the book of Jonah – reviewing eight scenes in it – might be viewed as a missional reading of it.

David Bosch is another scholar who sees the value of an approach that reads Scripture in an integrated way to build a biblical foundation for mission. He (1978, 439) points out the problem of using the Bible as 'a mine from which "missionary texts" could be extracted'. He also warns about the awkwardness of a hermeneutical approach which tries to find mission-related texts and concepts from isolated Scripture verses. He illustrates the gymnastics that this approach requires (439):

> Most of the Bible, especially the Old Testament, was undoubtedly 'particularistic' and therefore hardly usable as a foundation for a world-wide mission. If, however, we searched carefully and persistently among the rocks and rubble we would find small nuggets of real gold-stories of pagans such as Ruth and Naaman, who accepted the faith of Israel, 'universalistic' expressions in the Psalms and in Deutero-Isaiah, encounters between Jews and non-Jews, such as the Roman centurion, etc. Sometimes there are no such clearly visible nuggets of gold; then the ore would have to be melted carefully and the invisible gold meticulously extracted from it via the elaborate processes of exegesis.

His illustration precisely exposes the problem of a traditional approach to exploring the biblical basis for mission. The biblical basis for mission should mean more than gathering isolated texts from Scripture; it should mean studying the essence of the message of Scripture. As Bosch (1978, 440) summarizes, 'What is decisive for the Church today is not the formal agreement between what she is doing and what some isolated biblical texts seem to be saying but rather her relationship with the essence of the message of Scripture'. Instead of referencing those 'missionary texts', Bosch (1978, 442–451) proposes four important elements to show the missional significance in both the Old and the New Testament: compassion, history, suffering and conduct. I will discuss elements of a missional hermeneutic in a separate section.

In conclusion, it is necessary to distinguish these two different approaches. Since the 'proof-text' approach has been closely linked with the phrase 'a biblical basis for mission' for such a long time, it is better to use a new phrase for the other approach. Chris Wright (2006, 21–22) proposes 'a missional basis of the Bible' for this new approach. To read the Bible from a missional perspective, I propose a working definition of mission for this thesis as 'God expanding the fellowship of the Trinity by inviting people to be reconciled and transformed into a worshipping community'.[2] Therefore, mission is firstly the

---

[2] In June, 2011, the leadership team of Wycliffe Asia-Pacific developed a foundation statement as follows: 'We understand mission as God expanding the fellowship of the

mission of God (*missio Dei*) and mission is secondly we as disciples participate in His mission.

A Missional Hermeneutic as a Valid Hermeneutic

Before I develop the content of a missional hermeneutic, the question of whether or not it is adequate as a framework for reading Scripture should be addressed. One of the leading scholars in the area of missional hermeneutics is Christopher Wright. He had faced the challenge of the validity of the missional hermeneutic he proposed when Antony Billington (1998, [2]) questioned 'the relationship between the missiological framework and the text':[3]

> It's not that the bringing of a framework to a text is necessarily wrong in and of itself, nor even that the text may not be illuminated in significant ways when we do – for it frequently is. The question is more what sort of control the framework exercises over the text, and whether the text is ever allowed to critique the framework at any point.

Billington is asking if the process is properly self-critical. The point is whether the hermeneutic is changed by the reading process – can Scripture challenge the hermeneutic?

Wright's (2006, 68) first answer to the question is that the missional framework he offers would 'be evaluated for its heuristic fruitfulness', thus '[o]nly the reader can answer, if he or she can stay with [him] through the long biblical journey ahead'. There is no question about the 'heuristic fruitfulness' as he stated, if one uses the framework he proposed for reading Scripture. The 'heuristic fruitfulness' itself, however, cannot be used as a justification for the validity of it. It might be an outcome of a valid framework, but it cannot be used to validate it. In fact, 'heuristic fruitfulness' could even be obtained from a distorted framework, such as a prosperity Gospel framework.

Wright's (2006, 68) second answer to Billington's question is that '*any* framework necessarily distorts the text to some degree'. He claims that '[t]he only way not to distort the biblical text is simply to reproduce it as it is' and '[a]ny attempt to summarize or provide some system or pattern for grasping it, or some structure to organize its content, cannot but distort the givenness of the original reality – the text itself' (68). To illustrate this, he (2006, 69) uses the

---

trinity by inviting people to be reconciled and transformed into a worshipping community. We realize that the Holy Spirit initiates, sustains and completes this mission for God's glory. We participate with Him through the offering of self'. (Wycliffe Asia-Pacific Statements, updated June 2013).

[3] Chris Wright gave a lecture on a missional hermeneutic on Ezekiel at London Bible College in February 1998, when Billington, an official respondent in the meeting, asked this question as a sort of prepared response to the lecture.

London Underground map as an example of how some degree of distortion of reality can be justified.

> It [the map of the London Underground] distorts and omits in order to simplify and clarify. And indeed that iconic diagram provides a much more comprehensible framework for understanding London by Tube (subway) than any map would do that showed all the Underground lines in their actual twists and turns, distances and directions. Furthermore, we all know that the Underground map is a distortion of reality of the Tubes simply and safely'.

With this analogy, he (2006, 69) justifies the missional hermeneutic thus:

> A missional hermeneutic such as I have sketched seems to me to fulfil some of these mapping requirements. It does not claim to explain every feature of the vast terrain of the Bible, nor to foreclose in advance the exegesis of any specific text. But when you encounter on your hike some feature of the landscape that is not marked on your map, you do not deny its existence because it has no place on your map. Nor do you necessarily blame the map for choosing not to include it.

In my view, however, Billington's (1998) comment is not that there should not be any distortion in the map. He even agrees with Wright regarding the 'fruitfulness' of any framework. Rather, his question is why the proposed hermeneutical framework is valid for reading Scripture, and furthermore, what relationship exists between hermeneutic and the text since an invalid hermeneutic or a one-way imposition of it might control the given text to gain a desired outcome, which can be another version of the 'proof-text' way of reading the Scripture. The distortion of a framework over a certain text, which Billington raised, does not refer to some degree of distortion in a map, which Wright explained. Rather, I observe that Billington is asking whether the missional framework is a valid bird's-eye view of all of London (Scripture) or just a specific part – like a map of the sewers of London or the London underground map. Billington asks '*why*', and Wright answers '*how'*. Thus, the question should be answered with the proper reasons that explain why a missional framework is a valid bird's-eye view for reading the Scripture.

In fact, Wright (2006, 29) already implied why he chose the framework by renaming 'the biblical basis of mission' as 'the missional basis of the Bible':

> Mission is what the Bible is all about; we could as meaningfully talk of the missional basis of the Bible as of the biblical basis of mission. Now this is a bold claim. One would not expect to be able to turn the other way any phrase that began "The biblical basis of..." There is, for example, a biblical basis for marriage, but there is not, obviously, a marital basis for the Bible. There is a biblical basis for work, but work is not what the Bible is all about.

Why is it that 'the missional basis' does not distort the Bible while 'the marital basis' and the occupational basis do? According to his explanation above, it is because 'mission is what the Bible is all about'. If the claim is accepted, a missional framework can be supported as a valid one from which to read the Bible. To sum up what has been said so far, Billington's question about the possible distortion of the text can be answered, not by legitimizing some degree of distortion on a map, but by stating that 'mission is what the Bible is all about'.

Then, on what basis can one make such a statement? There are at least two main reasons that support the claims that a missional framework for reading Scripture is valid.

First, it could be justified by the missional character of the ultimate author of the Bible. Christian tradition affirms that the Bible was written by various human authors, but it is not merely a human book. The Bible says, 'All Scripture is God-breathed' (2 Tim 3:16a). As Wright (2009a, 4) comments, 'the Bible is not *partly* the word of God and *partly* the words of human beings, but *wholly both*'. God is not one of the authors but the ultimate author of the Bible. Though the Bible is a collection of sixty-six books from a human perspective, it is one integrated book from a divine perspective and has a central, penetrative, overarching nature throughout. Since God is the author of authors, understanding God's character as the author must not be excluded. Saying that God is the ultimate author of the Bible means not only that the reader needs to depend on the author for guidance through prayer and faith in him, but also that the reader should understand the overall elements of the whole Bible, which are related to the missional character of God. Those elements combine to create one of the key structures that form a missional hermeneutic, so I will discuss this in a later section.

Wright (2006) starts a section called 'Shaping a Missional Hermeneutic' in his book subtitled 'The Bible as the product of God's Mission'. He asserts that 'the whole canon of Scripture is a missional phenomenon in the sense that it witnesses to the self-giving movement of this God toward his creation and us, human beings in God's own image, but wayward and wanton' (48). God is a missionary God, and the Bible is the record of that missionary God. The Bible is the self-revelation of God. God reveals his plan for his creation through the Bible. Hesselgrave (1993, 17) insists that 'the missionary purpose of God is so much an expression of his nature, so much in evidence in the giving of his revelation, and so interwoven with the entire fabric of God's plan as revealed in the Bible that it becomes a pre-understanding for the interpretation of the whole Bible'.

Köstenberger (1999, 349) uses different terminology for this perspective. He prefers a 'salvation-historical' approach as opposed to a 'religion-historical' approach which 'focuses on the development of *humankind's* understanding of God, leading to particular concepts of God, forms of worship, and moral codes'. According to the 'salvation-historical' view of Scripture, the Bible is 'not merely a human witness to the emergence of human religious consciousness, but rather the inspired record of God's revelation and redemptive acts in human history' (350). This missional character of God and 'salvation-historical' nature of Scripture provide support for a missional hermeneutic as a valid framework for reading and interpreting Scripture.

Secondly, further support for a missional hermeneutic can be inferred from recognizing that the Bible originated in missional circumstances. The Bible, including the Old Testament, is a product of mission – something the people of God produced in the context of their struggle to understand and live out their identity as 'a kingdom of priests' (Exod 19:5) and 'a royal priesthood' (1 Pt 2:9). Wright (2006, 49) points out that many Scripture texts 'emerged out of events or struggles or crises or conflicts in which the people of God engaged with the constantly changing and challenging task of articulating and living out their understanding of God's revelation and redemptive action in the world'. Paul's letters were given to people who were struggling to find their new identity as Christians in a new community. Most of the letters were written during his missionary journeys. Flemming (2011, 9), who views Paul's letters as 'missional documents', points out that '[a]lthough Paul is not physically present, the apostle continues to fulfil his God-given mission among the Philippians [and others] by means of written correspondence'. Other books in the New Testament are no exception. Brownson (1994, 482) supports this, saying, 'the early Christian movement that produced and canonized the New Testament was a movement with a specifically *missionary* character'. The New Testament was recorded as a reflection on the early church's missional context and practice. This missional seedbed for the birth of Scripture justifies a missional hermeneutic as a valid framework for reading and interpreting the Bible.

To summarize the discussion to this point, a missional reading of Scripture can be seen as valid because 1) the Bible as a whole reveals the mission of God and 2) the Bible has been produced in missional circumstances. As Chris Wright (2006, 51) summarizes, 'a missional hermeneutic proceeds from the assumption that *the whole Bible renders to us the story of God's mission through God's people in their engagement with God's world for the sake of God's purpose for the whole of God's creation*'.

Current Developments in Missional Hermeneutics

I have introduced several scholars who have attempted to overcome the 'proof-text' way of reading Scripture. They pointed out that mission should be based on the whole of Scripture and the essence of its message, even though no specific term for the approach was suggested. Hesselgrave (1993, 17) calls this approach 'a missionary hermeneutic', saying as follows:

> Without doubt the Bible is the basis for missions. But how about the other way around: Is missions also the basis for the Bible? If this is true then we have a new

> hermeneutic – "a missionary hermeneutic." Without this specific mission pre-understanding much of the Bible will remain a mystery, or be misinterpreted.

From the mid-1990s onward, the term 'missional hermeneutics' has become the phrase of choice for expressing this approach. A missional hermeneutic does not necessitate that every single verse be interpreted as missional. Instead, it means that mission is a hermeneutical key to reading Scripture. Wright (2006, 31) affirms this when he cautions, '[t]o say that the Bible is "all about mission" does not mean that we try to find something relevant to evangelism in every verse'. Bauckham (2016, 28–29) explains a missional hermeneutic as follows:

> … a way of reading the Bible for which mission is the hermeneutical key… a way of reading the whole of Scripture with mission as its central interest and goal… a way of reading Scripture that sought to understand what the church's mission really is in the world as Scripture depicts that mission, and thereby to inspire and inform the church's missionary praxis.

Since this term was introduced, different scholars have developed their ideas about what a missional hermeneutic is, what it should be, what elements it has and so on. Missional hermeneutics in its various forms is more a process than a fixed framework. As Flemming (2011, 5) points out, 'no consensus has emerged on precisely what a missional reading of the Bible entails'. Hunsberger, a coordinator of the current discussion of missional hermeneutics in North America, categorized the different proposals about missional hermeneutics into four streams.[4] The four streams are (Hunsberger, 2016, 49–62): 1) the missional direction of the story, 2) the missional purpose of the writings, 3) the missional locatedness of the readers and 4) the missional engagement with cultures. I will examine these streams to determine the extent to which each stream relates and contributes to reading the Fourth Gospel missionally.

First, some scholars have developed a missional hermeneutic as an interpretive framework of the whole Bible as one story. Hunsberger (2016, 50) calls this view 'the missional direction of the story', that is to say, '[t]he *framework* for biblical interpretation is the story the Bible tells of the mission of God and the formation of a community sent to participate in it'. This approach asks what the Bible story as a canonical whole is about and how it affects us. Chris Wright is one of the active pioneers of this approach. He claims that the Bible is one grand universal narrative that is 'moving in the

[4] He has presented the paper at a meeting of the American Academy of Religion and the Society of Biblical Literature for the first time in 2008, then published the article in many different places including *Missiology* (39:3, 2011) and a recent book edited by Goheen (2016).

same direction ultimately – towards Christ at its centre and the new Creation at its end' (2009a, 37). Therefore, he recommends reading any passage in the Bible 'not only within its immediate literary and historical context, but also within its canonical context in the flow of the Bible' (38). Hesselgrave (1993, 18) calls this 'mega-context', while Goheen (2006, 1) uses 'a macro-framework for a missional hermeneutic'. Chris Wright (2006, 41) also suggests that a missional hermeneutic entails a Christ-centred reading of Scripture:

> *Jesus himself* provided the hermeneutical coherence within which all disciples must read these texts, that is, in the light of the story that leads *up to* Christ (messianic reading) and the story that leads *on from* Christ (missional reading). That is the story that flows from the mind and purpose of God in all the Scriptures for all the nations. That is a missional hermeneutic of the whole Bible.

Kelly (2010, 62) uses *Christotelic* and *missiogenic* instead of the 'messianic reading' and 'missional reading' – the terms suggested by Chris Wright. Kelly (2010, 64) elaborates on Christ-centred reading with the new term *Christotelic,* claiming 'Jesus Christ functions as the end point, or the goal, of the OT, and the center of the NT'. He adds that *missiogenic* reading means 'Scripture, obediently read, should also generate a response that will call the reader to align himself or herself with the mission of God in the world' (72).

Secondly, other scholars insist that Scripture had been written to equip the missional community in a missional context. A missional hermeneutic in this circle reads Scripture with an understanding of the missional context in which both the human authors of the biblical texts and the hearers of the texts were situated. This also means that the biblical writings served the purpose of forming the missional community. Guder (2015, 90) sees this in the ministry of Jesus' disciples. He states that the apostles' 'strategy was the formation of witnessing communities whose purpose was to continue the witness that had brought them into being'. Thus, '[w]e observe especially how the apostolic strategy of continuing formation of missional communities became the motivation of their writings' (91).

Michael Goheen (2006, 7) also points out that Scripture is a tool of God's mission as follows:

> The Old Testament Scriptures were written to "equip" God's people for their missional purposes… The New Testament Scriptures tell the story of God's mission through Israel as it climaxes in Jesus, and bring that story to bear in various ways on the early church to form and equip them for their missional calling in the world.

He claims that 'if we are to "hear" the text aright today our own involvement in God's mission will be a necessary prerequisite' (2). Hunsberger (2016, 53) calls this stream 'the missional purpose of the writings' explaining that '[t]he *aim* of biblical interpretation is to fulfil the equipping purpose of the biblical writings'. If the first stream of a missional hermeneutic is related to the ultimate authorship of God and his mission, the second has to do with the human authors and the missional situation they faced.

Thirdly, some scholars emphasize the importance of the context of the readers as a hermeneutical community. Michael Barram (2007, 58), one of the leading scholars in this view, focuses on questions from each community's social location, which he calls '"located" questions'. He insists that 'the "social location" of the people of God is at the very heart of a missional hermeneutic' (58). He (2006, 3) argues that a missional hermeneutic is not just a methodological framework which a grand narrative approach might pursue. Rather, it is characterized by 'its relentless commitment to articulating critical questions aimed at faithfully articulating the *missio Dei* and the community's role within the purposes of God'. Thus, he (2006, 3) defines a missional hermeneutic as 'an approach to the biblical text rooted in the basic conviction that God has a mission in the world and that we read Scripture as a community called into and caught up by those divine purposes'.

Hunsberger (2016, 55) titles this stream '[t]he missional locatedness of the readers', summarizing that '[t]he *approach* required for a faithful reading of the Bible is from the missional location of the Christian community'. Each missional community commits to reading Scripture in its own location, and those communities need to share with each other what they have learned to broaden their perspective on *missio Dei*. Brownson (1994, 483) insists that multiple interpretations of Scripture by various contexts of the interpreter as individual or community is inevitable, but 'a missional hermeneutic must be committed to dialogue with other readers of the biblical text'. David Bosch (1991, 187) summarizes this hermeneutical communities' sharing as follows:

> Scripture comes to us in the shape of human words, which are already "contextual" (in the sense of being written for very specific historical contexts) and are, moreover, open to different interpretations… No individual or group has a monopoly here. So, the Christian church should function as an "international hermeneutical community" (Hiebert 1985b:16) in which Christians (and theologians) from different contexts challenge one another's cultural, social and ideological biases.

Fourthly, there is a view that a missional hermeneutic is an '*interpretive matrix* – a set of interpretative "rules" or assumptions' (Brownson, 1994, 493) that is generated in a missional moment when text meets context by a reader of Scripture as an interpreter. Hunsberger (2016, 59) calls this stream '[t]he missional engagement with cultures'. He adds that '[t]he gospel functions as the interpretive *matrix* within which the received biblical tradition is brought into critical conversation with a particular human context'. Brownson (1994, 495), who holds this view, points out that the interpretive matrix is 'what the New Testament calls "the gospel"'. He (1994, 499) summarizes the Gospel as 'the story of Jesus' identity, death and resurrection as a story of salvation', adding that 'this summary of the gospel provides the hermeneutical perspective or matrix through which the Christian tradition and specific historical contexts are *interpreted*'.

Even though there are four different streams, as Hunsberger has summarized and others may add more in the future,[5] it is important to understand how these different streams are related to each other. Essentially, they could be characterized as tributaries rather than streams, all feeding a single river – a missional hermeneutic.

These four proposals on missional hermeneutics could be grouped under two main categories. Hunsberger himself affirms these two categories in his recent reflection (2016, 66). It is worth quoting his reflection:

> The accents of the first two are more located in the text (the spaces behind and within the text, as Lois Barrett suggests), and the accents of the latter two are more located in the readers (the spaces before the text). This, of course, highlights the "two horizons" in biblical interpretation: then and there – here and now. The first pair focuses on the missional dimensions of the text (direction and intent), and the second pair focuses on the missional dynamics of the church's life and social situation into which those texts are speaking (context-probing, and gospel as matrix).

I view the first two as being connected with building a methodological framework through which the missional purpose of the Bible could be read, while the other two are linked with the attitude and context of the reader of the Bible either as an individual or as a community. '*The missional direction of the story*', for which Chris Wright is mainly searching, provides a bigger, coherent picture of the Bible. It is naturally connected with the mission of God. Others such as Bosch with his four important elements, Goheen with his seven overall points of Scripture,[6] and Kelly (2010, 62) with his *Christotelic* and *missiogenic* explanations are also trying to engage with this big story. '*The missional purpose of the writings*' contributes another aspect of the framework. It pursues the interpretive framework of the human author and the hearers of the texts.

---

[5] Chris Wright (2009b, 2) already added another one called 'the missional cost to the messenger' in his missional reflection on the book of Jeremiah.

[6] Goheen (2006, 2–6): 1) The Bible is the true story of the world in which we find our place and role. 2) God's mission to redeem [the] world is the main storyline of the narrative that the Bible tells. 3) In [the] Old Testament God chooses and forms Israel as a people with a view to bringing salvation to the whole world. 4) In Jesus, God's purpose to restore the creation comes to a climax. 5) Church taken up into God's mission to continue the mission of Israel and Jesus. 6) The 'already-not yet' period of the kingdom is an eschatological era of the missional in-gathering of the nations. 7) The mission of God's people involves a missional encounter with culture which both embraces the treasures and opposes the idolatry of all cultures.

Within the coherent direction of the story in the Bible, this second aspect allows us to see how the contemporary people of God in the text are equipped and how they engaged with their given context. The third stream, '*The missional locatedness of the readers*' emphasizes the importance of the reader's location and context, which is related to the attitude and context of the reader. As the scholars in the third stream recommend, however, each community needs to communicate with other communities its own interpretation of a text in order to form a 'universal hermeneutical community'. The process of the universal hermeneutical community includes certain implicit criteria, which could be called an interpretive framework. The fourth stream, '*The missional engagement with cultures*' is linked to both categories. It belongs to the first category in that it tries to find the '*interpretive matrix*' influencing the minds of the writers of the biblical texts. At the same time, it belongs to the second category for it insists that the framework occurs only when the texts interact with a context.

In conclusion, the current missional hermeneutic proposals are classified broadly into two categories. The first one looks for an interpretive framework by studying the divine author's narrative and the human authors' and hearers' interpretive matrix. The other category addresses how we, as readers of the biblical texts, could be a missional community reading the texts contextually in our missional situation, and communicating with other hermeneutical communities in our reading of the biblical texts. To read the Fourth Gospel with a missional hermeneutic, I view that the first two streams, the missional direction of the story and the missional purpose of the writings, are relevant since they are related to the text. In this thesis, missional hermeneutic is an unassuming process of reading the text itself rather than a deductive process of reading mission into the given text. I will discuss what a missional hermeneutic is, particularly for reading the Fourth Gospel, in section 2.4.

The Fourth Gospel as a Missional Document

More than a Collection of Memories

I have argued that a missional hermeneutic is a valid lens with which to read the Bible. The assumption for my insistence is that 1) the Bible reveals the mission of God, and 2) the Bible was produced in the context of mission. It is necessary to discuss how reading particularly the Fourth Gospel with a missional lens could be justified. In other words, I will examine the extent to which the Fourth Gospel accommodates such a reading. For instance, if a document is about cooking, then a missional reading of it is hardly justified. I am not saying that the Bible – the Fourth Gospel for this study – is a handbook or a manual for mission. However, the given document needs to be clarified as having missional aspects in it. Chris Wright (2006, 24) defines the word 'missional' as 'simply an adjective denoting something that is related to or characterized by mission, or has the qualities, attributes or dynamics of mission'. I will examine the extent to which the Fourth Gospel may be read from a missional point of view.

Chris Wright (2003, 3) insists that 'the Bible is the product of God's engagement through God's people in God's world for God's ultimate purpose for the nations and the world'. He continues, '[t]he documents which now collectively form our canon of Scripture emerged as God's people (in both Testaments) wrestled with the issues thrown up by their identity, role, and mission in the context of a fallen world of surrounding nations, cultures and religions'. If Scripture is the product of the missional engagement of God with his creatures, it is necessary to read the product from a missional point of view; the Fourth Gospel is no exception.

In the Fourth Gospel, the missional heart of God is expressed in the verse that tells us '[t]he Word became flesh and made his dwelling among us' (1:14). Thus, grasping the deeper meaning of who Christ is, and what and how he has spoken and has lived among us, is crucial for understanding the missional purpose of God. The Gospel records what Jesus is saying and doing in the world, but Jesus is revealing the Father (1:18) and the Father's will (cf 4:34; 5:30; 6:38, 39, 40). Thus the missional nature and purpose of God are being expressed by the existence of Jesus, including what he says and does. The Evangelist uses the verb ἐξηγέομαι (to explain) in 1:18, which is the only occurrence of that word in the Gospel. Köstenberger (2004, 50) points out that '[i]n its Lucan occurrences (Luke 24:35; Acts 10:8; 15:12, 14; 21:19), the term regularly means "to give a full account" in the sense of "telling the whole story"'. Olson (1999, 143) explains this view: '[t]he Gospel of John is in form a narrative about Jesus, but its contents are in fact a narrative about what God has done and continues to do through Jesus'. To reach the goal of understanding the missional heart of God through the life of Jesus Christ in the Fourth Gospel, I argue that the Gospel is not just a collection of memories focusing on the history of the life of Jesus itself. Thatcher (2006, 24) claims that 'John's theory of the nature of memories and the persistence of memory makes it unlikely that he wrote a Gospel primarily to preserve information about Jesus, and this perspective is reflected in the explicit purpose statements in his book'.

The Fourth Gospel was considered by the early church as a 'spiritual Gospel'. Origen, who emphasizes the deeper meaning of Scripture, claims that 'the Gospel has a special admixture of the unhistorical' (Wiles, 1960, 22). Clement of Alexandria also contends that the Fourth Gospel had been written to reveal 'the deep spiritual/christological truth behind the events of history' (Thatcher, 2006, xii). We may find evidence for such arguments from the Evangelist's own statements in the Gospel. The Evangelist says that 'Jesus performed many other signs in the presence of his disciples, which are not recorded in this book' (20:30). He suggests that his recorded selection is minimal, 'Jesus did many other things as well. If every one of them were written down, I suppose that even the whole world would not have room for the books that would be written' (21:25). It affirms that the Evangelist's purpose of writing the Gospel was not intended to preserve the whole memory of what he had experienced during his time with Jesus. Billington (1995, 111) supports this view, saying, 'John has not written an exhaustive historical account of the life of Jesus (cf 20:30; 21:25); he has shaped his narrative on a deliberate artistic plan. Scholarly separation of "historical" and "literary" aspects of gospel criticism would more than likely bemuse the author of the Fourth Gospel'. Thatcher (2006, 45) also points out that 'the Fourth Gospel was produced in service of specific rhetorical objectives' and the rhetorical objectives the Evangelist mentions are that 'you may believe that Jesus is the Messiah, the Son of God, and that by believing you may have life in his name' (20:31). In this sense, the Fourth Gospel has a deeper meaning behind the history. There are, however, two distorted views on 'spiritual Gospel' or 'the deeper meaning behind the history', which might lead to a misunderstanding of the Evangelist's purpose.

First, there is a view that the Fourth Gospel has only a theological intention, implying that the history set forth in the Gospel may not be trustworthy. According to the Evangelist's explanation (20:30; 21:25), he chose a few signs Jesus performed to fulfil the purpose of his writing, which is for the audiences (recipients) of the Gospel to believe and have life. This does not mean that he only has theological intentions at the expense of history. Scholars who emphasize the theological intention of the Evangelist seem to overextend their assertion. It is difficult to agree with what scholars such as Scott (1908, 3) contend when he says, 'Sayings are ascribed to Him [Jesus] which He may not literally have spoken, but which express His essential thought, as the Evangelist conceived it'. Thatcher (2006, xiii) points out that applying the label 'spiritual Gospel' to the Fourth Gospel leads us to overlook two facts:

> First, John is the only early Gospel that explicitly claims (and more than once) to offer the reader a direct, firsthand witness to the preresurrection Jesus… we have to come to a definite conclusion about John's historical consciousness before we can discuss the Gospel of John's historicity, rather than vice versa… Second, John is the only evangelist, and one of the very few Christian writers at any point of history, who articulated a distinct theory about what "the Jesus tradition" was and how it operated. Whatever else he may have thought about Christ, John had a very clear sense that his presentation of Jesus was based on someone's memory, and an explicit theory of how that memory worked.

Secondly, another distorted view that arises from the term 'spiritual Gospel' is the assumption that every single word or phrase of the Fourth Gospel has symbolic or allegorical meaning. Wiles (1960, 23) gives an example of such cases in Origen's interpretation of John 13:30:

> 'He… went out straightway, and it was night'. Judas went out not simply from the house in which the supper was being held, but altogether from Jesus himself, like those of whom it is said in the epistle that 'they went out from among us'. The night into which he went was symbolic of the darkness in his own soul, or the darkness which pursued but could not overtake the true light.

Regardless of whether or not the above interpretation is accurate, this individualistic analytical approach for discovering the 'deeper meaning' of the text, while it may result in unveiling many 'spiritual meanings' here and there, may also fail to reveal the intrinsic and original purpose of the whole narrative. The Fourth Gospel is a 'spiritual Gospel' and has a 'deeper meaning' or 'theological intention' in the sense that it is not just a collection of memories but is also a selection and reflection of those memories purposely chosen to achieve a specific goal. Furthermore, the selection of the memories is based on an eyewitness account and the Evangelist's own experiences with Jesus. Thus, the Fourth Gospel is both historical and theological (spiritual).

A Reflection of the Evangelist

The Fourth Gospel is historical in the sense that it was written by the Evangelist who was an eyewitness of what Jesus had done and said from the beginning of Jesus' public life. It, however, was not written simply to preserve memories, which might be called a 'historical' purpose, but rather for conveying a message which the Evangelist believed important, a message that would eventually lead audiences into faith. Therefore, it is also theological and spiritual, which indeed affords a deeper meaning behind the history, not because of an allegorical meaning of each word but because of the deeper goal of the Evangelist for the Gospel writing. Augustine (in Adams, 2005, 16) affirms that the Gospel is the outcome of deep reflection, saying

> [The Evangelist] soared beyond the flesh, soared beyond the earth which he trod, beyond the seas which he saw, beyond the air where birds fly; soared beyond the sun, beyond the moon and the stars, beyond all spirits which are unseen, beyond his own intelligence and the very reason of his thinking soul. Soaring beyond all these, beyond his very self, where did he reach, what did he see? 'In the beginning was the Word, and the Word was with God, and the Word was God'.

The Gospel itself testifies that it is the result of the writer's reflection in many ways. It is the Evangelist's post-resurrection reflection on what he had experienced during the years he shared with Christ, paying particular attention to how Jesus expressed a new understanding of Scripture (the Old Testament). It is also a reflection of the Evangelist who selected choice memories for the purpose of understanding the deeper meaning of what Jesus was doing and saying.

First, it is a reflection of the Evangelist after Jesus' resurrection. In many places of his Gospel, the Evangelist adds his interpretation of what happened or what the people around the event including the disciples either misunderstood or could not understand. In John 2:22, he adds his interpretation regarding what Jesus had said about the temple, 'After he was raised from the dead, his disciples recalled what he had said. Then they believed the scripture and the words that Jesus had spoken'. In 7:39, he explains, 'By this he meant the Spirit, whom those who believed in him were later to receive. Up to that time the Spirit had not been given, since Jesus had not yet been glorified'. In 8:20, he adds that 'He spoke these words while teaching in the temple courts near the place where the offerings were put. Yet no one seized him, because his hour had not yet come'. In 12:16, he again interprets the situation, 'At first his disciples did not understand all this. Only after Jesus was glorified did they realize that these things had been written about him and that these things had been done to him'. There are many more verses[7] showing the author's own interpretation of situations. Those comments indicate that even the disciples of Jesus did not understand what their teacher was talking about and that the Evangelist eventually understood the meaning of what his teacher had said and performed previously, but only after the resurrection or even after his ascension. Thatcher (2006, 27) explains this 'as a complex cognitive interaction between (a) the disciples' autobiographical recollections of an ambiguous event involving themselves and Jesus, (b) their subsequent awareness of Jesus' destiny, and (c) a messianic reading of a passage from the Hebrew Bible'.

Secondly, the Fourth Gospel is a reflection of the Evangelist on the signs performed by Jesus Christ. The Evangelist knew that 'Jesus performed many other signs in the presence of his disciples, which are not recorded in this book [the Fourth Gospel]' (20:30). However, he selected a few signs[8] for fulfilling his writing purpose. A significant expression of the events in the Fourth Gospel is the word 'sign' (σημείον); the Synoptic Gospels use the word 'miracle' (δύναμις) for such events. The 'signs' in the Fourth Gospel are more than merely miraculous acts of Jesus. The signs in the Fourth Gospel are not a collection of different 'miracles' but are signs that reveal *meaning* through the subsequent discourses. Köstenberger (1998, 63) says that '[a] sign is a symbol-laden, but not necessarily 'miraculous', public work of Jesus selected and

---

[7] See 2:24, 24; 4:9; 6:64,71; 7:1, 5, 30, 39; 8:27; 9:22; 11:13; 12:6, 33; 13:11; 18:9, 28, 32; 21:19, 23.

[8] The numbers commonly accepted by Johannine scholars as signs in the Fourth Gospel are six (1. Changing water into wine at Cana, 2. Healing a royal official's son at Cana, 3. Healing a lame man at Bethesda, 4. Feeding five thousand on a mountainside, 5. Healing a blind man at Jerusalem, and 6. Raising Lazarus from the dead at Bethany). Different scholars add different events as a seventh sign of the Fourth Gospel. Smalley adds the catching of 153 fish (21:1–14), Dodd sees Jesus' walking on the water as the seventh (6:16–21), and Köstenberger suggests Jesus' cleansing of the temple (2:14–17).

explicitly identified as such by John for the reason that it displays God's glory in Jesus, who is thus shown to be God's true representative, even the Messiah'.

It is ultimately to reveal God's glory that Jesus performs the 'signs', but a significant feature of the signs is that they are sometimes followed by a discourse in the Fourth Gospel and include the Evangelist's own reflections on the subject. For example, the account of Jesus feeding five thousand is followed by the discourse on 'the bread of life' and the Evangelist's conclusion that '[f]rom this time many of his disciples turned back and no longer followed him' (6:66). The intention of the Evangelist in selecting those 'signs' in the Fourth Gospel needs to be interpreted in the context of the subsequent discourses, making this one of the critical points to understanding the purpose and the character of the Fourth Gospel. Morris (1989, 42) points out that '[e]very sign can be linked in some way with a discourse, and such links are part of the way John carried out his plan'.

Thirdly, the Fourth Gospel is a reflection of the Evangelist on the Old Testament. The Fourth Gospel reveals that the Evangelist had a new understanding of Scripture. The new understanding of Scripture, based on what he had received from Jesus Christ, enabled him to interpret it reflectively. In that sense, the Fourth Gospel includes reflections of Christ from the Old Testament. It is true that 'the number of direct quotations from the O.T. given in the [Fourth] Gospel is small when compared with those of the other Gospels' (Barrett, 1947, 155). Barrett, however, points out that the Evangelist uses the Old Testament 'in a novel manner, collecting its sense rather than quoting' (156). The Old Testament permeates the Gospel, which is only possible when a person understands the given text and the intention of the ultimate author of the entire Scriptures.

Christ himself taught his disciples in that manner. The Jewish disciples, undoubtedly, would be able to quote from the Old Testament since they were expected to memorize it from their childhood, according to Jewish tradition. Nevertheless, they were not able to grasp the essence of the whole message of the Old Testament. Jesus points out this discrepancy of the Jews, saying, 'You [the Jews] study the Scriptures diligently because you think that in them you have eternal life. These are the very Scriptures that testify about me, yet you refuse to come to me to have life' (5:39). The disciples of Jesus were no exception. One of the significant changes in the disciples after their interaction with Jesus was their change of perspective when looking at the Scriptures through the lens of Jesus. There is some evidence in the New Testament that supports this change. According to Luke, two disciples on the road to Emmaus experienced their 'hearts burning' after Jesus 'explained to them what was said in all the Scriptures concerning himself beginning with Moses and all the Prophets' (Luke 24:27, 32). A similar thing happened to other disciples (cf Luke 24:46–47). That was the turning point for them, the moment in which they understood the prophesied Christ and began to penetrate the Old Testament with this new understanding. It is natural for 'the disciple whom

Jesus loved', as a close friend of Christ, to understand the Old Testament in this new way rather than randomly quoting some isolated verses. As Barrett (1947, 168) points out, 'the whole body of the O.T. formed a background, or framework, upon which the new revelation rested' in the Fourth Gospel.

The word 'Lamb' (John 1:36) in the Gospel is a suitable example. Some scholars say that it is a mistranslation of the word 'servant' since it seems to be a clear reference to Isaiah 53 where it is translated as 'servant'. Jeremias (1964, 339) insists on this point of view, saying, 'the original reference thus [refers] to Jesus as the servant of God'. There are, however, other scholars who see the text as it is and insist that the word 'Lamb' is evidence of the Evangelist having a holistic understanding of the Old Testament rather than just quoting a few verses from it. The holistic understanding and the reflective citation of the Old Testament by the Evangelist in the Gospel is the outcome of his new reading of the Scriptures through the lens of Jesus. Schuchard (2015, 41) points out as follows:

> The evangelist's chief purpose in citing the Old Testament is to elucidate the person and the work of Jesus, especially the death of Jesus. His principal goal in his late first-century sociocultural context is that the hearer of his Gospel would be persuaded steadfastly to believe that Jesus is the Christ, the Son of God, so that, believing, the hearer would have life in his name (20:30–31). If the enduring popularity of his Gospel is any indication of the success of his efforts, we may say with some confidence that the evangelist's intention for his Gospel was in the end accomplished.

The Missional Aspect of the Reflection

I have discussed the view that the Fourth Gospel is the Evangelist's reflection on his experiences with Jesus as an eyewitness, including several selected events performed by Jesus and his new understanding of the Scripture (Old Testament) intertwined into the reflective process. Then, what caused the Evangelist to write the Gospel? An immediate answer to this question would be to compel the audience and readers to believe. The Evangelist says that '[e]ven after Jesus had performed so many signs in their presence, they [the Jews] still would not believe in him' (12:37). Nevertheless, he selects some of the signs, linking them with a discourse or discourses which have an interpretive function for the signs, so that 'you may believe that Jesus is the Messiah, the Son of God and that by believing you may have life in his name' (20:31). It demonstrates that the reflection of the Evangelist has a missional purpose. The Fourth Gospel is a missional document in the sense that it is written in a missional situation and the real 'spiritual/christological' purpose is missional. Of course, what it means to be a missional document should be identified. Since it is related to the word 'to believe' (πιστεύω), it can only be known first by what the word 'to believe' in the Gospel conveys. This will be discussed in detail later (see 6.3.3).

In the current Johannine discussion, there are arguments about whether or not it is a missional document on the basis of 'evangelistic' purpose. Those in favour of the argument insist that it is a missional document because it is written for non-believers. They use the Hellenistic evidence in the Gospel, such as *logos* and other Hellenistic expressions, to support their claim. On the other hand, those opposed insist that the Gospel is not missional because it was written for the so-called Johannine community. According to their argument, the criterion for this being a missional document is based on whether or not it is written to non-believers directly, that is to say, whether it is evangelistic. Holding to a view of the Gospel as a missional document, however, does not require its purpose to be limited to the direct evangelism of non-believers. It also includes raising awareness of and persuading believers to know and understand the missional identity of the Christian community. When Jesus articulated the missional statements in different places such as Matt 28:18–20 or John 20:21, the audience of the statements was his disciples. The discussion on whether the Fourth Gospel is missional should not solely depend on whether it was written for non-believers directly. Instead, it needs to be examined to determine whether or not it is talking about the missional identity of believers, especially the new community. Köstenberger (1998, 17, 27–29) offers probing questions for studying mission in the Fourth Gospel, questions such as, 'How can one avoid reading one's own conception of mission into John's Gospel? How can one be sure to have grasped the entire scope of John's teaching on mission?' Nevertheless, he still chooses only 'terms of activity' and 'terms of accomplishment' in the Fourth Gospel as his 'semantic field survey of mission' to ascertain the mission of Jesus and the disciples, which reveals his concept of mission.

The Evangelist's reflective quotations of the Old Testament are another missional aspect of the Gospel. The Evangelist's referential use of the Old Testament is one of the arguments utilized in the study of the Fourth Gospel to determine if it is a Hellenistic Gospel or a Hebrew one. Beasley-Murray (1999, [xxxii]) notes the dispute saying, 'Whereas many scholars have spoken of it as the gospel for the Greek world, others have seen it as firmly rooted in Judaism by upholding the good news of Christ among Christians from the Synagogue'. One possible solution for this problem is to look at this from a missional perspective. In his study on the apostle Paul's use of the Old Testament, Jung (2010) proposes a shift of focus from Paul as a theologian or Bible interpreter to Paul as an intercultural communicator. He insists that 'biblical books are missional phenomena not only because they were written in missional context but also because, more specifically, the biblical authors' formulation and communication of the messages vividly reflect their missionary communicative, rhetorical strategies for achieving their missional agenda' (317). Moloney (2002a, 648) extends this perspective into the whole story of Jesus in the Fourth Gospel, saying, '[t]he Gospel of John told the old story of Jesus in a radically different fashion without betraying the roots of the original

Christian tradition … One of the reasons for these remarkable differences, might I suggest, was an awareness of the new world into which Jesus' story had to be announced'.

Shaping a Missional Hermeneutic for Reading the Fourth Gospel

An Interpretive Lens and Guiding Questions

I have discussed that a missional hermeneutic is a valid framework for reading the Bible, and also the Fourth Gospel is worthy of being read with a missional hermeneutic. In this section, I will discuss a missional hermeneutic particularly for reading the Fourth Gospel. I have introduced the four 'streams' of a missional hermeneutic identified by Hunsberger (see 2.2.3). I agree with Dean Flemming (2011, 6) that '[a]lthough all four of these "streams" are relevant to missional interpretation, the first two seem to be foundational'. Hunsberger (2016, 66) points out that the first two are 'more located in the text', while the other two are 'more located in the readers'. The first two are 1) the missional direction of the story and 2) the missional purpose of the writings. Flemming observes that the former 'reads Scripture as a witness to the gracious mission of the triune God' (2016, 213), which 'relates to what Scripture is *about*' (2011, 6), while the latter 'asks how the biblical writings function to equip and energize God's people to participate in the *missio Dei*' (2016, 213), which 'concerns what Scripture *does*' (2011, 6). Joel Green, who reads James missionally, points out as follows:

> From this perspective, we are encouraged to read James within the context of the Christian Scriptures, guided by a different set of questions – especially these two: How does the letter of James locate its readers within the scriptural narrative of God's mission? How might James's letter shape its readers in their formation as participants in God's mission?

In this study, I will consider Hunsberger's first two 'streams' of a missional hermeneutic as foundational viewpoints for reading the Gospel. One is reading the Gospel in the context of the grand narrative of the Bible, and the other is reading it with an equipping aspect in mind. The questions or themes raised from my missional journey were relationship, missional identity and self-initiative. According to the Hunsburger's categorization, those themes constitute my 'locatedness' for reading the given text. Rather than establishing a third viewpoint with those themes, however, I will include them in the two perspectives already mentioned. Before each viewpoint is discussed, I highlight two prerequisites to the viewpoints.

First, Jesus should be an interpretive lens in this reading of the Gospel since the Gospel always has Jesus as the focus of its discourse. For instance, Flemming (2011, 15) explores how Paul's letter to the Philippians shapes and equips 'its readers for their missional calling in the world'. That is what Scripture *does* in his explanation above, which relates to the missional purpose of the writings. However, the Gospels – the Fourth Gospel for this study – account for the life and public ministry of Jesus on earth including his interaction with his disciples. It means that studying how Jesus shapes and equips his discipleship community has to precede searching how the Gospel does the same for its readers. The latter can be an application or implication of the former.

The Gospel could be seen as an interpretation of the grand narrative of the Hebrew Bible (a witness of God's mission) and of the newly formed community (equipping them for God's mission) as viewed through a lens the Evangelist acquired from Jesus Christ, or more precisely, using Jesus himself as the lens. Schneiders (1999, 35) uses John 5:39[9] for her insistence that 'Jesus is the hermeneutical key to their [Jewish Scriptures] meaning'. The contemporary Jews of Jesus' day, including the Jewish disciples, interpreted the grand narrative without Christ. In the Fourth Gospel, Jesus pointed out the problem of the Jews regarding the reading of the Scripture in that way, saying, 'You study the Scriptures diligently because you think that in them you have eternal life. These are the very Scriptures that testify about me' (5:39). Those who read Scripture without Christ had a problem not in what they were reading but how they were reading. It was a matter of their lens and their interpretation. Barrett (1978, 268) supports the idea of Jesus as the lens for the reading, saying, '[t]he fact is that Jesus illuminates the Old Testament more than the Old Testament illuminates him'. In a sense, Jesus is not only the lens through which Scripture is to be read but also an interpreter himself. This Christ-centred and *Christotelic* (Kelly, 2010, 62) reading of what was already known in the grand narrative and in the new community enabled the Evangelist to write with new understanding. Kelly (2010, 76) emphasizes this aspect, saying, 'Missional hermeneutics aids biblical theology from falling into a merely descriptive undertaking, reminding those engaging in biblical theology of the necessity of other perspectives and other voices in seeing *how* Jesus functions as the center of the Scripture'. In a missional reading of the Fourth Gospel, the recognition of Jesus as the interpretive lens is key to understanding both Jesus' revealing of the will of the Father and his encounters with the Jews, individuals and his discipleship community.

Secondly, the two viewpoints of a missional hermeneutic, a grand narrative view and an equipping view, should be guiding questions rather than fixed frameworks for reading the text. The 'proof-text' way of reading is just one step away from a missional reading. The moment a person merely uses those two viewpoints (or any others) as a solid framework and then searches only to

---

9 'You diligently study the Scriptures because you think that by them you possess eternal life. These are the Scriptures that testify about me'.

see how the themes in the given text fit the framework, that person has surrendered to a 'proof-text' methodology in another sense. The perspectives or viewpoints are intended for readers to keep in mind in the process of reading the given text rather than providing blinders. Gorman (2009a, 156) suggests five key questions that 'readers operating with a missional hermeneutic will want to ask of the biblical text and themselves' as follows:

> What does this text say, implicitly or explicitly, about the *missio Dei* and the missional character of God?
>
> What does this text reveal about humanity and the world?
>
> What does this text say about the nature and mission of God's people in the world, that is, about the church understood as an agent of divine mission rather than as an institution, civic organization, or guardian of Christendom?
>
> How does this text relate to the larger scriptural witness, in both testaments, to the *missio Dei* and the mission of God's people?
>
> In what concrete ways might we deliberately read this text as God's call to us as the people of God to participate in the *missio Dei* to which it bears witness?

In short, a missional hermeneutic of this study attempts to read the Fourth Gospel with viewpoints of a grand narrative and an equipping of the discipleship community through Jesus as an interpretive lens. In the next two sections, I will examine those two viewpoints of a missional reading.

A Grand Narrative Viewpoint

First of all, one of the most critical components of the hermeneutical framework is a grand narrative view of the Bible. The grand narrative provides a backbone and a big picture of the whole Bible and also relates to the missional direction of the Bible. The Gospels and letters in the New Testament could be described as a new exegesis of the grand narrative through the interpretive lenses of those writers, and the Fourth Gospel is no exception.

Then, what is the grand narrative view for reading the Bible missionally? The traditional and typical grand narrative structure of the Bible has been described as encompassing four elements: creation, fall, redemption and restoration (or consummation). Among those four elements, fall and redemption have been emphasized excessively compared to the other two. The selective emphasis has caused a reductionism of Christianity, plunging it into a private realm, placing the focus on individuals and making mission a matter of just soul-winning and, therefore, very task-oriented. It is necessary to emphasize the other elements equally. Further, the grand narrative elements need to be redefined from a missional perspective. Some have suggested looking at the grand narrative of the Bible from a missional point of view, which elevates the narrative approach above the four elements model. N. T.

Wright (2013a, 122) reads the grand narrative as a five-act model: creation, fall, Israel, Jesus and the church, while Bartholomew and Goheen (2004b) explain the grand narrative with six acts: creation, sin, Israel, Jesus, mission and new creation. Chris Wright (2006, 61–68) identifies five elements of the Bible, each having a mission, which collectively emphasize 'God's mission'. Those five elements are God (with a mission), humanity (with a mission), Israel (with a mission), Jesus (with a mission) and the church (with a mission). Referring to those grand narrative elements introduced by various scholars, I suggest that the grand narrative in a missional reading of the Fourth Gospel can be viewed as a God-initiated story with five different elements: creation, fall, Israel, Jesus and new community. The expression, 'God-initiated' means that God is not just an element in the narrative but the one who owns and initiates the whole story.

The first element, *creation*, could include many different meanings in the grand narrative. In the missional narrative of the Bible, it could mean God's creation purpose, which is still relevant for God's people and needs to be recovered. Goheen (2011, 25) points out that God's people need to 'look *backward* to creation, embodying God's original design and intention for human life'. The importance of the creation purpose in a missional reading would be validated since the goal of mission is not to go back to the stage of creation but to fulfil the original purpose of creation.

The second element, *fall*, reveals the brokenness of the relationship between God and all humanity. This alienation between God and the world caused God to start the redemptive and recovery work for the world, but the whole mission of God is greater than the redemptive work. The element of *fall* in a missional reading needs to be viewed as a blockage that prevents humanity from understanding 'heavenly things' (John 3:12) rather than simply as something from which to be restored.

The third element, *Israel*, has its position as a chosen community in the grand narrative since God chose or, more precisely, *formed* (cf Isa 43:1) the nation Israel for his purpose. Goheen (2011, 25–26) describes the obligation of Israel as follows:

> To be a distinctive people displaying an attractive lifestyle to God's glory before the surrounding nations, Israel was obliged to face in three directions at once: to look *backward to creation*, embodying God's original design and intention for human life; *forward to the consummation*, bearing in its life God's promise of the goal of universal history, a restored humanity on a new earth; and *outward to the nations*, confronting the idolatry of the nations for whose sake it had been chosen.

The fourth element, *Jesus,* is more than an episode in the grand narrative. Unlike the other elements, Jesus needs to be viewed as the fulfilment of the first three and the creator of the fifth – the new community. The relationship between Jesus and the other elements is also found in the Fourth Gospel. The

Word, *Jesus*, is the one '[t]hrough [whom] all things were made; without him nothing was made that has been made' (1:3). He is not introduced as the creator itself, but he is the agent through whom God the Father created all things (cf 1 Cor 8:6; Heb 1:2). With regard to *fall*, he is introduced as 'the Lamb of God, who takes away the sin of the world' (1:29). Further, he is the life-giver for the world: 'In him was life, and that life was the light of all mankind' (1:4), and he came that people 'may have life, and have it to the full' (10:10). Regarding his relationship with *Israel*, Jesus is confessed as 'the King of Israel' by Nathanael (1:49) and described as 'the King of the Jews' by Pilate (19:19). Smalley (1978, 60) insists that '[f]or him [John] Jesus is the true Israel, through whom Judaism is transformed and universalised'. At the end of the Gospel, Jesus is sending the disciples (20:21). It signifies that Jesus relates to the fifth element of the narrative – *Jesus* and *new community*. By this reasoning, Jesus functions not only as the fourth element of the narrative but also as the hermeneutical lens for all the elements. That Jesus-view of things will eventually provide a new identity for the contemporary readers as a new community in Christ.

The fifth element of the grand narrative, *new community*, which was formed by Jesus and sent by him, is revealed as the discipleship community in the Gospel, then expanded beyond the community (cf Acts 2:41; 6:7).

The grand narrative, with those five elements in it, will provide a diachronic context in which the Fourth Gospel is read and interpreted. It will also provide a broader and more coherent perspective through which the Gospel narratives are seen as a continuation of certain themes rather than as detached iterations. For instance, from the grand narrative viewpoint, creation-related narratives (1:3; 1:19–2:11; 20:19–23) of the Gospel are seen as a coherent story rather than isolated episodes, enabling readers to see the new community as a new creation. Another example is Jesus' encounters with the Jews. The grand narrative viewpoint allows these to be read not merely as a conflict between Jesus and the Jews or between a hypothetical contemporary Christian community and the Jews. Instead, they are seen as Jesus' comments to the Jews on the proper identity of chosen people and his teachings on that to the new community.

The missional hermeneutic I propose in this research is an approach that comes from outside the Fourth Gospel rather than one developed from the text of the Gospel itself. As I noted in the previous chapter (1.5.1), both Okure and Gorman chose the latter approach. Their differences are that Okure developed a pattern from the Samaritan episode (4:1–42) and applied that pattern to the whole Gospel, while Gorman chose a theme, 'missional theosis' from the Gospel, and explored the presence of that theme throughout the Gospel. Despite seeming to be inductive, even this approach is in danger of becoming a deductive process of imposing a pre-formulated missional hermeneutic onto the given text. I chose to follow the approach commended by Chris Wright (2009a, 38), namely to read the Gospel itself 'within its canonical context in the flow of the Bible'. This approach does not control the given text with a fixed pattern, does not create a grid into which the Gospel must fit, but does provide a boundary within the wider canonical context. If one assumes that the Gospel was written only in response to its immediate historical context, then a purely deductive approach would hold validity. However, the Gospel, from the outset, responds to its immediate historical context by referring back to the wider canonical context through allusion to Old Testament texts, themes and characters. Thus, I have developed a potential missional hermeneutic drawn from the wider canonical context and will seek to show that it can help us understand the Gospel missionally.

An Aspect of Equipping a Discipleship Community

The second viewpoint for reading the Gospel is its equipping aspect. This is based on the assumption that the Bible is the product of mission. Howard Marshall (2004, 34–35) addresses this aspect as follows:

> New Testament theology is essentially missionary theology. By this I mean that the documents came into being as the result of a two-part mission, first, the mission of Jesus sent by God to inaugurate his kingdom with the blessings that it brings to people and to call people to respond to it, and then the mission of his followers called to continue his work by proclaiming him as Lord and Savior, and calling people to faith and ongoing commitment to him, as a result of which his church grows. The theology springs out of this movement and is shaped by it, and in turn the theology shapes the continuing mission of the church. The primary function of the documents is thus to testify to the gospel that is proclaimed by Jesus and his followers.

N.T. Wright (2016, 176) points out that 'the purpose of the New Testament emerges from the entire missional agenda of the early church'. Darrell Guder (2007, 108) maintains that '[t]he actual task of these scriptures [he refers to the New Testament, particularly the Epistles], then, was to deal with the problems and the conflicts, the challenges and the doubts as they emerged in particular contexts, so that these communities could be faithful to their calling'. The Scriptures, particularly the books in the New Testament, are written to equip their readers to be a witnessing community. Thus, the question of how the given text contributes to shaping and equipping its readers to participate in God's mission is a key aspect of a missional reading. Then, how does this aspect need to be applied in this study?

As I mentioned earlier, the Fourth Gospel – the Synoptics as well – should stand in contrast from the Epistles with regard to the second question. Since the Epistles speak directly to the recipients, they perform this shaping and equipping function directly. Thus, the question about how the text functions to equip its readers naturally becomes an important aspect in reading the text. Guder (2007, 108) points out that '[t]he Epistles carry out this formation through direct engagement with the challenges arising out of the contexts of the addressed communities'. I agree with his statement that 'the Gospels are about the same fundamental task' (108), but I do not agree that the Gospels 'are carrying out this formation of witnessing communities as they engage congregations that are already shaped by Easter' (108). One does not need to buy into views around a specific community, the Johannine community in particular, in order to reflect on how the story of Jesus told by the Evangelist was designed to shape early Christian witness. Specifying the recipient community or even viewing the text from the perspective of the community is likely to distort the Gospel intentions and is not the way of a missional reading. Byers (2017, 3) points out that the focus should not be 'on the community that produced John's Gospel, but on the sort of community John's Gospel seeks to produce'.

I view that the Gospels, the Fourth Gospel in particular, carry out the formation by describing the way Jesus himself formed the disciples. Guder addresses this point, saying, '[t]he story begins with the earthly ministry of Jesus, with the invitation for us to join the disciples as they respond to Jesus' summons to "follow me." In this preparation of disciples to become apostles, missional formation is happening in the Gospels' (108). For this reason, the second question in a missional reading of the Fourth Gospel should be: How does Jesus engage, shape, and equip his disciples? The study about how the Gospel does the same for its readers can be an application or an implication of the reading rather than a guiding factor for a missional reading itself.

In short, a missional reading of the Fourth Gospel includes an equipping viewpoint in a way that accounts for how Jesus shapes and equips his disciples to participate in God's mission. Jesus' ministry as the interpretation of the story of God, his encounters with the Jews, and his interactions with individuals all function for the equipping of the disciples as a new missional community.

Chapter Summary

In this chapter I have discussed an approach for reading the Fourth Gospel. It is a missional hermeneutic. I have demonstrated how this approach could be justified as a valid one for reading the text. It has its basis in the fact that the Bible is the product of mission. This indicates two aspects. One is that the Bible reveals the mission of God and the other is that it originated in missional circumstances to shape and equip its readers to participate in the mission of God. I have also argued that the Fourth Gospel is worth reading with the approach discussed since it is a part of the grand narrative of God's mission, and I proposed a few characteristics of it.

Finally, I have presented what I mean by a missional hermeneutic, particularly for reading the Fourth Gospel. I proposed two dimensions of it. One is a grand narrative viewpoint. The Gospel will be read from this point of view. Since the Evangelist begins the Gospel with a grand narrative to provide background to the incarnate Word, the viewpoint will provide a valid position for reading the text. The other is an equipping aspect of the Gospel for its readers. I pointed out that studying how Jesus shapes and equips his disciples precedes searching how the Gospel does the same for its readers. In this respect, I insisted that Jesus should be an interpretive lens for examining those two dimensions. Furthermore, the missional hermeneutic I proposed should not be a fixed framework but rather guiding questions for a reader to keep in mind in the process of reading the text.

The two guiding questions would be: 1) What does the Gospel reveal about the mission of God and the missional God through Jesus? and 2) What does the Gospel reveal about Jesus' shaping and equipping of his disciples? These guiding questions will illuminate the Gospel allowing the main themes to be exposed. I anticipate that the themes raised during my missional journey will be included in them since the Gospel reveals the relationship between the Father and the Son, and also between the Son and his disciples. The missional identity issue will be exposed through Jesus' shaping and equipping of his disciples. I believe all of those findings from a missional reading of the Gospel will contribute to the biblical understanding of mission.

PART II

A MISSIONAL ANALYSIS OF THE FOURTH GOSPEL

Preconditions for a Missional Reading of the Fourth Gospel

In Part II, the Fourth Gospel will be analysed from a missional point of view. In doing this, several preconditions need to be considered.

First, the study refers to the Fourth Gospel as it is in the final text.[1] It has been suggested by various scholars that certain parts of the text have been added and edited later. While not denying the possibility of early editions of the text, it is my intention to focus on the current accepted text (NA28) as a complete and coherent story, which is now called John's Gospel, rather than see the Gospel as a less coherent collection of different stories. As Culpepper (1983, 5) put it, this study will focus on 'analysis and interpretation rather than upon the construction of hypotheses or critique of methods'.[2] For instance, I include the episode of 'an adulterous woman' in 7:53–8:11. I am aware that the story is not found in some early manuscripts.[3] Nevertheless, I will treat the

---

[1] By the 'text', I mean what is recorded in NA28 for the Greek Bible. I also refer to NIV for the English Bible, and New Korean Revised Version (NKRV) for the Korean Bible.

[2] He insists that the subject of his book, *Anatomy of the Fourth Gospel* (1983), is 'the gospel as it stands rather than its sources, historical background, or themes' (5). I see that this missional reading shares a similar perspective with his approach even though the angle might be different. Phillips (2006, 3) says that 'whatever position is taken on reading as retrieval or creation of meaning, the text is still a given to be encountered by the reader'.

[3] Michaels (2010, 461) observes that 'the passage is omitted by the earliest papyri (P^{66} and P^{75}), by the earliest of the parchment manuscripts (א, B, L, W, Θ, and most others), and by the old Syriac and some of the old Latin and Coptic versions. It appears first in so-called "Western" manuscripts (the fifth-century Codex Beza [D] and most of the Latin versions), and then comes to be rather consistently present in the majority of later manuscripts and versions'. Many commentaries include the episode, yet treat it

story as an integral part of the Gospel in its present place not because I stand on any side of the textual criticism but because this study is a missional reading of the text found in the Bibles to which I refer.[4] Michaels (2010, 461) points out that 'because it has been considered an integral part of John's Gospel for so many centuries, and has been routinely included in English versions (often in brackets, which I have used as well), it has become very familiar to modern readers'.[5]

Chapter 21 of the Gospel is another case. Scholars have disputed whether it is an epilogue[6] or a later addition to the original text,[7] and whether it is written by the Evangelist or someone who edited the text later.[8] Regardless of the merits of the dispute, the chapter will not be treated as an addition to the text in the analysing process. Instead, it will be considered as part of the complete text. After examining three main conclusions on the issue,[9] Minear (1983, 98) concludes that 'in the original design of the Gospel the last two verses of chapter 20 served only as the conclusion of that chapter and that the last chapter served as the conclusion of the entire document'. This view is naturally connected to the second precondition – the authorship of the Gospel.

I do not designate any specific person or community as the author of the Gospel. It is not the purpose of the study to find the person or the community that produced the Gospel. Whether it has been written by a single person or by several people through the ages, I argue that they – if there are several – all share the consistency and same direction rather than each of them bringing

---

independently, Brown (1966, 332–38) and Schnackenburg (1980b, 162–68) with a subtitle, 'A Non-Johannine Interpolation', Barrett (1978, 589–92) as an appendix, Carson (1991, 333–37) as an excursus, and Lincoln (2005, 524–36) as an appendix. Phillips (2013): 'The Woman Caught in Adultery: Nameless, Partnerless, Defenceless' in Character Studies in the Fourth Gospel, (WUNT 314, Mohr Siebeck, 2013, 407–21)

[4] Most of the Bible versions include the episode even though they place it in brackets or in smaller size font, NA28 in double brackets, NIV in smaller size font, and New Korean Revised Version (NKRV) in single brackets.

[5] Michaels (2010, 493–500) addresses the larger section (7:37–8:30) in two ways: one without the story and the other with it as an excursus. In the excursus, he treats the story not as an independent episode but as a part of the larger section.

[6] Lincoln (2005, 508) insists that 'it should be seen as an integral part of the final form, as the Gospel's epilogue, and not simply as material that was attached to it much later'.

[7] Brown (1970, 1078) says 'the clear termination seems to preclude any further narrative'. Barrett (1978, 577) says 'Ch 20 is a unit which needs no supplement'.

[8] Brown (1966, xxiv) says Ch 21 'differs from the rest of the Gospel in small stylistic details that betray difference of authorship'.

[9] Minear (1983, 86) summarizes three main positions on the issue as follows: 1) 'There is no manuscript evidence whatsoever that the Gospel of John was ever circulated without chapter 21'. 2) 'Scholars must raise the question whether the vocabulary of chapter 21 is homogeneous with that of the earlier chapters'. 3) 'Scholars examine the grammatical habits and style of the chapter to see if there is substantial divergence from the rest of the gospel'.

their own agenda to the Gospel. As Newbigin stated (1982, xiii), '[o]ne should rather ask what is the purpose for which the evangelist both brings this witness before us and refuses to identify him by more than the repeated statement that Jesus loved him'. Since the purpose of the study is to read the Gospel from a missional perspective rather than seeking to uncover what the hidden agenda of the possible author or authors might be, the text will not be read from any specific author's perspective.

Thirdly, the study is not going to analyse the text from an assumed context such as a 'two-level drama'[10] or a 'polemic and apologetic' perspective.[11] It is correct to say that any given text has been written in a certain context, not in a vacuum. Therefore, it is acceptable to analyse a text and interpret the contemporary context based on the message obtained through the text analysis but not vice versa. In other words, I am going to read the final version of the text and not get involved with various theories of how the text ended up in this state. If we regard the Bible as just a record of a certain community's hidden agenda, it would be a complete disregard for the Bible as it stands. Barth (1956, I.2, 473) points out that 'what we hear in the human expression is more than a human expression. What we hear is revelation, and therefore the very Word of God'.

Structure of the Gospel for a Missional Reading

The most popular analysis for the structure of the Fourth Gospel is the one Beasley-Murray (1999, xc) suggests, dividing the Gospel into four parts as follows: 'after the prologue of 1:1–18 an account is given of the public ministry of Jesus to the end of chap. 12; the latter half of the Gospel portrays the last week of the life of Jesus, including his ministry to the disciples in the Upper Room, his arrest, trial, death, and resurrection, and an epilogue in chap. 21'.[12] Carson (1991, 105–08) slightly modifies it dividing the second part into two sections.[13] Dodd (1963b, 289) has a different analysis of the structure of the Gospel. He sees the first chapter of the Gospel as 'The Proem', and divides the rest of the Gospel into two parts. The first part, he calls 'The Book of Signs

[10] Martyn (2003).

[11] Brown (1979).

[12] Beasley-Murray (1999, xci-xcii) entitled them Prologue (1:1–18), Public Ministry of Jesus (1:19–12:50), The Passion and Resurrection of Jesus (13:1–20:31), and Epilogue (21:1–25)'. Köstenberger (2004, 10–11) calls them as 'Prologue (1:1–18), The Book of Signs (1:19–12:50), The Book of Glory (13:1–20:31), and Epilogue (21:1–25).

[13] The Prologue (1:1–18), Jesus' Self-Disclosure in Word and Deed (1:19–10:42), Transition: Life and Death, King and Suffering Servant (11:1–12:50), Jesus' Self-Disclosure in His Glory and Exaltation (13:1–20:31), and Epilogue (21:1–25).

(2:1–12:50)', and the second part 'The Book of the Passion (13:1–20:31 or 21:25)'.[14]

As to the structure of the Gospel, however, I have found that Michaels' analysis (2010, 30–37) has something in common with the structure that I will propose. He divides the Gospel into five parts as follows (36):

> PREAMBLE (1:1–5).
> THE TESTIMONY OF JOHN (1:6–3:30), with a transition on the lips of John (3:31–36) corresponding to the preamble.
> JESUS' SELF-REVELATION TO THE WORLD (4:1–12:43), with a transition this time on the lips of Jesus (12:44–50).
> JESUS' SELF-REVELATION TO THE DISCIPLES (13:1–16:33), with a much longer transition in the form of Jesus' prayer to the Father (17:1–26).
> VERIFICATION OF JESUS' SELF-REVELATION IN HIS ARREST, CRUCIFIXION, AND RESURRECTION (18:1–21:25).

It is interesting that he reads the first five verses only as 'preamble' and the Baptist's testimony as a separate part in his structure analysis. However, I read the first chapter of the Gospel together with the Cana story in the following chapter as the first part of its structure (1:1–2:12). The Cana story completes the first part of the Gospel as an introduction of the entire Gospel revealing the formation of the new community.

Then, the second part employs the feasts as the background plot structure from the first Passover to the beginning of the last Passover (2:13–12:50). In this part, Jesus encounters the Jews mainly in Jerusalem and Judea, and partly in Galilee. At the same time, Jesus interacts with individuals. It shows Jesus' mission to continue his Father's work as Jesus said: 'to do the will of him who sent me and to finish his work' (John 4:34). Those encounters and interactions function as an education for the disciples about the identity and the scope of the new community Jesus forms.

The similarity between what Michaels suggests and what I propose is found in the following two parts. I read the next five chapters (13:1–17:26) as Jesus revealing something to his disciples. From a missional point of view, I read this third part as the *equipping of the new community*. Jesus is teaching the characteristics of God's mission to the disciples. The narrative in this third part follows the pattern of the 'sign' narratives of the previous part. An action is performed by Jesus, then a related discourse follows. The uniqueness of the action in this part is that the disciples are required to follow the example of Jesus.

Then, the last part includes the passion narrative and the last chapter of the Gospel not as an appendix but as a confirmation of the mission (18:1–21:25). The mission of the new community commissioned by Jesus begins where the

---

[14] He sees the final chapter (21) of the Gospel as an 'appendix'.

Gospel ends. The preceding discussions provide the following structure of the Fourth Gospel in this study:

1. A JOHANNINE GRAND NARRATIVE (1:1–2:12).
2. ENCOUNTERING THE JEWS AND INTERACTING WITH INDIVIDUALS (2:13–12:50).
3. EQUIPPING THE DISCIPLESHIP COMMUNITY (13:1–17:26).
4. THE ACCOMPLISHMENT OF JESUS AND THE COMMISSIONING OF THE DISCIPLESHIP COMMUNITY (18:1–21:25).

3. A Johannine Grand Narrative (1:1–2:12)

Introduction

In this chapter, the first part of the Fourth Gospel (1:1–2:12) will be discussed as a grand narrative setting out a missional agenda for the whole Gospel. The first part of the Gospel is an introduction to the rest of the Gospel.[1] Dodd (1963b, 292) calls Chapter One of the Gospel 'a proem' and divides it into two parts, 'Prologue' (vv1–18) and 'Testimony' (vv19–51). From a grand narrative perspective, the part flows naturally without any division regarding the storyline. Newbigin (1982, 1) points out that '[t]here is no break, in the Gospel as it now stands, between verses 18 and 19 [of the chapter]'. Smalley (1978, 96) also remarks that 'John 1 *in toto*, it is being claimed, provides an important introduction to the Fourth Gospel; as a unity in itself, this chapter is intimately related to the rest of John, and has a vital part to play in the Gospel's careful over-all structuring'.

The first part of the Gospel sets out, in Johannine terms, a missional grand narrative. The narrative begins with an introduction to who the Word is in relation to God. This Word, who later becomes incarnate, plays a central role in all following events, which include Creation, Incarnation, and the formation of a discipleship community. For this reason, the first statement in the Gospel holds the key to understanding the whole Gospel in terms of a missional reading.[2] I will discuss this statement in Section 3.2. Section 3.3 will examine how the foundational statement relates to the following three events: Creation (v3), Incarnation (v14) and Formation of a discipleship community (vv37–39). A man sent from God, John the Baptist, also plays a significant role. Therefore, it is essential to understand how John the Baptist is used in those episodes. I

---

[1] For the introductory role of the first part of the Gospel, Phillips (2006, 5) insists that 'the Prologue actually operates as part of the frame, part and parcel of the Gospel which it begins'. On the contrary, Harris (1994) and Genette (1997) read the Prologue from outside of the frame.

[2] Beasley-Murray (1992, 1867) points out that 'the Prologue may be seen as *an anticipatory description of the Mission of the Logos-Son to the World*, in preparation for the extended exposition of the theme in the Gospel'.

will discuss the Baptist in section 3.4. In section 3.5, the formation of the new community will be examined through the Cana story.

The Foundation of the Grand Narrative

Ἐν ἀρχῇ ἦν ὁ λόγος

Ἐν ἀρχῇ ἦν ὁ λόγος, καὶ ὁ λόγος ἦν πρὸς τὸν θεόν, καὶ θεὸς ἦν ὁ λόγος (John 1:1, NA28).[3] The first statement of the Gospel provides essential information about ὁ λόγος (the Word). Although the Greek noun λόγος is used 40 times in the Gospel, only four refer to the Word as an existing being.[4] Three of them appear in the first statement and the fourth in verse 14 in the first chapter. In verse 14, ὁ λόγος becomes flesh, then the noun is complemented by μονογενοῦς παρὰ πατρός (one and only Son who came from the Father, NIV)[5] and later in verse 17 by Jesus, the Christ/the Anointed One. Therefore, in order to understand the use of λόγος, it is necessary to examine the first statement where λόγος appears three times. It is essential to understand the first statement because it lays the foundation for the whole of the first part, which lays the foundation for the whole Gospel. The three repetitions of ὁ λόγος in the statement appear within three different clauses, and all of them are used with the verb εἰμί[6] (to be). The first two verbs are intransitive meaning 'to exist' while the third one functions as a link between two nouns.[7] Kanagaraj (2005, 35) observes that the εἰμί in those three clauses respectively 'implies the eternal *existence* of the Word', 'denotes His eternal *relationship* with God', and 'exhibits the *identification* of the Word as God'. Since the clauses provide important information on ὁ λόγος, the statement will be discussed clause by clause in this section to understand ὁ λόγος in relation to God.

The statement starts with the first clause: ἐν ἀρχῇ ἦν ὁ λόγος (in the beginning was the Word). The opening ἐν ἀρχῇ recalls the first words of the book of Genesis.[8] In spite of the parallel between those two, there are also

---

[3] All Greek Scripture quotations are taken from *Novum Testamentum Graece*. 28th Edition (NA28) unless otherwise noted, Stuttgart: Deutsche Bibelgesellschaft. 2012.

[4] After exploring the normative form of λόγος in the Fourth Gospel, Phillips (2006, 82) points out that those four 'are references to Hebrew Bible understandings of the "Word of God"' and 'all other uses fit the general category of expressing what someone has taught or said'.

[5] The Greek phrase itself can be interpreted as 'the unique one from the Father'.

[6] ἦν in the text, the imperfect indicative third person singular form of εἰμί.

[7] Like the 'to be' in English, the Greek εἰμί also has two different meanings or functions. One is just a linking function called copulative and the other is an intransitive verb meaning 'to exist'. (Black, 1998, 32).

[8] ἐν ἀρχῇ ἐποίησεν ὁ θεὸς τὸν οὐρανὸν καὶ τὴν γῆν (God made the heaven and the earth, LXX).

significant differences between them. First, the Genesis account begins with the creation of the world while the Gospel narrative begins before the world is created. The Johannine opening is unique even when compared to the Synoptics. Flemming (2015, 54) points out that 'John immediately paints God's mission with broad brushstrokes on a cosmic canvas', '[u]nlike Matthew, who opens his Gospel with a Jewish genealogy, or Mark, who introduces Jesus as a fully grown preacher, or Luke, who starts with an extended birth narrative'. The opening of the Fourth Gospel goes further than the Synoptics, stating that the mission of God through his Son can be traced back to the beginning or the source of all things. Secondly, the character present at each of the two beginnings is, on the surface of things, different. God is the subject in Genesis, but the Word is the subject in the Gospel. As Beasley-Murray indicates (1999, 10), 'one expects to read "In the beginning… God"', but the Gospel says 'In the beginning… the Word'. Thirdly, the ἀρχή of Genesis is followed by an acting verb, ποιέω (to make), while it is followed by a being verb εἰμί at the ἀρχή of the Gospel. Michaels (2010, 47) explains the reason saying, '[p]erhaps, this is because God in the book of Genesis needs no introduction. God can be safely presupposed, but the same is not true of the Word in the Gospel of John. The Word must be identified, and can only be identified in relation to God, the God of Israel'.

The use of ἀρχή in Genesis provides a background for God's act of creation. However, the use of ἀρχή in the Fourth Gospel provides the context for what was going on before the world was created focusing on the existence of ὁ λόγος. This Johannine ἀρχή reappears at the end of Jesus' public life on earth (17:5; 17:24). Jesus himself mentions the ἀρχή such as πρὸ τοῦ τὸν κόσμον εἶναι (before the world began, 17:5) and πρὸ καταβολῆς κόσμου (before the creation of the world, 17:24).

In the ἀρχή before the world was created, ὁ λόγος existed. The verb ἦν (εἰμί), which is used for ὁ λόγος, contrasts with the verb ἐγένετο (γίνομαι) in verse 3, πάντα δι' αὐτοῦ ἐγένετο (through him all things were made), which is used for the creatures. According to Kemp (2002, 111), this means that 'in the beginning the Word was already in existence' and '[t]here never was a time when he was not'. This statement is a preparation for the following events in which ὁ λόγος will play a significant role. The three following events in the chapter are Creation (v3), Incarnation (v14) and the formation of a new community (vv37–39). The Evangelist will lead the readers into a deeper understanding of the existence of ὁ λόγος in the ἀρχή through the Gospel, yet the first clause is good enough to draw the attention of various readers. Phillips (2006, 149–50) points out as follows:

> The Johannine text is a multivalent text – different people can read it at different levels. It has been constructed in such a way that it can be read and understood at different levels, by readers experienced in different cultural contexts. So, a reader of Koinē, perhaps ignorant of Jewish scripture, could have understood the phrase

> as a general reference to the existence of λόγος (divine reason?) at the beginning. A reader who knows Genesis could read it as a specific reference to the Jewish creation narrative, and a reader versed in rabbinic teaching could be encouraged to think of the seven things existing before creation in rabbinic tradition. We could then add to these possibilities the multiple intertexts sparked off by the use of λόγος.

To those various readers, the Evangelist provides an explanation of how ὁ λόγος exists in relation to ὁ θεός in the next clause.

Ὁ λόγος ἦν πρὸς τὸν θεόν

The second clause, καὶ ὁ λόγος ἦν πρὸς τὸν θεόν (and the Word was with God) in the statement explains the relationship which ὁ λόγος has with ὁ θεός. It is not easy to understand the relationship since the clause is as awkward in Greek as the literal English translation of it: the Word existed toward God. The awkward part of the clause is ἦν πρός where the stative verb εἰμί is used with the transitive preposition πρός plus the accusative. The combination of the two words, εἰμί and πρός with the accusative make the relationship between ὁ λόγος and ὁ θεός mysterious. Many scholars have noticed the use of the preposition πρός in the sentence.[9] Dalcour (2005, 57), who has researched the use of the preposition πρός, insists that '[t]o highlight the intimate loving fellowship that the Word shared with the Father, the Apostle John specifically used the preposition *pros* in John 1:1b'. Köstenberger (2004, 27) also introduces various scholars' explanations of the preposition πρός as follows:

> The preposition πρός (*pros*, with) indicates place or accompaniment, but also disposition and orientation (Ridderbos 1997: 25 n. 23). What is expressed is "not simple co-existence, but rather the idea of active relationship or intercourse 'with'" (Pollard 1977: 364-65). In terms of relationship, not only does πρός establish a relationship between God and the Word, but also it distinguishes the two from each other (R. Brown 1966: 5).

Newman and Nida (1980, 8) also support the idea saying that 'there existed a mutual and reciprocal relationship between the Word and God'. It is necessary to examine how those two words, εἰμί and πρός are used within the Fourth Gospel to understand what the relationship looks like.

---

[9] Cited from Dalcour's (2005, 57–58, 70–73) book. '*Pros* with the accusative presents a plane of equality and intimacy, face to face with each other' (A. T. Robertson, 1932, *Word Pictures in the New Testament*, 4:4), 'The preposition pros means more than static "with." It has a sense of motion toward the person or thing that follows' (F. J. Moloney, 1998, *The Gospel of John*, 4:35) 'the term [pros] speaks to a personal relationship, in fact, to intimacy'(R. White, 1998, *The Forgotten Trinity: Recovering the Heart of Christian Belief*, 52).

First, the English translation, 'was with' in many Bible versions does not express the meaning of the relationship between ὁ λόγος and ὁ θεός. The reason why the preposition πρός is interpreted as a stative preposition 'with' even though the πρός itself is a transitive preposition is because of the general observation of Greek grammar. Wallace (1996, 359) explains a general principle in Greek: '*[s]tative verbs* ***override*** *the transitive force of prepositions*. Almost always, when a stative verb is used with a transitive preposition, the preposition's natural force is neutralized; all that remains is a stative idea'. However, it is incorrect to apply the general principle to this verse because the internal evidence within the Gospel does not support the general principle. Whenever the stative verb εἰμί needs to take a preposition to express 'to be with' in the Gospel, it takes the preposition μετά followed by a genitive word without any exception.[10] Therefore, ἦν πρός does not simply mean 'was with'.

Secondly, the preposition πρός never occurs with the stative verb εἰμί except on the first two occasions (1:1b; 1:2) in the Gospel.[11] Within the Gospel, the preposition πρός is used 102 times.[12] Out of the 102 occurrences, 98 times are followed by an accusative, and four times with dative. When the preposition is followed by a dative, it has a proximate meaning translated as 'near' or 'beside'.[13] The preposition πρός followed by a dative case is not used in the above clause probably because the meaning of proximity, 'near' or 'beside', does not reveal the relationship between God and the Word. All of the other 98 usages of the preposition are followed by an accusative in the Gospel. When the preposition is used with an accusative, it mainly has a directive meaning such as 'to' or 'toward'. For this reason, the preposition with an accusative word is used together with motion verbs in the Gospel such as ἔρχομαι (to

---

[10] 3:2, 26; 7:33; 8:29; 9:40; 11:31; 12:17; 13:33; 14:9, 16; 15:27; 16:4, 32; 17:12, 24; 18:18; 20:24. There are two more prepositions expressing 'with' in the Gospel, σύν (with dative, 12:2; 18:1; 21:3) and παρά (with dative, 1:39; 4:40; 8:38; 14:17, 23, 25; 17:5 (2); 19:25). None of them, however, occurs with the intransitive verb εἰμί in the Gospel. For this reason, Bultmann's suggestion (1971, 32–33, cited in Köstenberger, 2004, 27) that 'ἦν πρός is a Semitism equivalent to παρά plus the dative' is not persuasive, at least in the Gospel of John.

[11] There is one other place which has a similar form where the preposition followed by an accusative is used with the verb εἰμί directly (11:4). αὕτη ἡ ἀσθένεια οὐκ ἔστιν πρὸς θάνατον (this sickness is not toward death). In this case, the prepositional phrase functions as an adjective, so εἰμί is a link rather than intransitive or stative.

[12] The numbers might be slightly different according to the different versions of the Greek text. I refer to NA28.

[13] In the Gospel of John, the preposition πρός followed by a dative case is used with only two static verbs, ἵστημι (to stand, 18:16, 20:11) and καθέζομαι (to sit, 20:12 (2)). Since the εἰμί is also an intransitive or static verb, it could be claimed that the preposition πρός in 1:1b and 1:2 in the Gospel has the proximate meaning as well, regardless of what case is following it (Wallace, 1996, 380). This claim, however, does not explain why the first two prepositions plus accusative words do not follow the other four with dative words and vice versa within the Gospel.

come, 37 times),[14] λέγω (to talk, 19 times),[15] ὑπάγω (to depart, 5 times),[16] and so on.[17] Therefore, if the Evangelist intended to focus on πρός presenting the directive sense of ὁ λόγος toward ὁ θεός, he should use a transitive verb such as 'to come' or 'to talk' rather than the stative verb εἰμί. On the contrary, if he desired to highlight the intimate co-existence of the two by using εἰμί, then he should change the preposition to εἰς plus accusative as in 1:18b, ὁ ὢν[18] εἰς τὸν κόλπον τοῦ πατρὸς ([who] is in closest relationship with Father). The preposition εἰς also has a directive sense, yet provides an intimate place in the sentence. Based on the above internal evidence in the Gospel, it can be summarized that εἰμί μετά with genitive is used to express 'to be with', εἰμί εἰς with accusative shows the intimate togetherness and then εἰμί πρός with the accusative carries a deeper meaning regarding the relationship than the previous two combinations. In this sense, the use of εἰμί πρός in the first two sentences of the Gospel is unique, thus intentional.[19]

Then, how could the relationship be described?

First, it reveals 'oneness' of God and the Word. In the previous clause, it was declared that ὁ λόγος existed before the world was created, and now the Gospel says that the existence of ὁ λόγος is not alone but being together with God. The Word is not just with God, nor even being in the bosom of God but rather being as one without losing its own existence. Carson (1991, 116–117) says that 'the "Word" he [John] is talking about is a person, *with* God and therefore distinguishable from God, and enjoying a personal relationship with him'. Jesus himself testifies to this relationship saying ἐγὼ καὶ ὁ πατὴρ ἕν ἐσμεν (I and the Father are one, 10:30), καθὼς σύ, πάτερ, ἐν ἐμοὶ κἀγὼ ἐν σοί (Father, just as you are in me and I am in you, 17:21) and so on.

---

[14] 1:29, 47; 3:2, 20, 21, 26 (2); 4:30, 40; 5:40; 6:5, 17, 35, 37, 44, 45, 65; 7:37, 45, 50; 8:2; 10:41; 11:19, 29, 45; 13:6; 14:6, 18, 23, 28, 16:7; 17:11, 13; 19:3, 39; 20:2 (2).

[15] 2:3; 3:4; 4:15, 33, 48, 49; 6:5, 28, 34; 7:3, 35, 50; 8:31, 57; 11:21; 12:19; 13:28; 16:17; 19:24.

[16] 7:33; 13:3; 16:5, 11, 17.

[17] ἄγω (to bring, 4 times, 1:42; 9:13; 11:15; 18:13), ἀπέρχομαι (to go after, 4 times, 4:47; 6:68; 11:46; 20:10), πορεύομαι (to travel, 4 times, 14:12, 28; 16:28; 20:17), ἀποστέλλω (to send, 5:33; 11:3; 18:24), ἐξέρχομαι (to go out, 18:29, 38), ἀναβαίνω (to ascend, 20:17 (2)), ἀγαλλιάω (to rejoice, 5:35), κατηγορέω (to accuse, 5:45), ἥκω (to have come, 6:37), μάχομαι (to argue, 6:52), ἀποκρίνομαι (to answer, 8:33), γίνομαι (to come to be, 10:35), πίπτω (to fall, 11:32), ἑλκύω (to draw, 12:32), μεταβαίνω (to depart, 13:1), παραλαμβάνω (to take, 14:3), and πέμπω (to send, 16:7). There are few exceptions, which are not used with motion verbs such as εἰμί (copulative, 4:35; 11:4), τί with omitted εἰμί (copulative, 21:22, 23).

[18] The present participle-nominative singular masculine of the intransitive or static verb εἰμί.

[19] The same usage (εἰμί πρός plus accusative) is found in 1 John 1:2. ἦν πρὸς τὸν πατέρα (was with the Father).

Secondly, it is a perfect doing together or communicating with each other. The directive preposition πρός indicates that the relationship of ὁ λόγος and ὁ θεός is beyond the spatial oneness. Bearing in mind the noun λόγος is derived from the verb λέγω, and considering the frequent use of the verb with πρός within the Gospel, the use of the preposition with the subject λόγος is hardly surprising. Phillips (2006, 152) addresses the issue as follows:

> they [Louw and Nida] also mention the use of πρός with speech verbs to designate the addressee. However, the idea that πρός is used with verbs of speech provides an interesting intertextual diversion in that one could speculate that τὸν θεόν has been attracted into the accusative because of its link with λέγω. However, this begs more questions than it answers – for example, who is doing the speaking? But *Louw-Nida*'s suggestion does raise the possibility that the use of the preposition with the accusative here signals the focus of the subject's attention. In other words, rather than focus on Barrett's harsh concept of proximity, this phrase could suggest a reference to a relationship between λόγος and θεός – "and the Logos was turned towards God". Clearly a first reader of the Gospel will find nothing strange in a simple reference to the presence of "λόγος with God". However, for others the reference here may well suggest a relationship between λόγος and θεός that goes beyond the spatial placement of the two.

Thus, the εἰμί πρός is revealing the integration of intimate being and intimate communicating between ὁ λόγος and ὁ θεός. In this integrated relationship, Jesus declares that he is the only one who knows the will of God (4:34, 5:30, 6:38), who saw the Father (1:18, 6:46, 8:38. cf 14:9) and who is one with God (17:22).

In the previous section, I pointed out that the missional God could be traced back to the Johannine ἀρχή, and the Johannine ἀρχή is a preparation for the following three events. What provides the background is not the ἀρχή itself (left unexplained, with no definite article), but the communicative relationship ὁ λόγος has with ὁ θεός in the ἀρχή. This communicative relationship within the missional Godhead is the foundation for the following events in the Gospel. The relationship is not only a point of departure for the following events but also the goal of the mission of Jesus. Jesus himself mentions the relationship in the ἀρχή that he used to have ἡ δόξα (the glory) with God (17:5)[20] and God loved him (17:24).

Θεὸς ἦν ὁ λόγος

Ὁ λόγος existed before the world was created, and ὁ λόγος has the integral relationship with ὁ θεός regarding being together and doing together.

---

[20] In the Gospel, παρὰ plus dative means 'with' (1:39; 4:40; 8:38; 14:17, 23, 25, 17:5(2)) or 'near' (19:25).

Nevertheless, it has not been clarified what or who ὁ λόγος is. The first two clauses have provided the information about the eternal existence of ὁ λόγος and his relationship with ὁ θεός but not his identity. The third clause provides an answer to the curiosity, καὶ θεὸς ἦν ὁ λόγος (and the Word was God). The answer, however, raises more curiosity about ὁ λόγος. The combination of the two words, εἰμί πρός within a clause (1:1b) is now extended across the clause making the two clauses (1:1b and 1:1c) seem to contradict each other. How can the same λόγος be both 'was with God' and 'was God' at the same time?

The third clause needs to be examined from the Greek grammatical point of view to eliminate various interpretations. First, θεός is not the subject of the clause but a predicate even though it comes before the verb. When two normative words are linked by a linking verb εἰμί and only one has a definite article, the one with a definite article is the subject and the other one without it is the predicate.[21] Therefore, it should be translated as 'the Word was God' not as 'God was the Word'. Secondly, θεός should be emphasized because it comes in front of the clause. Michaels (2010, 47–48) points out that 'the placement of "God," or *theos*, first in its clause, before the verb, gives it a certain definiteness, warning us against reducing it to a mere adjective'. So, it should not be translated as 'the Word was divine', rather θεός needs to be emphasized such as 'it was God that the Word was'.[22] Thirdly, it should be noticed that θεός of the previous clause has a definite article, i.e. ὁ θεός[23] while the one in 1:1c appears without it. Newman and Nida (1980, 9) explain that there are two different types of equational sentences. One indicates 'complete identity'[24] and the other 'the class of persons to which he belongs'[25] and insists that the third clause (1:1c) belongs to the latter. If θεός in the third clause were used with a definite article such as ὁ λόγος ἦν ὁ θεός (the Word was the God [whom he was with]), it would belong to the former, 'complete identity'. In that case, it might mean that 'no divine being could exist apart from the Word' as Carson observes (1991, 117).

The third clause does not mean that the Word is God, the Father (whom he was with), rather it says the Word is God. Phillips (2006, 154) argues that 'Θεός is used here qualitatively, as an anarthrous predicate describing the nature of the subject ὁ λόγος: "In the beginning was λόγος and λόγος was in the company of θεός and λόγος had the nature of θεός"'. The nature of λόγος as θεός strengthens the relationship of the ὁ λόγος with ὁ θεός. By saying that θεὸς ἦν ὁ λόγος, the third clause denies that the relationship of the two is either just an intimacy of different beings or simply that the two are identical. The

---

[21] Black, 1998, 46.

[22] Black, 1998, 46.

[23] τὸν θεόν in the text, the accusative of ὁ θεὸς.

[24] Such as 'John Smith is my husband' where the two parts of the sentence are completely equivalent.

[25] Such as 'John Smith is a teacher' where the teacher just qualifies him.

relationship is the complete oneness of them denying not only the entire identical being of the two but also any separation of them.

Through the first statement, the Gospel shows that the λόγος existed before the world was created, the λόγος has an inseparable integral relationship with God, and the λόγος shares the nature of God. This intimate oneness of ὁ λόγος and ὁ θεός before the world was created is the point of departure for the upcoming events. Barrett (1978, 156) also sees the importance of the first statement in the Gospel saying 'John intends that the whole of his gospel shall be read in the light of this verse. The deeds and words of Jesus are the deeds and words of God; if this be not true the book is blasphemous'.

Considering the integral relationship the Word has with God as expressed in this statement, it might be more accurate to say that the deeds and words of Jesus came out of his relationship with God. Therefore, the first statement of the Gospel lays the foundation for the first part immediately and ultimately for the whole Gospel. The cornerstone of the foundation is the integral relationship between the Word and God. This signifies that *relationship* is key to understanding the mission of God, that 'relationship' and 'oneness' provide the core element of the following three events: Creation, Incarnation and the Gathering of a New Community. I will discuss how the relationship revealed in the foundational statement is related to those events in the next section. Through this discussion, the position of relationship in those Johannine grand narrative themes, that is, the missional story of God, will be clarified.

Relationships Revealed Throughout the Grand Narrative

The Relationship in Creation

How is the integral relationship between the Word and God related to the following first event that appeared in verse 3? The existence of ὁ λόγος and his relationship with ὁ θεός is expressed by the verb εἰμί in the first two verses suggesting description of a state of being. However, in the third verse the verb is changed to γίνομαι, a verb which suggests a process or action initiated by ὁ λόγος (πάντα δι' αὐτοῦ ἐγένετο) (Phillips, 2006, 159). As mentioned above, the divine relationship between the Word and God lays the foundation for the event and is the very basis for it. The relationship in the first statement is reaffirmed in the following verse (1:2), which connects the relationship and the following first activity (1:3). Verse 2, which summarizes the first statement, thus restates the divine relationship in the beginning; it is not merely a 'repetition' of the previous verse. Newman and Nida (1980, 9) point out that 'here he [the Evangelist] is careful to affirm that the two [Word and God] existed simultaneously'. Furthermore, it is to affirm that the Word and God have an intimate relationship. From a semantic perspective, verse 2 functions as the basis for the following sentence in verse 3, which explains that the first event happened through the Word. Carson (1991, 118) says that 'v.2 reiterates the middle clause of v.1, thus prepares the way for v.3'. The relationship reaffirmed in verse 2 alludes to the quality of the two in the event. The first event happened through the Word who had an intimate relationship with God in the beginning.

Then, what is the first event? It has been understood that πάντα δι' αὐτοῦ ἐγένετο (1:3a) refers to *creation*. Brown (1966, 6) says 'from the 2nd century on, this has been taken as a reference to creation'. Phillips (2006, 159-60) points out that 'most lexica and commentators understand this verse as a reference to creation and commonly translate it along the lines: "all things were created through him"'. Phillips goes on to point out that there are different views on the interpretation of the verb. So, Ashton (1986, 170–73), following Lamarche, argues that the verse does not indicate 'creation' but signifies 'the divine plan'. The alternative view relates to how the verb γίνομαι (come into being) in the verse is interpreted. Lamarche (1964, 51) insists as follows:

> If the central perspective of the Prologue is indeed God's universal plan, it is clear that the very wide meaning of his Logos throughout the history of the world, starting of course, from the creation, right up to the incarnation, and including Israel's election and the natural law of the Gentiles. Everything that has happened – the history of salvation as well as the creation – happened through the Logos.

Scholars following the wider meaning of the verb often cite the potential parallel between this verse and a passage in the Dead Sea Scrolls (1QS 11.11).[26] With all of these references, I agree that the verb could be interpreted both 'to create' and 'to happen'. However, as Phillips (2006, 161) points out, 'the author would probably have affirmed that λόγος brings about creation and also governs history', thus 'the readers can make their own choice how to read an ambiguous text'. No one can claim that the verb has the meaning of creation only, nor that there is no reference to creation. The meaning should be decided in the context of the text itself.

My own understanding is that the verb in verse 3 is more likely to refer to creation than to the divine plan for the following reasons.

First, the Evangelist uses the verb with the meaning of 'to create' in a similar context elsewhere in the Prologue. It is right to assert that the verb can be translated as 'to happen' throughout most of its occurrences in the Prologue. However, the verb means 'to create' or 'to make' in verse 10 where ὁ κόσμος

[26] Lamarche (1964, 52) uses that passage as one of his argument supports, Brown (1966, 6) mentions the passage but he adds 'is made' to show the creation connection, Ashton (1986, 171) uses the passage and quotes Pollard saying 'the context of this passage in The Manual of Discipline "has no reference to creation, but rather to the doctrine prominent in the Scrolls, that God is in control of everything, and particularly of human destiny".

replaces πάντα of verse 3 making ὁ κόσμος δι' αὐτοῦ ἐγένετο (the world was made through him). With this reasoning, it is natural to interpret the verb as 'to make' or 'to create' rather than 'to happen' in verse 3.

Secondly, the strong allusion of Genesis creation in the opening of the Gospel provides the creation context of the verb in verse 3. As mentioned above, the opening ἐν ἀρχῇ recalls the first words of the book of Genesis (The same phrase is used in Genesis in LXX). Frey (2016, 210) points out that '[t]he reference to the beginning of the (Greek) Bible is quite obvious in the beginning of John, and readers are immediately led to look for further connections with the creation account in Gen 1'. Lincoln (2005, 98) affirms that 'in the context of the preceding allusion to Gen. 1.1 it is more natural to see a reference to the role of the Word in creation rather than to the Word's providential control of history'.

Thirdly, the verb γίνομαι is used repeatedly in the creation episode in Genesis in LXX.[27] In LXX, the preceding clause of the verb provides contextual support for the creation, so the verb occurs together with καὶ (καὶ ἐγένετο) indicating that things are created as God says, while the verb in John 1:3 does appear neither in the immediate creation context nor with καὶ. With this reasoning, Ashton (2014, 146) argues that '[t]he opening of John 1, 'Ev ἀρχῇ, is unquestionably a reference to the opening of Genesis, but subsequent translators were mistaken when they concluded that what follows must also concern creation'.[28] Since the Genesis creation account is a narrative, it makes sense that the verb appears with καὶ, but the Gospel relates the Logos and creation. Thus, it should be read in a larger context than at a sentence level. Michaels (2010, 51) points out that the use of the verb is 'conspicuous in the LXX of the Genesis account'. By using the 'conspicuous' verb after the parallel context to the Genesis opening, I see that the Evangelist implies 'creation' of all things through the Logos in verse 3. Therefore, it is more reasonable to relate the verb in verse 3 of the Gospel to the creation meaning.

As seen above, verse 3 recalls the creation story in Genesis where God created the world.[29] God is the creator, and the Word is the agent of the creation, through whom all things came to be. The apostle Paul (1 Cor 8:6) describes 'God, the Father' as the one 'from whom all things came', while 'Jesus Christ' is the one 'through whom all things came'. By emphasizing that 'without him nothing was made that has been made' (1:3), the Fourth Gospel enlarges on the role of the Word compared to the same story in Genesis. This emphasis together with the foundation in the previous verse indicates that the Word in creation is not merely an instrument of God. Instead, he is the only

---

[27] Gen 1:3, 5, 8, 9, 11, 13, 15, 19, 20, 23, 24, 30

[28] For the argument between Ashton and Phillips, see Ashton (1986, 171), Phillips (2006, 160–61) and Ashton (2014, 146–47).

[29] Schnackenburg (1980a, 238) thinks that 'all realms of creation owe their existence to the Logos'.

agent of God, and the act of creation is a product of the divine relationship between him and God. The creation episode in the Fourth Gospel is not merely a repetition of the story in Genesis but reveals that all things came into being out of the divine relationship.

In this sense, God's desire, purpose or mission in creation through the Word is his willingness to share the relationship in the divine community with humanity whom he has created in his image (cf Gen 1:26). God's divine community is the permanent prototype and goal for any community formed from creation onward. Johnson (2002, 37) indicates that '[a]t the center of the universe is a community. It is out of that relationship that you and I were created and redeemed. And it is for that relationship that you and I were created and redeemed'. Barth (1960, 218 III.2) also points out:

> God repeats in this relationship *ad extra* a relationship proper to Himself in His inner divine essence. Entering into this relationship, He makes a copy of Himself. Even in His inner divine being there is relationship. To be sure, God is One in Himself. But He is not alone. There is in Him a co-existence, co-inherence and reciprocity. God in Himself is not just simple, but in the simplicity of His essence He is threefold – the Father, the Son and the Holy Ghost. He posits Himself, is posited by Himself, and confirms Himself in both respects, as His own origin and also as His own goal. He is in Himself the One who loves eternally, the One who is eternally loved, and eternal love; and in this triunity He is the original and source of every I and Thou, of the I which is eternally from and to the Thou and therefore supremely I. And it is this relationship in the inner divine being which is repeated and reflected in God's eternal covenant with man as revealed and operative in time in the humanity of Jesus.

The universe has been created from the relationship, through the relationship and for the relationship. From this perspective, the creation 'in the beginning' was not a momentary or one-time event in terms of relationship between God and the creatures. Instead, creation is a start for their ongoing relationship. The *very good* (Gen 1:31) of God in creation includes the relationship with creatures to come. The purpose of creation is not ornamental but relational. For that purpose, the Word has life, which is the light for all humanity. The Word is the perfect agent for the creation act and also for the resulting relationship between God and creatures including humanity because of the relationship he has with God. The Fourth Gospel emphasizes the relational aspect of the creation.

The relational purpose of God in the creation and its missional aspect are expressed more clearly in the treatment of light and darkness (1:4–13). Two terms, τέκνα (children) and ἴδιος (own) in the treatment need to be noted in this respect. First, the term τέκνα θεοῦ in 1:12 implies the relational purpose of God: 'to all who did receive him, to those who believed in his name, he gave the right to become children of God' (1:12). It is true that the right to become the children of God will be given to those who believe in the name of the

Word, Jesus. However, it should be understood that the right to become the children of God is not just a compensation for believing in him, rather it is the recovery of the purpose of creation. God's desire and purpose to have a relationship with creatures are revealed in the term τέκνα θεοῦ. The Word through whom all things were made and without whom nothing was made that has been made (1:3) is reintroduced as the one who gives the right to become the children of God to those who believe in him (1:10–12). The relational purpose revealed in creation by the divine relationship of God and the Word is achieved when the same Word gives the right to the people who believe in him. The Evangelist uses the word τέκνα in two more places in the Gospel. In 8:39, Jesus talks to the Jews: 'If you were τέκνα τοῦ Ἀβραάμ... then you would do what Abraham did'. In this statement, the word τέκνα implies the one who does what his/her father did rather than simply biological children. The Evangelist affirms this by saying that the children of God are 'children born not of natural descent, nor of human decision or a husband's will, but born of God' (1:13). The third usage of the word τέκνα appears in 11:52. Caiaphas, the high priest of the year, says, 'it is better for you [the Jews] that one man die for the people than that the whole nation perish' (11:50). The Evangelist adds his comment saying, 'He did not say this on his own, but as high priest that year he prophesied that Jesus would die for the Jewish nation, and not only for that nation but also for the scattered children of God [τέκνα τοῦ θεοῦ], to bring them together and make them one' (11:51–52). The Evangelist enlarges the meaning of τέκνα inclusively revealing the mission of Jesus, and also pointing out the relational purpose of it.

This inclusive meaning of τέκνα helps readers of the Gospel to understand how the Evangelist uses the second term ἴδιος in the episode. The term is used twice in 1:11. It first appears in neuter form, τὰ ἴδια, and then again in masculine form, οἱ ἴδιοι. Phillips (2006, 188) says, '[w]hile the neuter refers to domain or property belonging to an individual, the masculine plural refers to people owned by an individual'. Since the world was made through the Word (1:10), the neuter form, τὰ ἴδια [his own things] refers to the world. Some scholars[30] see the masculine οἱ ἴδιοι as God's own people, Israel. Considering that ὁ κόσμος did not recognize him in the previous verse (1:10), and the right to become τέκνα θεοῦ is open for all in the following verse (1:12), οἱ ἴδιοι in 1:11 is more naturally linked with all humanity – or at least to Israel as a representative of all humanity – rather than being linked only with Israel. Michaels (2010, 65) claims:

> Just as "the world" in verse 10 was an undifferentiated whole, so there is not distinction here between "what was his own" and what was not, or between "his

---

[30] cf Carson (1991, 124–25), Köstenberger (2004, 37), and Köstenberger lists those who favour this view as follows: Dodd (1953, 402); R. Brown (1966, 10); Morris (1995, 85); Borchert (1996, 114); Burge (2000, 59).

> own people" (Jews, for example) and others who did not belong to the Light. Rather, "what was his own is simply another way of saying "all things," or "the world," while "his own" (masculine) refers generally to "humans" (v. 4), or "every human being" (v. 9) in the world.

He (2010, 67) continues, '[t]he point is that while the Jews are not viewed here as Jesus' "own" in a special sense in which the Gentiles are not, they may be in mind as representatives of the world to which Jesus came, with Judea or Jerusalem as the stage on which the drama of Jesus' confrontation with the world is to take place'. Phillips (2006, 189–90) takes a clearer stance on the issue, saying, 'There is no need to focus this upon the Jewish nation. The condemnation is there for all – it is the world of humanity that has rejected λόγος.... The point of this verse is not necessarily to focus down upon Israel but to draw all people into his possession and to indict all of us with his rejection'. As seen in the previous term τέκνα, the term οἱ ἴδιοι also has both relational and missional implications in it. The term οἱ ἴδιοι shows the relational aspect: the world of humanity is God's possession. It is also missional because the term οἱ ἴδιοι implies all of humanity, either directly (Phillips) or representatively (Michaels).

The Relationship in Incarnation

The second event in the first chapter of the Gospel is the incarnation of the Word (1:14). Καὶ ὁ λόγος σὰρξ ἐγένετο καὶ ἐσκήνωσεν ἐν ἡμῖν (1:14a). The first statement in verse 1 again is the basis for the incarnation of the Word. The previous verses (1:4–13) in the chapter provide a background for the incarnation of the Word. The narrative between creation and incarnation will be discussed in section 3.4. To state it briefly, the world was created through the Word, and the Word was in the world shining his light to the world, yet the world did not recognize him. In that context, the Word became flesh (1:14). The first word καὶ in this verse functions as a conjunction referring to the incarnation as a result of the previous paragraph. Because the world cannot recognize the light of the Word even though it was created through the Word, the Word becomes flesh and dwells in the world.

In the incarnation episode, the 'being together' element is essential to the event. The 'being together' of the incarnate Word with humanity is well expressed by the two terms σάρξ and ἐσκήνωσεν in the statement.

First, the term σάρξ (flesh) reveals that the Word became human. The Word through whom all creatures, including humanity, were created now takes the nature of the created one. Paul describes this as follows: Christ, 'being in very nature God, did not consider equality with God something to be used to his own advantage; rather, he made himself nothing by taking the very nature of a servant, being made in human likeness' (Phil 2:6–7). The intimate relationship of the Word with God revealed in the beginning is now transferred to the relationship with humanity.

Secondly, the term ἐσκήνωσεν reveals another aspect of the relationship. Just as the Word was with God in the beginning, so now the Word is with humanity, dwelling among us, pitching his tent in our backyard. Bernard (1929, cxlv) insists that 'He became Incarnate, not as a momentary Epiphany of the Divine, but as an abiding and visible exhibition of the Divine Glory'. The verb ἐσκήνωσεν (made his dwelling) in verse 14 is derived from the Greek verb σκηνόω. It means 'to tabernacle' or 'to tent' referring to the Old Testament 'tabernacle' which God asked Moses to build (Exod 25:8–9) and which Moses called the 'tent of meeting' (Exod 33:7). The Evangelist uses the verb only once in the Gospel[31] while he uses another verb μένω (stay) in most cases to express 'to stay'. Coloe (2001, 23) points out that 'the use of the word σκηνόω draws attention to many older traditions of God's presence dwelling in Israel'. N. T. Wright (2002a, 18) also insists that '[t]he thought of a tent in which God lived would send Jewish minds back to the tabernacle in the wilderness at the time of the Exodus, and from there to the Temple in Jerusalem where God's presence was promised'.

The connection with the Old Testament use of the word is not only reminding the readers of the tabernacle and temple but more importantly, opening a new perspective on the incarnate Word. Köstenberger (2004, 41) points out that '[t]his rare term [σκηνόω], used elsewhere in the NT only in the Book of Revelation (7:15; 12:12; 13:6; 21:3), suggests that in Jesus, God has come to take up residence among his people once again, in a way even more intimate than when he dwelt in the midst of wildness Israel in the tabernacle (Exod. 40:34–35)'. The Evangelist identifies the incarnate Word as the tabernacle and temple. The Evangelist affirms this later in the temple account, when he says, 'the temple he had spoken of was his body' (2:21). The dwelling of the incarnate Word among humanity is not simply a representation of the divine relationship between the Word and God to humanity by Jesus. Rather, for the Word himself to tabernacle among humanity denotes the place where God would meet humanity. Jesus becomes the focus of God's presence among the people as the tabernacle was the focus of God's presence before. Brown (1966, 33) confirms this, saying '[w]hen the Prologue proclaims that the Word made his dwelling among men, we are being told that the flesh of Jesus Christ is the new localization of God's presence on earth, and that Jesus is the replacement of the ancient Tabernacle. The Gospel will present Jesus as the replacement of the temple (ii 19–22), which is a variation of the same theme'. The relational element should not be ignored in the incarnation of the Word, nor be treated as merely an instrument to achieve something. The relationship is the ultimate goal of the incarnation. The Word became incarnate in order to

---

[31] The word is used only in two books in the New Testament, one here in the Fourth Gospel and the other four times in Revelation (7:15; 12:12; 13:6; 21:3).

be with humanity to achieve eternal relationship. In a sense, the relationship, or being together, is the basis, the process and the goal of the incarnated Word.

The Relationship in a New Community

The third event based on the first statement in the chapter is the calling of a new community. The incarnate Word, Jesus, formed a discipleship community with those who came to him and those whom he called. In the process of forming the new community, the 'being together' of the Word with God is reflected. The divine relationship in the beginning has been expressed by the special verb σκηνόω in the second event, the incarnation of the Word, and now the specific 'being together' of Jesus with the new community begins within the bigger picture of σκηνόω of the incarnate Word among humanity.

In the narrative of forming a new community (1:37–51), two verbs (ἀκολουθέω and μένω) need to be noted. The narrative begins with the first verb ἀκολουθέω (to follow). The two disciples of the Baptist follow Jesus after they were introduced to 'the Lamb of God' (1:36) by their master. The verb ἀκολουθέω appears four times[32] in the narrative. The first three times are used for the two disciples who follow Jesus, and the fourth one is used when Jesus calls Philip to follow him (1:43). The verb ἀκολουθέω appears again in the last chapter of the Gospel when Jesus commands Peter to follow him (21:19, 22). Even though the same verb ἀκολουθέω is used both in the beginning (1:37) and in the last scene of the Gospel, the disciples' understanding of 'following' would be very different. Newbigin (1982, 19) describes the whole Fourth Gospel 'as an exposition of what it will mean to "follow Jesus"'. Bauckham (2015, 146) also supports this, saying:

> The literal following prefigures the true following that is possible only after the passion week. The two momentous weeks correspond in that the disciples become disciples of Jesus in the first week, but only in the passion week are they taught what it will mean for them truly to follow Jesus on the way through the cross to glory that he himself takes in that week.

The true meaning of the first verb ἀκολουθέω, however, needs to be supplemented by the second verb μένω (to remain) in two ways.

First, the true meaning of ἀκολουθέω can be achieved by remaining (μένω). The narrative shows a picture of the process through the first two disciples. They follow (ἀκολουθέω, 1:37) Jesus calling him 'Teacher', stay (μένω, 1:39) with him on the day they meet Jesus and tell Peter that they have found (εὑρίσκω, 1:41) the Messiah. The new community begins with ἀκολουθέω and works through μένω and eventually εὑρίσκω. This process can be applied to the whole narrative of the Gospel. The disciples follow (without fully

---

[32] 1:37, 38, 40, 43.

understanding what it means) Jesus, stay (being together) with him learning through the whole life of Jesus including the cross and resurrection, then understand what it means to follow Jesus. Without μένω, the new community cannot reach the point of understanding the true meaning of ἀκολουθέω. In this sense, the whole Gospel can be read as a process of the discipleship community 'being together' with Jesus, learning the true meaning of following him. The Evangelist uses the verb μένω 40 times in the Gospel. The 'to stay' or 'to abide' is an important theme of the Gospel not only because of the frequent use of the verb but also because of Jesus' intimacy with the Father and also with his disciples by being together with them.

Secondly, the ultimate purpose of ἀκολουθέω is associated with μένω. In other words, the new community follows Jesus to be with him forever. The 'being together' should not be seen just as a preparation for the following, rather it is the goal of the following. The Evangelist uses the noun form of μένω (μονή) twice in the Gospel. The μονή is the place the Father owns, which Jesus will prepare for the community (14:2) and also the place where God will abide with the one who loves him (14:23). In a sense, the 'being together' is the ultimate goal of God for the new community, and the Gospel could be described 'as an exposition of what it will mean to remain (μένω) with God through Jesus' (cf Newbigin, 1982, 19).

At the end of the new community section (1:44–51), which is the end of the chapter, Jesus presents what the new community will see. Jesus talks to Nathanael who came to him by the invitation of another disciple, Philip, and says to him, 'you will see heaven open, and the angels of God ascending and descending on the Son of Man' (1:51). In this verse, Jesus substitutes himself for the ladder (stairway in NIV) in Jacob's story in Genesis (28:12) meaning that he is the place where God meets humanity. The idea that Jesus is the meeting place in the incarnation episode (Tabernacle and Temple) is affirmed by what Jesus says to Nathanael. Those are the places where God enters into a personal relationship with his people. At the ladder, God promised Jacob that he would be with him and watch over him wherever he goes (Gen 28:15a). In the 'tent of meeting', '[t]he Lord would speak to Moses face to face, as one speaks to a friend' (Exod 33:11a). The relationship Jesus anticipates for the new community is to be friends with him. The meaning of *friend* is revealed in what Jesus says to his disciples after his being together with them. Jesus says, 'I have called you friends, for everything that I learned from my Father I have made known to you' (15:15b).

To summarize the discussion to this point, the relationship between God and the Word revealed in the first statement is represented by the Word, Jesus, in the following three events and provides the basis for them. Since those Johannine grand narrative themes show the missional story of God in the Gospel, I maintain that relationship is a central theme in the mission of God, and it is important to examine how Jesus reveals this relationship as he shapes and equips his disciples throughout the rest of the Gospel.

A Man Sent from God

John the Witness

In the first chapter of the Gospel, John[33] takes on an important role. Almost half of the chapter (24 verses[34] out of the 51 verses) are about John. Why does the Evangelist focus explicitly on one man named John, devoting such a significant portion of the chapter to him? In other words, what does the Evangelist want to say to the reader through the story of John? In this section, I will discuss how John needs to be understood from a missional reading of the grand narrative episode of the first chapter and also how the reading is linked with the rest of the Gospel.

John is first introduced in verses 6–8 before the incarnation of the Word; then he appears again in verse 15 and onward after the incarnation of Jesus. The Evangelist introduces him as follows:

> There was a man sent from God whose name was John. He came as a witness to testify concerning that light, so that through him all might believe. He himself was not the light; he came only as a witness to the light. (1:6–8)

Since many scholars read the first appearance of John in verses 6–8 as just an individual person, they believe those verses are 'an intrusion into the poetic structure and flow of thought of the rest of the Prologue' (Wink, 1968, 87). Beasley-Murray (1999, 11) says, 'The Evangelist interrupts his citation from the Logos hymn in order to present the Baptist's testimony to "the Light"'. Newbigin (1982, 5) also says, 'We might almost be in the timeless world of the Upanishads. And suddenly we are hearing a very ordinary, matter-of-fact piece of human story'. Bultmann is no exception. He (1971, 16) sees the verses as insertions into the original text, and insists that 'they are the Evangelist's own comments'. As evidence of the claim, he also says that '[i]f vv. 6–8 were originally in the text, vv. 9–13 would have to refer to them in such a way as to state that in spite of this witness the Logos found no faith'. However, the expression that 'his own did not receive him' does not necessarily mean that 'the Logos found no faith'. The Evangelist says, '[y]et to all who did receive him, to those who believed in his name, he gave the right to become children of God' and it did happen in the Gospel. This study reads the text as it is and sees how the description about John could be interpreted from a missional perspective.

John is introduced merely as John without any title in the Fourth Gospel, while the Synoptic Gospels commonly call him John the Baptist, except in a few cases (e.g., Matt. 11:2; Mark 2:18). In contrast, the Fourth Gospel

---

[33] In this section, John refers to the Baptist not the Evangelist.

[34] 1:6-8, 15, 19-37, 40.

identifies him as a witness (1:7). Brown (1966, 9) points out that '[t]he Fourth Gospel stresses more the role of John the Baptist as a witness than as a baptizer'. He is identified as a witness not only in the introduction (1:6–8) but also in his ministry later in the chapter. His role in the Gospel is ultimately to testify about Jesus. Because of his clear understanding of his relationship with Jesus, John is often viewed as an example of a Christian. Wink (1968, 105), one of the few scholars who has studied John in the Gospel, insists that 'John is made the normative image of the Christian preacher, apostle and missionary, the perfect prototype of the true evangelist, whose one goal is self-effacement before Christ'. He continues, saying, '[t]he determining motive in the Evangelist's use of John is the desire to placard before the eyes of the church the ideal relationship of evangelist to Lord' (106). It is hard to agree that the above interpretation is the purpose of the Evangelist's use of John with such a long description within the Gospel even though I agree that John sets an example of the ideal attitude for all Christians. The special expression about him, *sent from God* (1:6), particularly *ahead of the Son* (1:15, 27, 30), requires more explanation as to why it was inserted here to determine whether or not it was simply to serve as an example for Christians. Bennema (2009b, 271) says that 'John's characterization as a witness is complex and multifaceted – his single trait is not a simple trait'. Bennema (2009b, 282) explains the multifaceted roles as follows:

> John's characterization as a witness is seen specifically in his other roles as a baptizer, herald-forerunner, teacher, best man, and "lamp." These roles serve to *clarify* and *define* his role as witness. It is as baptizer that John reveals Jesus as the expected Messiah to Israel; as herald, he announces Israel's imminent restoration through Jesus as God's salvific agent; as teacher, he testifies about and directs his disciples to Jesus; as best man, he announces the arrival of the eschatological bridegroom; and as lamp, he testifies to the divine truth embodied in Jesus aiming to bring about belief. Thus, John's role as witness is not alongside or separate from his other roles; rather, he is a witness in or through those roles.

Through his ministry, John is always pointing to Jesus, and the role as a pointer reveals his identity. I will argue about his 'multifaceted' roles not regarding applications that Christians can learn from him but regarding his special introduction and what it means to the reading of the Gospel missionally.

John: His Sending and His Identity

The introduction or description about John in the Gospel has two notable features. One is honourable and the other is deprecating.

First, the introduction about John gives him a special status. The Evangelist says that John was *sent from God*. The word ἀποστέλλω (to send) first appears here in the Gospel. In the Gospel, he is the only person who is sent from God other than the Son (cf 3:17; 5:36; 6:57; 7:29; 8:42; 10:36; 17:18; 20:21) and the

Holy Spirit (cf 14:26; 15:26).[35] The other thing to note is that he is sent *ahead of Jesus*. He says to his disciples, 'I am not the Messiah but am sent ahead of him' (3:28). He is born before Jesus (cf Luke 1:57–63), and also starts his ministry before Jesus does (1:19–34). In other words, John is *sent from God ahead of the Son*. As John states, the Son existed before him (cf 1:15), but John was sent from God before the Son was sent. This is an honourable distinction. Why does the Evangelist introduce John using an expression similar to that used to introduce Jesus and the Holy Spirit regarding sending?

Secondly, the Gospel describes him not only in the introduction but also in many other places with a negative statement rather than an affirmative one, such as 'He… was not…' (1:8), 'I am not…' (1:20, 27) and so on. Barclay (1975, 49) points out, '[i]t is a strange fact that in the Fourth Gospel every reference to John the Baptist is a reference of depreciation'. Wink (1968, 98) summarizes such a description of John in the Gospel as follows:

> The denial that John is the light (1:8); John's violent refusal of the Christological titles (1:19ff.); the contrast between baptism in water (John) and in Holy Spirit (Jesus) in 1:31, 33; 3:22ff.; the implication in 3:31 that John is 'out of the earth' whereas Jesus alone is above all things because he is 'from above'; John's denial that he is prior (1:15, 30); the assertion that Jesus baptized more than John; John's confession of Jesus' superiority (3:22–4:2); the statement that John's witness is merely that of a human and is unnecessary (5:34, 36); and the comment that John did no sign (10:41).

Many scholars suggest that in the contemporary context of the writing, the Evangelist insisted on using negative statements about him because there was 'a group of people who contended that John the Baptist was himself the final revelation of God to mankind' (Carson, 1991, 121). Barclay (1975, 50) also says that '[i]t was simply John [the Evangelist] knew that there were certain people who gave John the Baptist a place that encroached upon the place of Jesus himself'. Such a context-based interpretation for the text is somewhat beneficial to understanding it, but it is in danger of limiting the interpretation of the text merely to responses to a contemporary context, thus overlooking the Evangelist's intention focusing on the context. It might be true that there was such a group that tried to put John in the place of Jesus. A group of people in Ephesus who knew only the baptism of John (Acts 19:3–4) might serve as evidence for such a claim. However, this study does not read the Gospel as written out of or for any specific hypothetical community. The deprecating description of John distinguishes between the sending of John from God and the sending of the Son from the Father.

The above two features, the honourable and the deprecating ones, point out that John succeeds the prophets of the Old Testament. John is a witness. His

[35] In 14:26 and 15:26 the verb πέμπω (to send) is used.

insertion in 1:6 could be because he has the role of a prophet testifying to God. He may fit into Hebrews' concept of bearing witness.[36] So John is therefore representative of the Jewish people since he is one of their prophets. Nevertheless, his role is different to that of the prophets. Thus, I will call him 'the forerunner' rather than 'the prophet'.

John as a Forerunner

The first two roles Bennema points out above, the baptizer and the herald, are related with John's connection to the Old Testament. Kanagaraj (2005, 46), who sees John as more 'God's ambassador' than simply 'the son of Zechariah', says that '[John] is in the same league as the OT prophets… whom God called and commissioned'. Westcott (1908, 19) says that '[t]he conjunction [Καὶ in verse 14] carries the reader back to v. 1, with which this verse is closely connected by this repetition of the title ὁ λόγος', thus the episode between creation and incarnation is 'in one sense parenthetical'. The insertion of John's first introduction in the midst of the grand narrative between Creation and Incarnation supports John's connection to the Old Testament. Phillips (2006, 175) points out that 'it is clear that the Jewish Scriptures do provide a conceptual backdrop to much of what is going on in the text [John's first introduction]'.

John identifies himself neither with Christ nor with any particular prophet (cf 1:20–21) but identifies himself with the role of prophets, in the words of the prophet Isaiah: 'I am the voice of one calling in the wilderness, "Make straight the way for the Lord"' (1:23). Myers (2015, 139) suggests that by '[b]lending John's ministry with that of Isaiah, the narrator continues building the argument begun in the prologue that Jesus is at the heart of Israel's sacred scriptural story'. The identification of John with the role of prophets shows that John is different from other prophets. The citation of the Fourth Gospel differs from that of the Synoptics. All three Synoptic Gospels quote the passage from Isaiah as follows: 'A voice of one calling in the wilderness, "Prepare the way for the Lord, make straight paths for him"' (Matt 3:3; Mark 1:3; Luke 3:4). The Fourth Gospel shortens it slightly by changing the word 'prepare' (ἑτοιμάσατε) to 'make straight' (εὐθύνατε). The Fourth Gospel is not just abbreviating the longer version, but as Dodd (1963a, 252) notes, there is 'cumulative evidence' that the Fourth Evangelist is 'not dependent on the other gospels for the choice or wording of the passage adduced'. Carson (1991, 144) explains how the verse shows a new meaning as follows:

> In the original context, the Old Testament prophet is calling for a (metaphorical) improvement in the road system of the desert to the east, a levelling of hills and

---

[36] 'In the past God spoke to our ancestors through the prophets at many times and in various ways' (Heb 1:1).

> valleys and a straightening of the curves, to accommodate the return of the covenant people from exile. But even in Isaiah, the end of the exile begins to serve as a model, a literary 'type', of the final return to the Lord far greater than a return to geographical Jerusalem.... It is this 'typological' connection, already established in the book of Isaiah, that the New Testament writers take up and understand to be fulfilled in the voice of John the Baptist, who cried in the desert, preparing the way for the Lord, and thereby announcing the coming of Jesus Messiah.

John came for the Messiah to be revealed to Israel (cf 1:31). This is more like the role of a forerunner. The prophets in the Old Testament were sent *for people to come to God*, but John came to prepare *for the Lord to come to Israel*. Brown (1966, 50) says that 'John the Baptist is to prepare a road, not for God's people to return to the promised land, but for God to come to His people'.

John as a forerunner provides significant meanings for the mission of Jesus within the Gospel.

First, the fact that God sent John for Israel ahead of Jesus shows God's desire for Israel to be recovered. John says, 'the reason I came baptizing with water was that he [Jesus] might be revealed to Israel' (1:31). The Evangelist uses the word *Israel* only four times in the Gospel referring to the whole nation in contrast to the title *the Jews*, which refers to the Jewish leaders and 'the Law-centred' Jews in most usages. In Jesus' mission and the forming of a new community, the recovery and participation of Israel are crucial even though it is not limited to the nation. Jesus says, 'salvation is from the Jews' (4:22). The Evangelist introduces many Jews who believe in Jesus. Not only the disciples of Jesus, 'the Twelve', but also other Jews came to believe in Jesus. For instance, the Evangelist describes the progressive change of Nicodemus, 'a member of the Jewish ruling council', through three appearances in the Gospel (3:1–21; 7:50–52; 19:39–42). Even though the overall assessment of the Evangelist regarding Jesus' encounters with the Jews in the first half of the Gospel (2:13–12:50) is not positive (cf 12:37), he points out that 'at the time many even among the leaders [of the Jews] believed in him [Jesus]' (12:42). There is no evidence revealing how the ministry of John influences the Jews directly to believe in Jesus. However, it is certain that John's appearance and his testifying about Jesus call the Jews' attention to the Messiah. The fact that the Jewish leaders sent a delegation to ask John whether he is the Messiah proves such an atmosphere.

Secondly, John as a forerunner prepares what Jesus will accomplish in the world, the forming of a discipleship community. John testifies regarding Jesus not only to Israel (1:29–34)[37] but also to his own disciples. By introducing Jesus to his own disciples, John takes on a significant role. Two disciples of

---

[37] It does not mention to whom John is testifying, but I assume that he is testifying to the Israelites based on what he is saying, 'he [Jesus] might be revealed to Israel (1:31).

John leave their own master to follow Jesus, eventually becoming his disciples. This connecting role is a highlight of John's ministry as a forerunner. It shows a glimpse of transition, from pre-Christ to post-Christ. John represents the voice in pre-Christ, *sent from God ahead of Jesus*, while the disciples represent the voice in post-Christ, *sent from the Son after his resurrection*. The fact that God sent John is not the object of John's testimony, but the sending of Jesus by the Father is the very object of Jesus' testimony. According to BDAG (756), 'John the Baptist was not, like Jesus, sent out from the very presence of God, but one whose coming was brought about by God'. The sending of the disciples by Jesus will be a continuation of the sending of Jesus: 'As the Father has sent me, I am sending you' (20:21). In that sense, the testimony of the disciples regarding Jesus is different from that of John.

By recognizing the incarnate Word when he comes into the world and by testifying about him to Israel, John fulfils his mission as a forerunner. He becomes a bridge between Jesus and Israel and between Jesus and the new discipleship community, at least for two of them. Of course, the disciples are also expected to testify of the Messiah, but the direction and meaning of their testifying are different from the testifying of John. John is supposed to testify of the Messiah before he achieves what is written in the Hebrew Bible, while the disciples are expected to testify to the world about what is achieved. What Jesus describes about John might be understood in this respect: 'among those born of women there has not risen anyone greater than John the Baptist; yet whoever is least in the kingdom of heaven is greater than he' (Matt 11:11; cf Luke 7:28). John is fulfilling the mandate of the chosen people by pointing out the incarnate Word – that he is the prophesied one and the Messiah for whom Israel has been waiting. John also lays a foundation for the new discipleship community by introducing his own disciples to Jesus.

In one sense, the first chapter of the Gospel ends with the formation of Jesus' discipleship community out of those Israelites. John is not representing a true Christian but is a stepping stone for the true Christian community. He knew his identity and mission. Dodd (1963a, 290) points out as follows:

> John the Baptist not only proclaimed the approaching advent of the Messiah, but also declared that he was at that moment present unknown, and might any day be identified. If this was his message, and not simply one more repetition of the age-long promise that the Messiah would appear in the future, even in the near future, it would go far to account for the immense stir which his preaching evidently caused.

The Formation of the New Community

Jesus forms a new community as part of the Word's creative work. As 'all things were made' through the Word in the first creation, the new community is being created through the same now incarnate Word, Jesus Christ. The final story of the first part, the Cana story, reveals the formation of the new community and its creation aspect in several ways. I will address the reasons I include the story in the first part of the Gospel and also argue its significance in the Gospel in relation to the creation process of the discipleship community.

First, the opening phrase of the story, καί τῇ ἡμέρᾳ τῇ τρίτῃ (and on the third day) supports the claim that the Cana story is part of the previous narrative. Michaels (2010, 140) points out that the phrase 'reminds us that we are still in the time-conscious world of 1:19–51, punctuated by the repeated expression, "the next day," in 1:29, 35, and 43'. Furthermore, the phrase indicates that the story completes Jesus' first week in his ministry. The first week of Jesus' ministry in the Fourth Gospel is often compared to the first seven days of creation in Genesis and thus considered 'a week of new creation'.[38] The Evangelist shows the time sequence of the story particularly in this narrative. He uses 'the next day' (1:29, 35, 43) three times, 'that day' (1:39) once[39] and 'the third day' (2:1) once. Carson (1991, 168) explains how these references constitute a week:

> This total of six days does not seem very significant. In fact, another day should be added. This is achieved, not by appealing to the variant at 1:41, but by observing that when the Baptist's two disciples attach themselves to Jesus it is already 4:00 p.m. on the third day – and they spent the rest of that day with him (1:39). That means Andrew's introduction of Simon Peter to Jesus takes place on the *next* day, the fourth; the Nathanael exchange occurs on the fifth; the changing of the water into wine on the seventh.... The week of days climaxing in the miracle at Cana may provide an echo of creation-week (Gn. 1).

Köstenberger (2004, 56) reconstructs the week as follows:

Day 1: John's testimony regarding Jesus (1:19–28)
Day 2: John's encounter with Jesus (1:29–34; "the next day")
Day 3: John's referral of two disciples to Jesus (1:35–39; "the next day")
Day 4: Andrew's introduction of his brother Peter to Jesus (1:40–42)
Day 5: Philip and Nathanael follow Jesus (1:43–51; "the next day")
[Day 6 not explicitly mentioned]
Day 7: Wedding at Cana (2:1–11; "on the third day")

---

[38] M.E. Boismard published a book on the theme (*Du Baptême à Cana*, Paris: Éditions du Cerf, 1956), and other scholars, such as Barrosse, have added to the theme. cf Lincoln (2005, 106–7).

[39] This phrase does not indicate a new day, but by saying that the two disciples spent *that day* with Jesus, the implication is that the following event – that of Andrew bringing his brother Peter to Jesus – happens on the next day. Those who see this as a total of six days insist that the bringing of Peter happens on the same day as when the two disciples meet Jesus (cf Michaels, 2010, 140).

Bauckham (2015, 133) points out that '[g]iven the biblical and Jewish significance of the week as a period of time, established by the Creator at the beginning (Gen. 1:1–2:4), there is an obvious appropriateness in beginning the Gospel's narrative of new creation with a week'.

Secondly, the Cana story makes the first part of the Gospel complete as an introduction to the Johannine grand narrative. The Johannine grand narrative begins with pre-Creation and ends with the formation of the discipleship community as a new creation. The incarnate Word, Jesus, calls his first disciples before he starts his public ministry. The disciples accompany Jesus to the wedding in Cana. The word μαθητής (disciple) first appears here in the Cana story, referring to the disciples of Jesus. Through the story, readers know that the gathering of his first disciples, 'the Twelve' in particular, is complete.[40] Bauckham (2015, 183) points out that 'Jesus performed this miracle [at Cana] before the beginning of his public ministry.... Shortly afterwards, in this Gospel's narrative, Jesus goes up to Jerusalem, where he inaugurates his public ministry to Israel at the heart of Israel, in Jerusalem and its temple (2:13–24)'.

The Cana story functions not only as the completion of the first part of the Gospel but also as a link between the first part and the rest of the Gospel. The story is introduced as the first of the signs performed by Jesus. The above-mentioned opening phrase, *on the third day*, attaches the story to the previous narrative while another phrase, ἀρχὴν τῶν σημείων (the first of the signs, 2:11) attaches it to the rest of the Gospel. Nevertheless, this first sign (and the last one, the resurrection of Jesus) is distinguished from the rest of the signs because Jesus performs this sign (and the last one) 'in the presence of his disciples' (20:30). Jesus' encounters with the Jews and his interactions with individuals in the second part of the Gospel could be parenthesized by the first and the last signs. Bauckham (2015, 183) claims, '[t]he public ministry begins in 2:13 and ends in 12:50.... The first sign precedes the public ministry, the seventh follows it'.

Since the first part of the Gospel functions as an introduction to the entire Gospel, the Cana story as the last story of the introduction is connected to the last main event (the resurrection of Jesus) of the Gospel.[41] Within the structural

---

[40] Lincoln (2005, 105) says that 'by emphasizing the reaction of belief on the part of the disciples, the evangelist shows that he has not forgotten the theme of evolving discipleship that was elaborated in ch. i'.

[41] As I mentioned, the Cana story functions not only as the completion of the first part of the Gospel but also as a link between the first part and the rest of the Gospel. Since I view the story as the completion of the first part, I compare the story with the last part of the Gospel. In the case of it being viewed as a link, the story might function as the beginning of his public ministry. Bennema (2009a, 71) points out that the first sign 'serves to lift the "not yet" from the messianic hour'. He says it 'marks Jesus' inauguration of the messianic age'.

parallel of the two events, there are two previews in the Cana story which will come true in the Gospel.

First, the Cana story signifies the resurrection of Jesus. Jesus changes water into wine. The fact that Jesus changes water into wine τῇ ἡμέρᾳ τῇ τρίτῃ (on the third day) recalls Jesus' resurrection ἐν τρισὶν ἡμέραις (in three days, cf 2:19) even though the Evangelist uses another phrase, 'on the first day of the week', in the resurrection story.[42] Bauckham (2015, 182) links the wine in the story with the resurrection of Jesus based on Isa. 25:6–8,[43] saying, '[h]ere the provision of the finest wine is linked with the abolition of death. The text provides a scriptural basis for connecting the miracle of Cana, the first of Jesus' signs, with the seventh sign, the resurrection of Jesus from the dead' (182). This connection between the Cana story and the resurrection of Jesus opens the second preview of the Cana story that will be accomplished in the resurrection narrative.

The second preview is the formation of the discipleship community. In the Cana story, the Evangelist ends the story with his own comment on it. The closing comment is 'his disciples believed in him [Jesus]' (2:11). Michaels (2010, 154) describes the story as follows:

> No one else is said to have seen Jesus' glory and believed – not the banquet master or the bridegroom, not Jesus' mother who seemed to know what was coming, nor even the servants who knew where the wine came from (v. 9) – only a handful of disciples watching from the sidelines. They are outsiders to the miracle, yet the revelation it brings is for them and them alone, not for those who actually participated in the miracle…. Now the disciples are beginning to see the "greater things" that will bring them to the next level of faith, and eventually, when Jesus' "hour" has come and he is raised from the dead, to yet another level.

Starting from this first sign of Jesus, the disciples progressively increase their faith in him. In the resurrection narrative, the Evangelist says that the disciples 'still did not understand from Scripture that Jesus had to rise from the dead' (20:9). As he mentions in the temple cleaning narrative, however, '[a]fter he [Jesus] was raised from the dead, his disciples recalled what he had said. Then they believed the scripture and the words that Jesus had spoken' (2:22). Therefore, the formation of the discipleship community as revealed in the Cana

---

[42] Bauckham (2015, 182) claims, '[a]lthough this formula [on the third day] is not used in John's Gospel to indicate the day of Jesus' resurrection, versions of it with such a reference are so common in New Testament literature (especially 1 Cor. 15:4; cf. Matt. 16:21; 7:23; 20:19; Luke 9:22; 18:33; 24:7, 46) that John's readers would be likely to recognize that usage'.

[43] 'On this mountain the Lord Almighty will prepare a feast of rich food for all peoples, a banquet of aged wine – the best of meats and the finest of wines. On this mountain he will destroy the shroud that enfolds all peoples, the sheet that covers all nations; he will swallow up death forever' (Isa 25:6–8).

story is a preview or just the beginning. It is achieved in the resurrection narrative when Jesus breathes on the disciples, commissioning them into the world (20:21–22). In this sense, the Cana story provides a guideline for how to read Jesus' public ministry in 2:13–12:50, which will be discussed in the following chapter of this study. The public ministry of Jesus, then, could be read as a new creation process of his disciples.

The new creation process was not limited to the disciples. The process reveals an ecclesiological dimension of the community as well. Barrosse (1958, 507), who supports the parallel comparison of both weeks, insists that the implication of the new creation should be 'ecclesiological'. According to him (1958, 507), '[i]f he [a discerning reader] reflects on this inaugural week of the public ministry in the light of the rest of the Gospel (or even in the light of the Synoptic tradition), he finds he has here in summary – or in symbol – the whole of Jesus' work: the establishment of His Church presented as the *new creation*'. This ecclesiological idea of Barrosse is based on the assembling of different groups into the new community. He (1958, 513) defines each assembled group as 'the Precursor [John the Baptist], the Savior Himself [Jesus], the disciples [two disciples of John the Baptist], the chief apostle [Peter], the apostles [Philip], and believing Israel [Nathanael]'. However, I argue that the ecclesiological dimension of the community will be shown to the disciples through the ministry of Jesus rather than through the gathering of the first disciples. Barrosse points out the ecclesiological aspect of this new community by listing different people. However, his list includes only Jews. I contend that the ecclesiological dimension will be revealed by his encounters with the Jews, Samaritans and other individuals. The first disciples in the Cana story might not understand this dimension, but the disciples in the resurrection narrative would have a different picture of the new community.

To summarize the argument to this point, the Cana story provides a picture of the formation of the discipleship community within the Johannine grand narrative. For that reason, I include the story in the first part of the Gospel. The story, however, functions as a link between the first part and the rest of the Gospel providing two previews for the events to come. One is the resurrection of Jesus and the other is the formation of the discipleship community before commissioning them into the world. Therefore, Jesus' public ministry between those two stories can be read as a new creation process of the community, that is, a shaping and equipping process of the community.

Chapter Summary

I have proposed that, in this first part of the Gospel (1:1–2:12), we can discover a Johannine grand narrative which is both missional and authentically Johannine. The narrative includes the story from Creation to the gathering of the disciples as a new community (1:1–2:12). The Evangelist views the Word as the centre of the narrative. The Word is introduced as the agent of Creation through whom everything was made. He himself becomes incarnate, becoming a human being. The incarnate Word, Jesus, calls his disciples. In short, God does everything only through the Word in relation to the world.

At the outset of the grand narrative, the Evangelist lays a foundation: the divine relationship between God and the Word. The intimate relationship of the Word with God functions as more than revealing who the Word is in relation to God; it provides the origin of Creation, the way of Jesus' ministry, and the goal of the new community. The essential role of the Word in the three main events (Creation, Incarnation, and forming a New Community) in the grand narrative is based on the divine relationship expressed in the first statement of the Gospel. By creating everything through the Word, God desires to extend the relationship he has with the Word into the world, and with humanity in particular. The incarnation of the Word into the world is also described as the dwelling of the Word among humanity, becoming the meeting place between God and humanity. The incarnate Word, Jesus, begins a new creation process by gathering a discipleship community, and the abiding together of Jesus and the disciples is not only the means of knowing who the Messiah is but also the goal of the community.

I have demonstrated that John, who is described more as a witness than a baptizer, is connected to prophets of the Old Testament. His role as a forerunner is to prepare for the Lord to come to Israel. He fulfils his role in two ways in the Gospel. First, he becomes a bridge between Jesus and Israel, signifying God's desire for Israel to participate in the new community. The Evangelist reveals it happening throughout the Gospel. Secondly, he contributes to the forming of the new community by introducing his disciples to Jesus. This distinguishes the role of the two agents. John fulfils his role as a preparation for the Lord to *come* to Israel, and the disciples will fulfil their roles as a witness for the Lord to *go* [through them] to the world. John represents the voice pre-Christ while the disciples do that post-Christ.

The Cana story closes the first part by revealing the last event of the first week of Jesus' ministry. This supports the reason as to why I include this episode in the first part of the Gospel. The first week of Jesus' ministry relates to the first week of Creation in Genesis signifying that the creation motif is one of the important aspects of the Johannine grand narrative. The story also reveals that Jesus gathers his disciples, 'the Twelve', before he inaugurates his public ministry in Jerusalem, signifying that his public ministry has an educational aspect for the accompanying disciples. In this sense, the Gospel prepares readers to anticipate learning what God expects for the new community. In other words, readers will discover the identity of the new community through the rest of the Gospel, which includes its mission in the world.

This first part of the Gospel provides several important themes in relation to a missional reading of the Gospel. First, it provides a grand narrative view in a Johannine way. It sets the readers' minds to read the rest of the Gospel within the context of the Johannine grand narrative theme, that is, the missional story of God. Secondly, it stresses relationship as a foundation of the mission of God. Thirdly, it provides a lens for reading those themes. The lens is the Word, Jesus. He is the agent of Creation, becomes incarnate and gathers his disciples. It signifies that the mission of God is represented by the life and ministry of Jesus. Fourthly, it reveals a creation aspect of the new community by comparing the first week of Jesus to the first week of Genesis. Finally, it highlights the discipleship community, causing readers to anticipate how Jesus will equip the disciples to participate in the mission of God. These missional themes will emerge through Jesus' encounters with the Jews and through his interactions with his disciples and individuals.

4. Encountering the Jews and Interacting with Individuals (2:13–12:50)

Introduction

This chapter will cover the story from the first Passover (2:13) to the beginning of the last Passover (12:50) in the Gospel. One of the significant differences of the Fourth Gospel to the Synoptic Gospels is that, in the Fourth Gospel, the stages where Jesus' ministry takes place are mainly Jerusalem and Judea.[1] The Synoptics record no visit of Jesus to Jerusalem during his public ministry until he comes to Jerusalem before his death. The Gospel of Luke alone records Jesus' visits to Jerusalem with his family when he was a baby (Luke 2:22) and a boy (Luke 2:42). This means that no encounters between the Jews in Jerusalem and Jesus during his public ministry are introduced in the Synoptics until the events associated with his Passion week. By contrast, the Fourth Gospel introduces several visits of Jesus to Jerusalem. In particular, the basic plot of the story in the portion between 2:13–12:50 is Jesus' encounters with the Jews mainly in Jerusalem and Judea and also partly in Galilee.[2] These encounters continue until the end of Chapter 12.[3] In the midst of his encounters with the Jews as a group, Jesus interacts with different individuals. Those

---

[1] Lincoln (2005, 28) says that 'while in the Synoptics the focus for Jesus' mission is Galilee, followed by one climatic visit to Jerusalem, in John the focus is Judaea with movements back and forth between Galilee and Jerusalem'. cf Carson (1991, 52), Milne (1993, 22). Schnackenburg (1980a, 16) thinks that 'after the public failure in Galilee, the whole interest is concentrated on Jerusalem'.

[2] Lincoln (2005, 8) says that 'the relation of Jesus to the symbols and institutions of Judaism will be dominant issues in his public mission'. Michaels (2010, 34) points out that 'the Gospel of John seems to divide Jesus' ministry into two parts, a "public ministry" to the crowds and the religious authorities in Jerusalem and Galilee (chapters 2–12) and a "private ministry" to his disciples in the setting of the last supper (chapters 13–17)'.

[3] Brown (1966, LXX) says that the first part of the Gospel (he refers to 1:19–12:50) 'shows the importance given to the theme of Jesus' replacement of Jewish institutions such as ritual purification, the Temple, and worship in Jerusalem (chs. ii–iv) and of Jewish feasts such as the Sabbath, Passover, Tabernacles, and Dedication (chs. v–x).

individuals are Nicodemus (ch. 3), a Samaritan woman (ch. 4), a royal official (ch. 4), a man at the Bethesda pool (ch. 5), an adulterous woman (ch. 8), a man born blind (ch. 9) and Lazarus and his sisters (ch. 11). The encounters of Jesus with the Jews and the interactions with those individuals will be examined and the missional implications of the encounters and interactions will be discussed in this chapter. One thing to note in this discussion is that his encounters and interactions are set during different Jewish feasts and are followed by various discourses.

In section 4.2 I will discuss who the Jews are in the Gospel, to understand what constituted the encounters and why Jesus encounters them. Then, the modifier τῶν Ἰουδαίων (of the Jews) for the feasts will be addressed to understand how the feasts are viewed in general in the Gospel, in order to understand the position of Jesus and the Evangelist regarding the feasts in section 4.3. In section 4.4, three pilgrimage feasts will be discussed along with the discourses that follow them. Those feasts are the Passovers, an unnamed feast and the feast of Tabernacles. There is a difference between the Jewish understanding of the feasts and Jesus' understanding of them. The former emphasizes *form* by following the Law itself while the latter reveals their *meaning*, which relates to the mission of God. The difference will reveal Jesus' identity in contrast to the lost missional identity of the Jews. Finally, Jesus' interactions with different individuals will be discussed in section 4.5.

Through Jesus' encounters with the Jews and his interactions with individuals, the missional nature of God will be addressed by Jesus, and the entire ministry of Jesus will function as an education for the accompanying disciples, shaping and equipping them as a missional community. By discovering those two key elements – the missional nature of God and the educational dimension for the disciples – the study will be able to identify the central concerns of God revealed by Jesus, which may contribute to a biblical understanding of mission.

The Jews

The ministry of Jesus described in the Gospel mainly occurs in Jerusalem and Judea where he encounters the Jews. Motyer (1997, 36) says that '[o]ne of the most pointed differences between John and the synoptics is the emphasis in the latter [I think it should be the former, John] on the Temple and the Jerusalem festivals. Not only is the cleansing of the Temple given a prominent position at the head of the narrative, but the festivals are closely woven into the structure of the Gospel'.[4] To understand what Jesus is pointing out through those encounters, it is necessary first to know who the Jews are in the Gospel. The

[4] Cf. also Brown (1966, 1:lxx), Yee (1989, 27), Wheaton (2015, 1-2).

adjective Ἰουδαῖος appears 70 times[5] in the Gospel and the noun Ἰουδαία, indicating the land of Judea, appears seven times. In the Gospel, Judea is mentioned a few times as the place Jesus leaves to avoid conflict with the Jews or a place he stays away from since the Jews are trying to kill him.[6] Under those circumstances, the Jews in the Gospel are associated with the land of Judea. However, it is insufficient to identify the Jews only as the people who are geographically located in Judea. The Jews appear not only in Judea but also in Galilee[7] in the Gospel. The fact that the Jews in Galilee know the father, Joseph, and the mother of Jesus[8] reveals that they are not from Judea, but from Galilee. Mason (2007, 511) points out that the term refers to an ethic group saying '[t]he *Ioudaioi* of the Graeco-Roman world remained an ἔθνος: a people associated with a place and its customs – no matter how far, or how long, they had been away from Judaea'. However, the Gospel adds that the people in Judea or Jerusalem are not referred to as Jews all the time. Instead, the Gospel differentiates between the crowd and the Jews there. It is recorded that the people who had a favourable view of Jesus in Jerusalem could not say anything publicly because they were afraid of the Jews.[9] Therefore, the term οἱ Ἰουδαῖοι represents something more than just geographical inhabitants of Judea.[10] The assumption that the Gospel uses the term οἱ Ἰουδαῖοι for a fixed group, labelling them with a definite character trait such as 'unbelief',[11] demands an additional explanation for the many exceptions in the text.[12] Porter (2015, 172–73) points out as follows:

---

[5] 1:19; 2:6, 13, 18, 20; 3:1, 25; 4:9 (2x), 22; 5:1, 10, 15, 16, 18; 6:4, 41, 52; 7:1, 2, 11, 13, 15, 35; 8:22, 31, 48, 52, 57; 9:18, 22 (2x); 10:19, 24, 31, 33; 11:8, 19, 31, 33, 36, 45, 54, 55; 12:9, 11; 13:33; 18:12, 14, 20, 31, 33, 35, 36, 38, 39; 19:3, 7, 12, 14, 19, 20, 21 (3x), 31, 38, 40, 42; 20:19. Some say 71 times. It depends on the interpretation of Ἰουδαίαν in 3:22 whether it is seen as a noun derived from Ἰουδαία or an adjective from Ἰουδαῖος. I see that it as a noun 'Judea' rather than an adjective 'Jewish', so this was not included in the number of Ἰουδαῖος. cf Matthew (five times), Mark (six times), and Luke (five times)

[6] 4:3; 7:1; see 11:7–8.

[7] 6:41, 52. cf Wahlde (1982, 44) says that 'the Ioudaioi of 6. 41, 52 are the only ones in the FG to appear outside of Judea'. Therefore he concludes that 'in the light of the literary peculiarities of that passage, it seems better to consider the usage in 6. 41, 52 simply as an "exception" possibly due to editorial activity' (45).

[8] 6:42.

[9] 7:13.

[10] Kierspel (2006, 13-36) introduces five different proposals on the issue, which are religious authorities, inhabitants of Judea, ethnic-religious term, fellow Christians, and religious term without empirical reference. He concludes that 'a broader definition for Ἰουδαῖοι (ethnic-religious term, religious term) fits the context better than very precise proposals (authorities, Judeans)' (35).

[11] Motyer (1997, 49) claims this view is because of Bultmann's influence.

[12] Culpepper (1983, 126) points out that 'the amount of discussion generated by John's varied use of the designation shows that the gospel does not attempt to distinguish and

> There has been much discussion of language regarding "the Jews" in John's Gospel. Much of the recent discussion has attempted to explain how it is that the author of John's Gospel can use what is often characterized as a blanket condemnation of the Jews…. My investigation indicates that the various major previous views regarding "the Jews" in John's Gospel all reveal themselves to be inadequate, for a variety of reasons. None of them presents an analysis that is comprehensive in scope…. If my analysis is plausible, then the author of John's Gospel, rather than having strong anti-Jewish tendencies, merely employed clear terms and used reasonable linguistic means to depict Jesus' opponents. In their opposition to Jesus, these opponents indicate a fundamental split between Judaism and what was to become Christianity, grounded in the language of the Gospel.

Reinhartz (2001, 73) suggests that 'by the time the Fourth Gospel was written toward the end of the first century C.E., the term was used to denote both an ethnic-geographic and a religious identity that was not limited to Jews who live in Judea or who were born of Judean parents'. Even though the term οἱ Ἰουδαῖοι does not always, without exception, denote a group of people in the Gospel, there is evidence that the term is mainly used for the people with whom Jesus has disputes on a variety of issues.

In this study, understanding οἱ Ἰουδαῖοι is not merely an attempt to know which group the term indicates.[13] Instead, the reader needs to understand who is referenced because knowing who the Jews are in the Gospel is a prerequisite for understanding what Jesus points out to them.[14] In other words, the focus of the question is not whether the Jews believe him or not, nor whether they oppose him or not, but what causes them to do what they do, precipitating Jesus' response and also what he teaches his disciples through these encounters. Motyer (1997, 56) points out that '[t]he *primary sense* of the term denotes those who identify themselves as Jews and adhere to the religion of Judea, whether living in Judea or not'. The explanation may include the neutral usages in the Samaritan woman's question[15] to Jesus and offer a further explanation to the text about the relationship between the Jews and the

---

separate these groups [the Jewish people in general, Judeans, or authorities hostile toward Jesus]; all are called Ἰουδαῖοι. They are one group in John'.

[13] There are two different approaches to the term, 'the Jews'. One is to search who the Jews are, and the other is to understand how the Evangelist uses the term in the Gospel. Ashton (1985, 57) calls the former, 'reference', while names the latter, 'sense'. Bennema (2009c, 240) thinks that 'while Bultmann defined the 'sense' of οἱ Ἰουδαῖοι, Martyn focused on its 'referent'.

[14] Culpepper (1983, 125) insists that the concern 'must be limited strictly to John's *characterization* of the Jews', and 'the "Johannine use" of the term has no nationalistic meaning since it distinguishes "Jews" from others of the same national, religious, cultural group and designates a group with a constant, unchanging hostility toward Jesus' (126).

[15] The woman wonders how Jesus as a Jew (singular) could ask for a drink from her, a Samaritan.

Samaritans.[16] Regarding reference he says that 'the term frequently designates adherents of the particularly strict, Torah- and Temple-centred religion' (56).[17] He continues that '[w]ithin the narrative it falls to the lot of these Ἰουδαῖοι to be the prime movers against Jesus, and so the word acquires a pejorative connotation as the narrative proceeds… particularly… in the passion narrative' (57). The 'Torah- and Temple-centred' Jews comprise one of two main counterparts to Jesus. The other is his disciples. For this reason, the overall structure of the Gospel is naturally divided into three sections demarcated with the appearance of the term οἱ Ἰουδαῖοι. The first section spans eleven chapters (chs. 2–12) during which Jesus encounters the Jews at different feasts. The next five chapters (chs. 13–17) are reserved for Jesus' discourse for his disciples.[18] The term then reappears in the passion narrative (chs. 18–19).

The plural form οἱ Ἰουδαῖοι occurs 43 times[19] in the first section (chs. 2–12). It refers to a particular group, the counterpart of Jesus, 34 times and also as a modifier for various feasts (five times)[20] and others (two times).[21] The former includes the temple cleansing (2:18, 20), Sabbath dispute in Bethesda (5:10, 15, 16, 18), bread from heaven dispute in Galilee (6:41, 52), the feast of Tabernacles episode (7:11, 13, 15, 35), heavenly belonging dispute (8:22, 31, 48, 52, 57), a blind man dispute (9:18, 22 (2x)), Dedication episode (10:24, 31, 33), the Lazarus episode (11:19, 31, 33, 36, 45; 12:9, 11) and so on. The encounters of Jesus with οἱ Ἰουδαῖοι happen mainly in the temple, on the Sabbath and during different Jewish feasts. The 'Torah- and Temple-centred religion' of Motyer (1997, 56) or 'the strict Torah- and temple-loyalists' of Bennema (2009c, 262) are well matched with the encounters in both time and place. They have a strong identity as God's people, believing that the role of God's people is to keep the Law given to them through Moses. As Wheaton (2015, 52) describes, the word Ἰουδαῖοι represents 'the people of God, the heirs of the institutions of Israel, and the people *through* whom salvation was to come into the world and *to* whom Jesus (as one of their own number) came'. Therefore, Jesus' encounters with the Jews encompass the conflict between the Jews' understanding of the identity of Israel and Jesus' presentation of it. The

---

[16] The text explains that Jews (plural) are not associated with Samaritans.

[17] After examining the term 'the Jews' with a combination of a historical (reference) and narratological (sense) approach, Bennema (2009c, 262) concludes that 'οἱ Ἰουδαῖοι in the Gospel of John are a particular religious group within Judaism – the (strict) Torah- and Temple-loyalists who are mainly located in Jerusalem and Judaea but could also have been present in Galilee'.

[18] The term οἱ Ἰουδαῖοι appears only one time in the five chapters (chs. 13–17) when Jesus referred to the Jews while he was speaking to his disciples (13:33).

[19] The term is used as a singular form twice in the sector (3:35; 4:9). Out of the 43 times of the plural usages, the term is used as a neutral twice (4:9, 22).

[20] 2:13; 5:1; 6:4; 7:2; 11:55.

[21] One is for the custom of purification (2:6) and the other for Nicodemus, one of the Jewish rulers (3:1).

conflict includes both redemptive and missional aspects. The redemptive aspect requires a fresh understanding among the Jews that Jesus fulfils what they believe and hold on to as the centre of their identity such as the temple, the Sabbath and so on. The missional aspect is related to the purpose of that identity. The Israelites are not expected to simply keep the Law in form but to understand the implied meaning of the Law. Since the 'Torah- and Temple-centred' Jews fail to understand both aspects, Jesus elucidates those aspects through the encounters. The dispute in the encounters regarding their redemptive and missional aspects will be discussed in the following section.

The Feasts τῶν Ἰουδαίων in the Fourth Gospel

One of the unique characteristics of the Fourth Gospel, when compared to the Synoptic Gospels, is the feast-centred narrative of the Gospel. The word 'Feast' and 'Passover' are frequently used[22] and the two feast terms, σκηνοπηγία (the feast of Tabernacles) and ἐγκαίνια (the feast of Dedication) only appear in the Gospel and nowhere else in the New Testament. Mollat (in Daise, 2007, 47) notes that '[t]he Jewish festivals are the "milestones" ("les jalons") of Johannine *kerygma*, which, in distinction to the Synoptics, center Jesus' activity in Jerusalem; further, they are the contexts in which the *semeia* and discourses of that *kerygma* receive their significance'. Flebbe (2009, 112) also proposes:

> The mention of feasts in John has a different, and substantially deep-seated purpose. It is therefore clear that feasts are revealing and qualifying events in the narrative sequence, in which dealings and dialogues of Jesus are reported. In this way it is shown that John's appears largely (if not almost exclusively) within the context of feasts, and his works have to be seen in conjunction with feasts.

Jewish feasts are mentioned six different times in the Gospel: three Passovers (2:13; 6:4; 11:55), an unnamed feast (5:1), the feast of Tabernacles (7:2) and the Dedication (10:22). Since Jesus in the Gospel makes a pilgrimage to Jerusalem in the season of the feasts,[23] most of the narratives in the Gospel happen in Jerusalem or somewhere in Judea, while the backdrop of his public ministry in the Synoptic Gospels is Galilee or somewhere in the North. In the encounters of Jesus with the Jews, the Jewish feasts not only provide the background of the scenes but also are woven into the content of the ensuing arguments.

---

[22] The word ἑορτὴ (feast) is used 17 times (7 times in the Synoptics) and πάσχα (Passover) 10 times (16 times in the Synoptics) in the Fourth Gospel.

[23] The only exception to Jesus not being found in Jerusalem at the time of the feast mentioned in the Gospel is the second 'Passover' (6:4).

Before each feast is discussed, it is necessary to examine how the feasts are viewed overall in the Gospel. The feasts in the Gospel function as the background for Jesus to reveal the contrasting and complementary role he fills in the Jewish traditions. Those who emphasize the contrastive aspect between Jesus and the Jewish traditions claim that Jesus himself replaces the Jewish traditions. Kerr (2002, 266–267) states that '[t]here seems to be an underlying critique of the festivals running through chs. 5–11 of the Gospel'. He supports this by pointing out that 'Jesus seemed to have little respect for the festivals. He scarcely attended them'. On the other hand, there are scholars who see the complementary or fulfilling feature of Jesus' relationship to the Jewish traditions. Wheaton (2015, 24) insists that '[a]s Jesus never adopts a negative attitude toward the Law but rather sees himself as the fulfilment of it, so he does not condemn the institutions of Judaism but participates in them'. It is true that there are disputes between Jesus and the Jews in the Gospel and, at the same time, it is also true that Jesus does not criticize the Law itself. The point, however, is not whether Jesus is the replacement or fulfilment of the Jewish traditions. Furthermore, even if Jesus is seen as the replacement of them, that does not necessarily mean that Jesus has a negative attitude toward them. Likewise, there is no straightforward equivalence between fulfilment and a positive attitude. Whether Jesus is the replacement, fulfilment or both, the point is that the Jews fail to keep the meaning of the traditions, particularly the inclusive attitude towards others, such as those individuals with whom Jesus interacts in the Gospel. The dispute between Jesus and the Jews on the traditions should be viewed from this perspective.

The Gospel uses the term τῶν Ἰουδαίων (of the Jews), the genitive of οἱ Ἰουδαῖοι to modify the feasts (2:13; 5:1; 6:4; 7:2; 11:55).[24] Porter (2015, 163) provides a syntactic function of the genitive form, saying, 'οἱ Ἰουδαῖοι is used within a genitive word group modifying a head term indicating a feature of Jewish religion-ethnicity. The governed genitive word group indicating the Jewish people as a whole restricts the meaning of the head term, often identifying it by restricting the range of options'. He means that the feast of the Jews indicates the feasts are only for the Jewish people themselves. This syntactic explanation provides a basis for both negative and positive reactions from scholars. Those who see the negative aspect of the phrase insist that it is evidence for a distance between the Jews and the Evangelist.[25] However, it is

[24] Out of six feasts in the Gospel, the Dedication (10:22) is the only feast introduced without the modifier. The Dedication is not one of the pilgrimage feasts, so the modifier functions to differentiate the pilgrimage feasts and non-pilgrimage one even though it is not the primary function of the modifier.

[25] Köstenberger (2004, 104) summarizes those claims as follows: 'Barrett (1978: 197) conjectures that the phrase may presuppose the existence of a Christian Passover at the time writing (so, earlier, Westcott 1908: 1.89; cf Borchert 1996:162). Schnackenburg (1991: 1.345 [1980a, 345]) and Beasley-Murray (1999: 39) suggest that the evangelist

hard to defend that distance considering both Jesus' participation in the feasts by ascending to Jerusalem and the feast-centred structure of the Gospel. The negative position, if there is one, does not come from renouncing the feasts by creating a gap between the Evangelist or Jesus and those referred to by the modifier τῶν Ἰουδαίων. Rather it comes from a desire on the part of the writer to recover the significance of the feasts through emphasizing participation in them and confronting the shift in their meaning (as Jesus did) and through focusing on the feasts in writing (as the Evangelist did). Others who interpret the phrase positively claim that the Evangelist kindly uses the term for the sake of his Gentile readers.[26] Furthermore, the positive interpretation is even used as evidence that the Gospel is a missional document for the Gentiles. Such shallow proof, however, only depreciates the deeper sense of the missional nature of the Gospel. For such an insistence, Carson (1991, 176) responds, saying, '[i]t is hard to believe that John's readers are Gentiles so ignorant of Judaism that they do not know the Passover is Jewish, when at several scores of points John's argument depends on his readers' grasp of subtle and detailed points of Old Testament history and Scripture'. The meaning-based quotations from the Old Testament by the Evangelist in the Gospel suggest that the Evangelist assumes his readers know the Old Testament well. Because of the seeming contradiction, Culpepper (1983, 221) questions, 'Are the comments added for the sake of the non-Jewish readers while the heart of the narrative is intended for readers who know a great deal about the festivals?' As an answer to the question, he (1983, 222) concludes that 'the reader is not Jewish but has extensive knowledge of the Old Testament', so 'the reader is either Christian or one familiar with Christianity'.

However, I argue that the modifier τῶν Ἰουδαίων should not be the basis for the claim that the reader is not Jewish. It should be noted that the term τῶν Ἰουδαίων is not used for all the feasts mentioned in the Gospel. The modifier is used only for the pilgrimage feasts given by the Lord in Leviticus 23 (cf Deut 16:16)[27] but not for the nation-made feast, the Dedication: 'Then came the Festival of Dedication [τὰ ἐγκαίνια] at Jerusalem' (10:22). This would indicate that the Evangelist uses the term τῶν Ἰουδαίων intentionally. For this reason, I argue that the Evangelist uses the modifier to point out the distortion of the original purpose and meaning of the feasts by posing a contrast between current attitudes (of the Jews) and what appeared in the Old Testament texts (of the

---

or the church had stopped participating in the Jewish Passover. Witherington (1995: 86-87) notes that the phrase indicates a certain distance between the author and Judaism and at least a partial Gentile audience (similarly, Morris 1995: 169)'.

[26] See Kruse (2003, 98), Anderson (2007, 49).

[27] In 5:1, the modifier is used for the unnamed feast; it could be supposed that the feast is one of the pilgrimage feasts mentioned in Leviticus 23.

Lord), regardless of who his readers are.[28] Brown (1966, 114) points out that the modifier 'may indicate a hostility to these feasts which are to be replaced by Jesus'.[29] The reason and purpose of the use of τῶν Ἰουδαίων, as it were, come from internal factors rather than external factors such as Gentile readers, even though that could be one of the outcomes. The internal factor is that the Jews lost the core meaning of the feasts and, instead, changed them into their own feasts, thus diminishing the missional purpose of God through them. According to Leviticus 23, what God repeatedly emphasizes when he establishes the feasts is that the feasts are ἑορταί μου (the feasts of me, Lev 23:2, LXX), that is ἑορταὶ Κυρίου (the feasts of the Lord).[30] As mentioned above, the Evangelist prefers meaning-based quotations from the Old Testament rather than direct quotations from the Greek version (LXX).[31] Wheaton (2015, 18) observes that 'it is not out of character for John to work directly from the Hebrew text when citing the Old Testament'. Then, why does the Evangelist change the modifier Κυρίου to Ἰουδαίων, *of God* to *of the Jews*? What meaning or sense does he suggest by the change? I propose the change implies that οἱ Ἰουδαῖοι reduced the meaning of the feasts by distorting them, shifting them from being God's to being their own, thus misrepresenting the meaning of the feasts.

The reductions and the distortions of the feasts have resulted in two problems.

First, οἱ Ἰουδαῖοι described in the Gospel lost their identity as a 'treasured possession' of God, a 'kingdom of priests' and a 'holy nation' (Exod 19:5–6). They kept the given Law, including the feasts and the Sabbath, on the surface but, in fact, they did not recognize that already they had lost the essence of these traditions. In the Gospel, the Jews keep focusing on the form of the Law, such as following the Law of the Sabbath day and the feasts, while Jesus keeps pointing to the meaning of the Law even by breaking the form of it. The Jews believed that they were still the descendants of Abraham (8:33, 39). However, Jesus said that they were no longer the descendants of him but of the devil.

---

[28] Michaels (2010, 158) points out that 'it signals that at this festival Jesus will confront "the Jews," that is, the religious authorities in charge of festival, and hints that there will be controversy'.

[29] Barrett (1978, 197) mentions that 'the feast is so defined partly because it is John's habit to set "the Jews" as a body over against Jesus and the church'. Lincoln (2005, 137) says that 'the narrator is not simply adding an explanation for Gentile readers; it is likely that he is also putting distance between himself and Jewish religious festivals'. Carson (1991, 176) insists on a geographical reason for the expression.

[30] Lev 23:2, 4, 37, 39.

[31] Barrett (1947, 156) finds that 'he [John] uses it [the Old Testament] in a novel manner, collecting its sense rather than quoting'. Wheaton (2015, 18) points out that 'full of grace and truth' (πλήρης χάριτος καὶ ἀληθείας) in John 1:14 is probably quoted from 'abounding in love and faithfulness' (πολυέλεος καὶ ἀληθινὸς, LXX) in Exodus 34:6 but comes directly from the Hebrew text (רב־חסד ואמת).

'You belong to your father, the devil, and you want to carry out your father's desires' (8:44). Jesus' encounters with the Jews were thus debates about their identity. Although they did not realize it, these became essential tools for educating the disciples who accompanied Jesus, helping them form the identity of the new community, which would be started with them shortly.

Secondly, an even bigger problem is misunderstanding the Messiah, since those feasts point to the Messiah. As the apostle Paul points out, one of the advantages 'in being a Jew' is that 'the Jews have been with the very words of God' (Rom 3:1–2). In a sense, they are the nation of 'revelation' of God. By being 'with the very words of God', they were expected to recognize the incarnate Word, Jesus. The Evangelist says, 'He came to that which was his own, but his own did not receive him' (1:11). As Jesus points out, the problem with the Jews is that they do not understand that the Scriptures testify about Jesus, even though they diligently study the Scriptures (5:39). Therefore, the attitude of Jesus toward the feasts should be read as his efforts to recover the meaning of them and the missional identity of the Jews (cf Matt 23:37).

In the Fourth Gospel, the reaction of Jesus to the distorted feasts, or more precisely, toward the Jews, grows progressively stronger. In the first feast (Passover), he enters the temple immediately, even though his visit precipitates his angry cry against the business people whom he drives from the temple. In the second feast (unnamed), however, he comes to Jerusalem but goes to Bethesda first, which is 'near the Sheep Gate', and comes to the temple later. In the third feast (Passover), no visit of Jesus to Jerusalem is mentioned. In the fourth feast (Tabernacles), 'he hijacked it for his own purposes' as Kerr (2002, 266) points out. In the last Passover, he eventually fulfils his purpose. To sum it up, the Evangelist uses the feasts and related traditions to demonstrate the way in which Jesus criticizes the distorted identity of the Jews and refreshes the missional identity of the people of God for the new discipleship community. He also uses them to point out their real meaning fulfilled in Jesus. It is a matter of the missional identity of the Jews, thus of the new community.

Jesus' Encounters with the Jews at the Feasts

Jesus in the Feast of Passover

Among the feasts mentioned in the Gospel, half are Passovers. Stibbe (in Porter, 2015, 204) says that '[t]he whole of the Gospel could be described as a Passover plot in that it moves through the three Passover festivals in 2:13, 6:4 and 13:1'. The Passover in the Gospel is not simply the name of a feast. The first three feasts of Israel are often collectively called either Passover or the Unleavened. The Synoptics use both terms,[32] but the Fourth Gospel uses only

[32] Matt 26:17; Mark 14:1, 12; Luke 22:1,7.

the term 'Passover'. For this reason, the term πάσχα refers to the whole Passover week, including the Unleavened and the Firstfruits, rather than just a day of Passover. The Passover is related to the redemptive aspect of the Messiah. Jesus is introduced by the Baptist as 'the Lamb of God who takes away the sin of the world' (1:29), so the final Passover, the passion narrative, is the fulfilment[33] by the Messiah of the paschal sacrifice of the Passover. The first two Passovers (2:13; 6:4), however, rather than repeating the same aspect, reveal instead the complementary aspects of the redemptive Messiah, which is the sacrifice for the Passover. In this section, the first two Passovers will be explored.

On the first Passover, Jesus cleanses the temple, identifying it with himself. He alludes to his death and resurrection in his answer to the Jews: 'Destroy this temple, and I will raise it again in three days' (2:19). The Fourth Gospel uses the verb ἐγείρω (to raise), implying the resurrection of Jesus,[34] instead of οἰκοδομέω (to build), which is used in the Synoptics.[35] Since the Passover and the Firstfruits symbolize the sacrifice and resurrection of the Messiah as the Firstfruits (cf 1 Cor 15:20) respectively, the destroying and raising of the temple perfectly identify with the body of the Messiah. The Evangelist adds a comment, saying, '[a]fter he was raised from the dead, his disciples recalled what he had said. Then they believed the scripture and the words that Jesus had spoken' (2:22). It should be noted that the temple cleansing episode in the first Passover reveals two other aspects of the redemptive mandate of the Messiah and the three following stories (Nicodemus, a Samaritan woman and a royal official) provide supplemental insights regarding these aspects. In this sense, the first Passover narrative spans all three chapters (chs. 2–4). The two other aspects of the redemptive Messiah, besides the sacrifice of Passover, are the fellowship aspect and the inclusiveness aspect.

First, Jesus is the reality of the temple.[36] Jesus is declaring that he is not only the true sacrifice but also the true temple where people can meet God. The temple identity of Jesus is developed within the Gospel. He was introduced as the incarnate Word who tabernacles among his people (1:14) and also as the ladder on which the angels of God are ascending and descending (1:51). Now he identifies himself as the true temple. The tabernacle, the ladder and the

---

[33] Evans (in Porter, 2015, 200) points out that the OT quotations in John 1:23–12:16 are 'regularly introduced or alluded to with "it is written", or the like, while in 12:38–19:37 [they are] regularly introduced with the formula "in order that [the Scripture or what was spoken] be fulfilled"'.

[34] The verb is used for resurrection in the Fourth Gospel. 2:22; 5:21; 12:1; 12:9; 12:17; 21:14.

[35] Matt 26:61; Mark 14:58.

[36] It is interesting that Paul uses the word σῶμα (body) meaning 'reality' compared to 'shadow' in Col 2:17 and the reality of the temple is the body of Christ in the Fourth Gospel. Therefore, the σῶμα of the temple is the σῶμα of Christ.

temple share one common feature – they are places where God meets his people and the meeting between God and his people is made possible in Jesus. The role of the redemptive Messiah is not just to be a victim *passively* to remove the sin of the world but also to be a place *actively* where his people can meet, worship and have fellowship with God. The fellowship aspect of the redemptive Messiah is emphasized in the Gospel through the following Passover narratives.

Secondly, the redemptive Messiah is not limited to the Jews only but is for all people. He is an inclusive Messiah. Jesus drives out those who were selling animals for sacrifice and the money changers in the temple. The probability is that the place spoken of here was the court of the Gentiles. No matter who the sellers and changers were, they were blocking the Gentiles' worship of God in the court of the Gentiles by occupying their space. Jesus is declaring that he is the redemptive Messiah for all by driving them out of the temple. These aspects – sacrifice, fellowship and inclusiveness – are affirmed and illustrated by the three following stories, each with different emphases, yet all aligned toward an explicit direction, which is for the people to πιστεύω (believe). The arrangement of the stories themselves shows the inclusiveness of the Messiah through whom anyone who believes shall have eternal life (3:16). Jesus encounters different individuals who represent different ethnic groups, one after the other, starting with a Jew, then a Samaritan and finally a royal official who might be a Gentile even though it is not specified in the Gospel. This will be discussed in detail in section 4.5.

In the second Passover narrative (6:4–71), Jesus is not ascending to Jerusalem; instead, he is staying in Galilee feeding a crowd. In the narrative, the feeding-a-crowd episode opens a new discourse describing Jesus, the sacrifice of Passover, as the bread of life. The significance of the unleavened bread in the feast is fully realized in Jesus, for he himself is the bread of life for the world. In the previous Passover feast, Jesus identified himself as a new temple where his people can have fellowship with God. Now he offers himself as a meal for his people to eat and have eternal life. Wheaton (2015, 88) observes that '[t]he significance of the sacrifice of Jesus *as paschal victim* lies not predominantly in any value intrinsic to the sacrifice itself, but rather *in its function as provision for the paschal meal, the eating of which is requisite for participation in the covenant community that is restored through the death of Jesus*'. In the discourse, πιστεύω is identified with eating and drinking the flesh and blood of Jesus (cf 6:40, 54). Jesus does the will of the Father (6:38) and the will of the Father is that everyone who believes in Jesus shall have eternal life (6:40). Furthermore, believing in him in the Gospel is to have fellowship with him. Jesus says: 'Whoever eats my flesh and drinks my blood remains in me, and I in them' (6:56). The fellowship verb μένω is used again. Through the first two Passovers, the Gospel introduces Jesus, the Passover lamb, not only as the traditional sacrifice aspect but also as the fellowship aspect – which requires that people participate in the meal of God – and as the inclusiveness aspect, indicating the meal is open to all.

Jesus in the Unnamed Feast

The anonymity of the feast, whether it was the Evangelist's intention or not, has caused conjecture by many commentators not only regarding the name of it but also regarding the broader structure of the Gospel. Michaels (2010, 287) proposes that 'this unnamed "festival of the Jews" could be any festival between the first Passover in Jerusalem (2:13) and the second Passover (presumably a year later) at the time Jesus fed the multitude in Galilee (6:4)'. There are a few things to be considered before assuming it is a particular feast. First, the modifier τῶν Ἰουδαίων is used in the Gospel only for feasts commanded by the Lord, so the unnamed feast of the Jews is probably one of the seven feasts mentioned in Leviticus. Secondly, for three feasts male Jews are required to ascend to Jerusalem, so the feast might be one of those three feasts since Jesus ascended to Jerusalem for the feast. Thirdly, three Passovers (2:13; 6:4; 11:55) appear in the Gospel and the name of each is mentioned without exception, so 'it is unlikely… that the author intends us to think it [the unnamed] as Passover' as Michaels (2010, 287) points out. The feast is located between two Passover observances, therefore it would be either Pentecost or Tabernacles. Fourthly, the feast of Tabernacles is also mentioned by name in the Gospel. Therefore, the probability is that the unnamed feast is Pentecost. Brown (1966, 206) points out that '[a]n early tradition in the Greek church identifies this unnamed feast as Pentecost'. Calvin (1961, 116) supports this claim, taking the 'four months to the harvest' as his evidence. He says that 'the order of time leads us to understand it as Pentecost' (116). Identifying the unnamed feast is not the point, however, though the story related to the feast is well matched with the missional nature of Pentecost.

The Evangelist describes Bethesda, the place into which Jesus entered, as ἐπὶ τῇ προβατικῇ (near the Sheep Gate). According to Nehemiah 3:1, the priest, Eliashib, and other priests rebuilt the Gate. It is probably so-named because the Gate is the place where 'the sheep were brought into Jerusalem for sacrifice' as Brown (1966, 206) describes and sacrifice is one of the main elements of the feasts no matter which feast it is (Num 28:19, 27; 29:2, 8, 13). In this sense, the Sheep Gate symbolizes religious fervour. The Jews' commitment to God could be measured at this Gate by the quality of the sacrifice without defect. The Sheep Gate is the appropriate place to be for all Jews who come to Jerusalem for the feast. Jesus, however, goes not to the Gate, but to Bethesda, a pool where a great number of the sick are gathered. This visit might be a surprise for his disciples primarily and, secondarily, for readers of the Gospel who knew the tradition. By going to the pool first instead of to the Gate or the temple, Jesus reveals that the important point is not how well the people of God keep the feast but whether the essence of the feast is still present. The essence of the feast is to know the meaning of it rather than simply to follow the rules. As Jesus says, quoting Hosea in Matthew, '[b]ut go and learn what this means: "I desire mercy, not sacrifice."[37] For I have not come to call the righteous, but sinners' (Matt 9:13). There are lots of people who need 'mercy' near the place of 'sacrifice'. The essence of the sacrifice is to enhance 'mercy' as a way of reminding the Jews who participate in the feast that they are to reveal the mercy of God to the world. The Sheep Gate in the Gospel, however, or more precisely, *the Jews*, did not fulfil their role. Alan Kerr (2002, 276), who suggests that the unnamed feast represents all feasts,[38] insists that 'John may be pointing in the subsequent verses to a picture of Judaism (including the festivals) in its weakness and impotence'.

Jesus does not stop there, though. If it is a passive challenge for the Jews that he goes to the pool first instead of to the Gate, now he challenges them actively by breaking the Sabbath Law. The day he heals a sick man at the pool is the Sabbath. Again, the primary concern for the Jews is to keep the Law rightly and thereby they have just cause to persecute Jesus because of this violation. Jesus justifies himself saying, 'My Father is always at his work to this very day, and I too am working' (5:17). The response of the Jews in answer to Jesus is not curiosity about what kinds of work God and Jesus are doing but displeasure at the blasphemy of Jesus claiming he is equal with God (5:18). It is interesting that a few recent Johannine commentaries[39] also interpret the verse (5:17) in the latter perspective. The thrust of the argument in the commentaries is that God does not cease his work in sustaining the universe, and that Jesus injects himself into the same level with God by saying so. When the argument goes in the direction of the latter perspective, the consequent questions may be similar to those Michaels (2010, 302) poses:

> Does it mean that after creating the world God continued working until now, but that now Jesus takes over in God's place? Or does it mean that God continued working and is still at work, only now through Jesus the Son? Or that God has been at work ever since creation, first through the pre-existent Son and now through the incarnate Son? Or is it simply that God is still at work, and Jesus is God's imitator, like a son apprenticed to his father?

However, I argue that the question should be regarding what kinds of work God and Jesus are doing, and that all this needs to be understood within the overall theme of the Gospel. In the previous chapter, the study has already discussed the relationship God and the Word had before the world was created.

---

[37] Hos 6:6a.

[38] Kerr, 2002, 206.

[39] Köstenberger (2004, 185); Michaels (2010, 301–302) uses 'life' instead of 'universe' saying 'God is at work constantly, giving and sustaining life, rewarding the righteous and punishing the wicked'.

Their relationship was the foundation for Creation, Incarnation and creating a New Community. Therefore, the work of God and Jesus in the Gospel should not be described in generalities such as sustaining the universe and so on. Instead, it should be understood within both a redemptive and a missional perspective. First, the work of God and Jesus is redemptive. God is doing his work by sending his own son into the world. The fact that the Son is in the world signifies that the Father is working at the moment, the work of salvation. Secondly, it is missional. The Father created all creatures through the Word. The Father sent the incarnate Word to the world, so the Father is creating something through the incarnate Word, Jesus, in the world. The whole life of Jesus reveals the process of the new creation. The discipleship community is the start of the new creation; the community is expected to continue the work. In that sense, it is missional.

I propose that the Evangelist uses the unnamed feast and the following narrative to reveal the missional identity of the chosen nation. If the analysis that the unnamed feast is Pentecost is plausible, then the narrative is well matched with the meaning of the feast. Pentecost is the feast requiring the Jews to bring the first fruits (of wheat), and it later signified the birth of the church. Acts records the church as birthed in the first Pentecost after the resurrection of Jesus (cf Acts 2).

Jesus in the Feast of Tabernacles

The feast of Tabernacles is mentioned only in the Fourth Gospel in the New Testament. As the feast of Passover represents three spring feasts, the feast of Tabernacles represents three autumn feasts, the feast of Trumpets, the Day of Atonement and the feast of Tabernacles. Because of the role of the trumpets for gathering the congregation in Israel (Num 10:1–10), the feast of Trumpets is associated with the return of the Messiah as the apostle Paul envisions (1 Thes 4:16; cf 1 Cor 15:51–52). The next feast, the Day of Atonement, is the day once a year when God cleanses his people from all their sins (Lev 16:29–30). It is written in the book of Hebrews that Jesus, who came as high priest, 'entered the Most Holy Place once for all by his own blood, thus obtaining eternal redemption' (cf Heb 9:7–12). This reference demonstrates Jesus' authority to forgive sins (cf Matt 9:6; Mark 2:10; Luke 5:24); this will be completed when he returns. The last feast has two different names. One is the feast of Booths or Tabernacles and the other is the feast of In-gathering. The former refers to the Israelites dwelling in temporary shelters during the feast; the latter derives its name from the time when all crops are harvested and gathered revealing the completion of the harvest. In the Fourth Gospel, the term σκηνοπηγία (Tabernacles) is used. The return of the Messiah (the feast of Trumpets), the atonement of sin (the day of Atonement) and the gathering of the harvest (the feast of Tabernacles) are the themes related with the autumn feasts.

The narrative of the feast of Tabernacles in the Gospel includes the episodes in the following chapters (7:2–11:46). The episodes in this section of the Gospel are 'a woman caught in adultery', 'a man born blind' and 'the resurrection of Lazarus'; then various discourses are attached to the episodes. One issue needs to be addressed before arguing the episodes are all related to the theme of the feast of Tabernacles. In 10:22, a new feast, the feast of Dedication, is mentioned. If the feast is introduced as a new feast to explain a new theme, and the following episode and discourse are attached to that theme, then it should be handled as a separate feast and theme. The feast of Dedication, however, does not appear to be the introduction of a new theme in the narrative for many reasons. First, the feast does not have the modifier τῶν Ἰουδαίων, which has been used in the Gospel for all the feasts prescribed in Leviticus 23 (cf Deut 16:16). This fact indicates that the feast of Dedication is not mentioned for the issues disputed by those Old Testament feasts in the Gospel. Secondly, there is no indication that Jesus or others ascend to Jerusalem for the feast. The verb ἀναβαίνω (to ascend) is used in the pilgrimage feasts in the Gospel[40] except for the second Passover during which Jesus remains in Galilee. Instead, the Gospel notes that Jesus is already there. Thirdly, this is the only feast in the Gospel for which a season (winter) is mentioned. This indicates that Jesus is in Jerusalem at the time between the feast of Tabernacles and the last Passover. Fourthly, what Jesus talks about after the feast is the same topic he talked about before the feast, which is the theme of the good shepherd. The introduction of the feast of Dedication does not serve to change the theme. Based on the above facts, the feast of Dedication serves merely as an indicator that Jesus was in Jerusalem (possibly remained there since the feast of Tabernacles) and the Jews were there gathered around Jesus because it was the time of the feast. It does not appear to signal that a new feast and a new theme are introduced in the narrative. Therefore, I view that the narrative of the feast of Tabernacles extends to 11:46.

In the feast of Tabernacles, for the first time Jesus mentions returning to the one who sent him (7:33), which aligns with the theme of the feast of Tabernacles as the completion of the harvest and the gathering of the harvest. Therefore, the episodes and their related discourses need to be viewed from this perspective. In this feast of Tabernacles and the following episodes, the encounters between Jesus and the Jews are intensified. First, the episode of 'a woman caught in adultery' and the following debate between Jesus and the Jews reveal a clearer identity of Jesus as the one who replaces and fulfils the Law. In the episode, it is not known what Jesus wrote on the ground twice, but it is important to note that he wrote with his finger. The picture reminds the reader of 'the tablets of stone inscribed by the finger of God' (Exod 31:18).

---

40 2:13; 5:1; 7:2, 6, 8, 10; 11:55 (cf for the last Passover, Jesus arrives at Bethany first, so ἔρχομαι is used in 12:1).

The Jews use the Law inscribed (γράφω, LXX) by the finger (δάκτυλος, LXX) of God for condemning the woman (8:5). In contrast to this, Jesus writes (γράφω)[41] something with his finger (δάκτυλος) to forgive the woman. Through the episode, it is revealed that the Law-centred Jews misunderstand and misuse the Law.

In the following debate with the Jews, Jesus goes even further and accentuates the Jews' misunderstanding of Abraham's descendants, saying, 'You belong to your father, the devil' (8:44) even though he knows that they are the descendants of Abraham (8:37). As the apostle Paul says, 'Scripture… announced the gospel in advance to Abraham: "All nations will be blessed through you"' (Gal 3:8). Jesus declares: 'Your father Abraham rejoiced at the thought of seeing my day; he saw it and was glad' (8:56). Descendants of Abraham are not those who have his blood in them but those who understand his missional purpose and know that it is fulfilled and will be fulfilled in Christ. Therefore, what is essential is not to be physical descendants of Abraham but to be disciples of Jesus. Jesus says to the Jews who believe him that they are really his disciples if they abide (μένω) by his teaching (8:31).

The next episode, 'a man born blind', reveals that the Messiah is the light of the world (9:5). In connection with the gathering theme of the Tabernacles, this episode introduces a new term ἀποσυνάγωγος (excommunicated). The term ἀποσυνάγωγος (9:22; 12:42; 16:2) provides the foundation for Martyn's 'two-level drama' of the Fourth Gospel. He (2003, 66) insists that '[i]n the two-level drama of John 9, the man born blind plays not only the part of a Jew in Jerusalem healed by Jesus of Nazareth, but also the part of Jews known to John who have become members of the separated church because of their messianic faith and because of the awesome Benediction'. Culpepper (1983, 3) critiques this approach saying that 'John has been used as a "window" through which the critic can catch "glimpses" of the history of the Johannine community'. The crucial error of this 'window-like' reading of the text is that it blurs what Jesus is pointing out, and shifts the focus to the conflict between the Jews and a Christian community called the Johannine community. Here, the man born blind confesses that he believes and worships Jesus (9:38). The contrast is that the distorted missional community excommunicates people because of Christ, while God gathers people because of Christ. The gathering activity of God is not just to assemble a collection of people but to build intimate relationships with people in the process.

The good shepherd discourse emphasizes this characteristic of the gathering. According to the discourse, the shepherd calls his own sheep by name, and the sheep know his voice (10:3–4). This intimate relationship reaches a depth that causes the shepherd to lay down his life in order for the sheep to have life (10:10–11, 15). Jesus goes even further and says to the Jews (Pharisees), 'I

[41] καταγράφω (to write down) in 8:6 and γράφω in 8:8.

have other sheep that are not of this sheep pen. I must bring them also. They too will listen to my voice, and there shall be one flock and one shepherd' (10:16). It needs to be noted that Jesus is making this missional statement to the Jews. It affirms that Jesus is drawing attention to the distorted missional identity of the Jews.

The last episode in the narrative of the Tabernacles is the resurrection of Lazarus. The themes in the feast of Tabernacles escalate through the narrative beginning with the forgiveness of sin, moving through the giving of the light and the good shepherd and climaxing in the episode of the resurrection of Lazarus through the giving of life back to him. The Lazarus episode is the only place where the Jews do not argue with Jesus directly nor among themselves, even though 'some of them went to the Pharisees and told them what Jesus had done' (11:46).

Through the feast-centred or feast-related narratives, the Evangelist points out that the Law-centred Jews, the Jewish leaders in particular, misunderstand the meaning of the Law, and the Jews as Abraham's descendants or the Jews who are Jews 'only outwardly' in Paul's term (Rom 2:28) are not the nation God intended to build even though the Jewish leaders worry about their 'temple and nation' (11:48). That does not mean that Jesus rejects the Jews. On the contrary, Jesus wants the Jews to join the new community by faith. Even though the Jewish authorities are overtly opposed to Jesus in this phase, there are also many people who believe in him. The progressive change of the Jews is remarkable in this phase. Unlike the prompt decision of Samaritans and a Gentile family, the Jew Nicodemus shows his progressive change[42] through the course of the Gospel. Likewise, the progressive change of the Jews appears throughout their encounters with Jesus. The phrase τοὺς πεπιστευκότας αὐτῷ Ἰουδαίους (the Jews who had believed him) appears for the first time in 8:31. The Evangelist comments that 'many of the Jews who had come to visit Mary, and had seen what Jesus did, believed in him [Jesus]' (11:45). The final assessment of the Evangelist for this second part regarding the Jews is as follow: 'Even after Jesus had performed so many signs in their presence, they [the Jews] still would not believe in him [Jesus]' (12:37). 'Yet, at the same time many even among the [Jewish] leaders believed in him [Jesus]' (12:42).

---

[42] The Evangelist depicts Nicodemus in three different appearances. At first, Nicodemus appears as one of many people who saw the signs Jesus was performing. (cf 2:23; 3:2) He probably believed in his name with the signs. Jesus did not entrust himself to those people (2:24; 3:3). Then, he appears again as a defender of Jesus in a meeting of leaders (7:50–51). Lastly, he appears with a disciple of Jesus, Joseph of Arimathea. The three appearances with different roles reveal that there was progress in his faith.

Jesus' Interactions with Different Individuals

The Characteristics of the New Community

The Evangelist introduces Jesus' interactions with different individuals throughout the second part of the Gospel. Those individuals are Nicodemus, a Samaritan woman, a royal official, a man at the Bethesda pool, an adulterous woman, a man born blind and Lazarus' sisters. Those interactions and their responses to Jesus contrast to the responses of the Jews in the Gospel. Jesus' interaction with a Samaritan woman and Samaritans in Sychar (4:1–26, 39–42) contrasts with his encounter with the Jews at the first Passover in Jerusalem (2:13–25). Jesus' interactions with a man at the Bethesda pool, an adulterous woman and a man born blind contrast with his encounters with the surrounding Jews. The contrasts between the Jews and those individuals in the Gospel demonstrate the characteristics of the new community that Jesus is forming and that his discipleship community will continue to extend.

First, Jesus' interactions with different individuals reveal that the new community is a diverse community. The diversity of the community is all-inclusive. Jesus' interactions in his first trip from Cana to Cana (2:13–4:54) reveal that the new community is open to all ethnicities, from Jews to Samaritans and possibly to Gentiles, should the royal official be a Gentile.[43] The narrative shows Jesus' ministry in Jerusalem, Judea, Samaria and at least the beginning of the ends of the earth (cf Acts 1:8; Matt 4:15), Galilee.[44] The new community that Jesus desires to form is not a community of a single ethnic group, the Jewish community, but a community of people from all over the world. As the Samaritans confessed, Jesus is 'the Savior of the world' (4:42). The interactions also show the inclusion of all social classes in the community. The scope of the new community includes both the leaders of a society and the marginalised people. It is all-embracing in its scope.

Secondly, the new community is a believing community rather than an entitled community. The Jews insist that they are 'Abraham's descendants' (8:33) and God is their father (8:41). But, Jesus says to them that they belong to the devil (8:44). The Evangelist already proclaimed in the first chapter that 'to all who receive him [Jesus], to those who believed in his name, he gave the right to become children of God – children born not of natural descent, nor of human decision or a husband's will, but born of God' (1:12–13). The Evangelist reports that those individuals believe in Jesus. The Samaritan woman believes in him and also many of Samaritans believe in him 'because of the woman's testimony (4:39). The royal official whose son was healed by Jesus and his whole household believe in him (4:53). The man born blind says

---

[43] It is unidentified whether the royal official is a Gentile.

[44] The royal official's family was in in Capernaum, a town in Galilee. It is called 'Galilee of the Gentiles' by Isaiah (9:1) quoted in Matthew 4:15.

to Jesus that he believes in him (9:38). It is unknown whether the man at the Bethesda pool and the adulterous woman believe in him or not, but there are positive signs suggesting they do.[45] Carson (1991, 300) points out that '[t]he dividing line, for John, is never race but response to Jesus'.

Thirdly, the interactions show the intimate characteristic of the new community. The intimate relationship between Jesus and those individuals is expressed in various ways. Nicodemus' seventy-five pounds of a mixture of myrrh and aloes (cf 19:39) could correspond to the expensive perfume Mary lavished on Jesus (12:3). Those are expressions of their love for Jesus. The Samaritan woman also feels intimacy with Jesus, saying, 'see a man who told me everything I ever did' (4:29). Because of the similar setting of this story with the well narratives in the Old Testament, such as Rebekah (Gen 24:1–27), Rachel (Gen 29:1–12) and Zipporah (Exod 2:15–21), the Samaritan woman is often interpreted as a bride. Bennema insists that 'Jesus indeed functions as a sort of bridegroom and the Samaritan woman as a bride – in that the woman's confession of faith in Jesus symbolizes a spiritual betrothal'. The intimate relationship between Jesus and those individuals climaxes in the narrative of Lazarus. The Gospel says Jesus ἀγαπάω the family (11:5) and Jesus himself calls Lazarus ὁ φίλος ἡμῶν (11:11). Jesus uses the word φίλος for the first time[46] in the Gospel. His intimate relationship with Lazarus is affirmed by what the Jews say, 'See how he [Jesus] loved him [Lazarus]!' (11:36) when Jesus weeps.

Nicodemus – A Ray of Light

Among those individuals, the position of Nicodemus is noteworthy since he appears as the only person who personally contacted Jesus from the group of Jewish leaders in the Gospel (3:1–2). As seen above (4.4), Jesus' encounters with the Jews in the Gospel bring certain debates in general between Jesus and the Jews around him, the Jewish leaders in particular. Unlike most individuals who show a change to believing in Jesus after their interactions with Jesus, Nicodemus does not show such a result after his first encounter with Jesus. Because of these two different pictures of Nicodemus, a positive picture that he visited Jesus and a negative picture that he did not confess his faith in Jesus, there is no agreed view on him in terms of his faith in Jesus. Bennema (2009a, 77) lists those different views saying 'from being someone who became Jesus' disciples, to "the true Israelite", "a well-intentioned representative of the ruling classes", a fearful "secret believer", a *tertium quid*, a pathetic character lacking

---

[45] The Evangelist uses the verb ἀναγγέλλω (to announce) in 5:15. Within the Gospel, the verb λέγω (to say) is used both positively (4:28) and negatively (11:46), but the verb ἀναγγέλλω is used positively taking the Messiah (4:25) and the Holy Spirit (16:13,14,15) as subject.

[46] Jesus uses the word φίλος (friend) one more time later for his disciples (cf 15:13–15).

courage and conviction, one who has come "to a dead end", or even the typical unbeliever'. Each of these views only describes a part of his identity. In a missional reading within the canonical context, I argue that the Evangelist uses him as more than 'a seeker' in general for the following reasons.

First of all, the Evangelist introduces Nicodemus as a representative of 'sign-based' believers. In Jesus' first visit to Jerusalem, 'many people saw the signs he was performing and believed in his name' (2:23). The Evangelist adds his comments that '[b]ut Jesus would not entrust himself to them' (2:24). Nicodemus' mention of 'signs' (3:2) signifies that he is one of those who saw the signs Jesus was performing. The dialogue between Jesus and Nicodemus shows that the 'sign-based' belief is not adequate. What he knows about Jesus is 'a teacher who has come from God' based on the signs, but what he must know is 'the kingdom of God' which he can see by being 'born again' (3:3). The 'sign-based' belief which Nicodemus represents is criticized by the 'kingdom-based' belief which Jesus introduces.

Nicodemus' identity as 'a Pharisee' (3:1), 'a member of the Jewish ruling council' (3:1), and 'Israel's teacher' (3:10) shows that no one, even the Jewish leaders who believe that they are saved by default, can enter the kingdom of God without believing in Jesus whom God sent to save the world through him (3:17). Nicodemus' first encounter with Jesus reveals that he is ignorant of 'heavenly things' even though he is 'Israel's teacher' (3:10–12).

Nevertheless, the Evangelist implies that there is hope for the Jews through the second appearance of Nicodemus in the Gospel (7:45–52). The Pharisees who got a report from the guards responded: 'Have any of the rulers or of the Pharisees believed in him? No!'. It indicates that those Jewish leaders believed that no believers of Jesus were known among the Pharisees and the Jewish leaders. They thought that the followers of Jesus were all from Galilee (7:52). However, the appeal of Nicodemus in the meeting signifies that there are believers from the group. Later, the Evangelist comments that 'many even among the leaders believed in him [Jesus]. But because of the Pharisees they would not openly acknowledge their faith' (12:42). Michaels (2010, 177) points out that 'the writer [Evangelist] quickly brings Nicodemus, both ruler and Pharisee, on the scene (7:50–51) as if in refutation of their claim, confirming the impression here that he belongs to those who "believed in his name" at this first Passover'. Through this second appearance of Nicodemus in the Gospel, the readers have a somewhat more positive stance on him than the first appearance. In that sense, the third appearance of Nicodemus in the Gospel is important to know how he is understood in terms of 'faith'.

He comes to the scene again after Jesus' death (19:38–42). He and Joseph of Arimathea came and took the body of Jesus for the burial. In this episode, there is no clear mention that Nicodemus is now a disciple of Jesus or believes in him. Bennema (2009a, 82) points out that 'John does not provide sufficient evidence that Nicodemus's action or understanding of Jesus is adequate for salvation'. Nevertheless, Nicodemus' third appearance needs to be understood in a larger context. First, his action with Joseph should be compared to the action of the disciples. Nicodemus and Joseph came to take the body of Jesus while most of the disciples flee from the place of his death. Secondly, Joseph is introduced as a disciple here, so Nicodemus who accompanies with him can be understood as a similar status. Schnackenburg (1982, 297) views that 'Nicodemus too in a similar way to Joseph of Arimathaea, is pictured as a man for whom Jesus' death leads to a breakthrough of a more decisive attitude in his death'. Thirdly, what he brings for the burial of the body is equivalent to the burial of a king which shows that Nicodemus understands the kingship of Jesus. Brown (1994b, 1261) points out that 'Jesus was accorded a burial fit for a king' and this 'would correspond well to the solemn proclamation that on the cross he was truly "the King of the Jews" (John 19:19–20)'. Fourthly, the Evangelist devotes the recovery of the disciples rather than pointing out the unbelief of someone in the narrative after Jesus' death (chs. 19-21). The recovery of the disciples starts from Nicodemus right after Jesus' death to Thomas (20:26–29),[47] Peter (21:15–19) and probably the beloved disciple (21:22–23).

Based on those observations, I argue that Nicodemus shows progressive changes throughout the Gospel.[48] Nicodemus's example shows how difficult the change of religious leaders is in comparison to the changes of the crowd, the people in need in particular. In that sense, Nicodemus is a ray of light for the potential change of the Jewish leaders.

The Samaritan Woman – Breaking Socio-Religious Impossibility

Jesus' encounters with the Jews and his interactions with those individuals are observed by the accompanying disciples, 'the Twelve' in particular. I describe those encounters and interactions as the breaking of *socio-religious impossibility* by Jesus. I have borrowed this term from Hoekendijk's use of it to point to the barriers which existed between different social classes in the Roman Empire.[49] Jesus' interactions with different individuals break various barriers including social or religious barriers in the eyes of the disciples. The Samaritan episode reveals this missional characteristic, thus I will examine the story from this perspective.

---

[47] Even though Thomas shows his doubt in the narrative since he was not present when Jesus visited the disciples (20:24) but the story ends with the recovery of him (20:26–29).

[48] Schnackenburg (1982, 295) supports this view saying, 'in clear contrast to the Jews (v.31, cf. v.38) they [Joseph and Nicodemus] represent the fellowship of Jesus which shows great honour to its Lord'.

[49] Johannes Hoekendijk uses the term 'sociological impossibility' in his book, *Kirche und Volk in der deutschen Missionswissenschaft* (1967, 245), and David Bosch quotes the term in his book, *Transforming Mission* (1991, 48).

The Samaritan episode consists of three separate but integrated stories: Jesus' interaction with a Samaritan woman (4–26), Jesus' dialogue with his disciples (27, 31–38), and the story of the Samaritans (28–30, 39–42). Okure (1988, 77) views 'vv 1–26(27) as the *thesis* or the *narratio* and vv 28–42 as the *consequential argument* composed of an *expositio* (vv 31–38) and a *demonstratio* (vv 28–30, 39–42)'.

The first part of the episode, Jesus' interaction with the Samaritan woman, reveals Jesus' example of how one could cross the barriers for communicating the salvation message. First, Jesus crosses various barriers to interact with the woman. The barriers he crosses are multi-faceted and accumulated through history for a long time. They are geographical, ethnic, social, cultural, gender, moral[50] and even theological barriers. Bennema (2009a, 87) points out that 'He [Jesus] crosses geographical, ethnic, religious, social and gender barriers in order to meet this complex character – a Samaritan, a woman and a social outcast'. The Jews did not socialize with the Samaritans. The strangeness of this interaction is expressed through the reaction of the woman: 'You [Jesus] are a Jew and I am a Samaritan woman. How can you ask me for a drink?' (4:9). The Evangelist comments on the reaction, explaining, 'For Jews do not associate with Samaritans' (4:9). For this reason, the disciples 'were surprised to find him [Jesus] talking with a [Samaritan] woman' (4:27).

Crossing such barriers is already a shocking experience, but we should pay attention to the overcoming of the internal barriers that Jesus shows through the process of dialogue with her; not just those external barriers. Jesus faces conversational barriers as expected. The Samaritan woman shows her resistance through the process of the conversation saying 'How can you ask me for a drink?' (4:9), 'I have no husband' (4:17), and 'Our ancestors worshipped on this mountain' (4:20). Jesus keeps his humility and listening attitude in this conversation starting with putting himself in a vulnerable position by asking for a drink. Okure (1988, 130) says that '[t]hough Jesus is the one with the "gift of God" to offer, he nevertheless approaches the woman as a beggar, thereby making himself most approachable, even putting himself at the woman's mercy at the start of the conversation'. The manner and attitude of Jesus in the conversation shows that his interaction with her basically proceeds in love. Nevertheless, he does not lose the focus, speaking the truth (cf Eph 4:15). While he maintains the humble attitude, he leads the conversation to the truth by mentioning 'the gift of God' (4:10), 'eternal life' (4:14), 'salvation' (4:22),

---

[50] Carson (1991, 217) points out that '[w]omen were more likely to come in groups to fetch water, and either earlier or later in the day when the heat of the sun was not so fierce'. My own life experience in a village in a Middle East country supports Carson's insistence. Not only because of the heat but also because women are not supposed to reveal themselves in daytime and so they tend to come in at the beginning or the end of the day in groups. If they need water urgently during daytime, they send their sons.

'worship the Father in the Spirit and in truth' (4:23), and 'I am he [Messiah]' (4:26).

The story does not end in this personal interaction since the woman went back to her village. While she brings the villagers to Jesus, the Evangelist introduces the second story of the Samaritan episode. The second story shows that the whole Samaritan episode has an educational purpose for the disciples – their mission to come, in particular. Even though they were not present when Jesus interacted with the woman, they will know the result soon when the Samaritans come to Jesus because of the testimony of the woman. As I mentioned above, one of the major purposes of the interaction of Jesus with the woman and also other interactions of him with different individuals is to equip the disciples to be a missional community so that they carry on their mission. The disciples of Jesus observe not only the performances of Jesus but also the contemporary meaning of Jesus' performances in their socio-religious context, particularly in light of the strong opposition of the Jews. From this perspective, his mission breaks *socio-religious impossibility*. Jesus says 'My food is to do the will of him who sent me and to finish his work' (4:34). This implies that the food of the disciples will be to do the will of Jesus who will send them, and to finish his work since Jesus will send them as the Father sent him (cf 20:21). Their mission will follow the same characteristics. Okure (1988, 76) points out that 'vv 31–38 deals with it [Jesus' mission] didactically from the standpoint of the disciples whom Jesus instructs on the nature of their own involvement in the mission'.

The third story of the Samaritan episode deals with the outcome of Jesus' interaction with the woman which is what Okure (1988, 77) calls a *demonstratio*. The confession of the Samaritans that 'this man really is the Savior of the world' (4:42) reveals that this Samaritan episode shows an overall picture of Jesus' mission from doing the will of the Father to equipping the disciples for their mission in the future and coming of the people through the testimony of his disciples (it is the Samaritan woman in this episode who believes in Jesus). In this sense, the Samaritan episode is 'a miniature of the whole Gospel' as Okure names (1988, 55). Michaels (2010, 270) points out that '[t]he Samaritan community speaks for all gentiles, acknowledging Jesus as "Savior" not simply of Samaritans in addition to Jews, but of the whole world'. The story does not end with the coming of the Samaritans to Jesus. The Samaritans ask him to stay (μένω) with them. They come through the testimony of the woman but they experience the fellowship with Jesus themselves and believe in him.

Disciples

Through Jesus' interactions with different individuals and also his public ministries, many people believed in him. The Gospel reveals the scope and quality of the new community Jesus is forming through the narratives. This fact raises some questions. What is the difference between those believers and 'the Twelve'? Are they all disciples? Was the contemporary discipleship community a community of many nations, including the Samaritans? What is the role of 'the Twelve', then? The answers will provide a perspective on how to understand these interactions of Jesus in terms of the discipleship community. To answer those questions, how the Gospel uses the term 'disciple' or 'disciples' needs to be examined.

As Bennema (2009a, 119) points out, 'the phrase "his [Jesus'] disciples" occurs frequently and mostly refers to Jesus' twelve disciples, or at least includes them (2:2, 11–12, 17, 22; 3:22; 4:2, 8, 27; 6:3, 8, 12, 16–17; 9:2; 12:16; 16:17, 29; 18:1; 20:26; cf 11:7, 54; 13:5)'. There are a few exceptions in the Gospel. Joseph of Arimathea is introduced as 'a disciple of Jesus' (19:38) even though he is not one of 'the Twelve'. The Gospel says that 'many of his [Jesus'] disciples turned back and no longer followed him' (6:66). In this usage, the twelve disciples are not included in the 'many of his disciples'. Rather, the twelve disciples are distinguished from those other disciples by the following question of Jesus to them: '"You do not want to leave too, do you?" Jesus asked the Twelve' (6:67). The Evangelist's use of the term 'disciple' could be divided into three categories: those who turned back, those who are not included in 'the Twelve' such as Joseph of Arimathea, and 'the Twelve' (οἱ δώδεκα).[51]

It is worth noting that the Evangelist calls all of them 'disciples', rather than distinguishing between just followers and disciples. By using the term 'disciple' for all of the followers of Jesus including 'the Twelve', the Evangelist emphasizes that the distinctive feature of 'disciple' is not in the term itself but in its essence. The essence of disciple is introduced by one of the important themes of the Gospel, μένω (to remain). It is revealed by what Jesus says to the Jews who believe in him: 'If you hold (μένω) to my teaching, you are really my disciples' (8:31). A true disciple defined by the Gospel is not the one who simply believes in Jesus but the one who believes in him and remains in his word. Carson (1991, 300) points this out as follows:

> At the most elementary level, a disciple is someone who is at that point following Jesus, either literally by joining the group that pursued him from place to place, or metaphorically in regarding him as the authoritative teacher. Such a 'disciple' is not necessarily a 'Christian', someone who has savingly trusted Jesus and sworn allegiance to him, given by the Father to the Son, drawn by the Father and born again by the Spirit, Jesus will make it clear in due course that only those who *continue* in his word are *truly* his disciples (8:31).

---

[51] The Evangelist uses the term four times referring to the twelve disciples of Jesus. (6:67, 70, 71; 20:24).

Considering the content regarding 'disciple' emphasized in the Gospel, Jesus' interactions with those different individuals should be understood more as revealing the scope and quality of the new community he is desiring to build through his disciples than as his own efforts to build a contemporary multi-ethnic discipleship community. The disciples who believe in Jesus and remain in his word are represented by 'the Twelve' in the Gospel. This affirms that one of the purposes of Jesus' encounters with the Jews and his interactions with different individuals, including the signs among them, is to equip his discipleship community as a missional community when he sends them into the world.

Chapter Summary

I have read the second part of the Gospel (2:13–12:50) with two aspects in mind. One is Jesus' encounters with the Jews, and the other is his interactions with different individuals. The Evangelist uses the term οἱ Ἰουδαῖοι to describe the 'Law-centred' Jews who come to the temple in Jerusalem for various feasts. They believe themselves to be the people of God as descendants of Abraham and try their best to keep the Law given through Moses, thus recognizing their identity as God's people in the world. The Gospel, however, shows that they are misunderstanding the identity of God's people by failing to understand the essence of the Law and failing to link the Law with the Messiah who came into the world, the one in whom the Law has been completed. The Messiah as the lens for reading the Hebrew Bible has two essential aspects.

First, the Jews fail to link the Law and the Jewish traditions with the redemptive aspect of the Messiah. Through the encounters with the Jews, Jesus keeps pointing out that the Law has been replaced in terms of form or place, and fulfilled in terms of its meaning by himself, the redemptive Messiah. He reveals that he is the true temple (2:21), the real paschal lamb (6:54) and the fulfilment of the redemptive meaning of all the feasts. Furthermore, he is the Law-giver (8:6–11), light-giver (9:5–7; cf 8:12), and life-giver (11:43–44).

Secondly, the Jews fail to connect the Law and the Jewish traditions with the missional aspect of the Messiah. The true temple, Jesus, is built not only for the Jews but also for other nations. This Messiah-for-all meets not only a Jew (Nicodemus) but also Samaritans (4:7, 40) and Gentiles (4:47) for their salvation. In particular, the Messiah bypasses the Sheep Gate of the temple to go to Bethesda and heals a man who has been sick for thirty-eight years (5:1–9). The narrative contrasts what the Jews are and do with what the Jews should be and should do as a missional community.

The failure of the Jews in the Gospel to understand their missional identity in the world as God's people is due to several reasons. First, the 'Law-centred' Jews focus on the rules themselves rather than reflecting on the meaning of the rules. As Jesus points out (5:39), they 'diligently study the Scriptures' but do not realize that the Scriptures testify about Jesus. By sticking to the form of the

Law, they fail to recognize the essence of it – the Messiah. Secondly, the Jews as 'Abraham's descendants' focus on themselves exclusively. Their exclusive understanding as God's people is based on the lineage of human beings. Of course, there is an exclusive aspect of God's people, but it is not based on ancestry; it is based on 'believing in him'. Furthermore, the exclusiveness of the discipleship community exists because of the inclusiveness for all people, which is missional.

What Jesus rejects is not the Jews, the people themselves, but their distorted understanding of the Law and of their identity as God's people. The new community that Jesus is building includes the Jews who believe in him. The Gospel shows this fact by the progressive change in Nicodemus and also in many other Jews who believe in him including the Jewish leaders. At the same time, the Gospel reveals that the new community includes other people, those who cannot be God's people from the traditional Jewish point of view. They are Samaritans and Gentiles in terms of ethnicity, and marginalised people in terms of social class. Throughout Jesus' interactions with different individuals in this part, two things need to be highlighted. One is that Jesus is 'the Saviour of the world' (4:42), as the Samaritans confess. The other is that Jesus crosses many socio-religious barriers to meet those individuals. Jesus is accomplishing the work of God through these encounters and interactions. However, Jesus focuses on the disciples, 'the Twelve' in particular.[52] They represent the Johannine disciples, those who believe in him and μένω (to remain) in his word. The above two things, 'the Saviour of the world' and 'breaking socio-religious impossibility', would be important aspects for the discipleship community to embrace in order to continue the ministries given them.

This second part contributes to a biblical understanding of mission by clarifying who the missional community of God is. The Johannine discipleship community is not limited to any particular ethnic group but consists of people who believe and follow Jesus. Furthermore, they are not merely those who follow but those who remain in Jesus and his word. It shows that the process of being a disciple and being a missional community go together. Jesus' shaping and equipping of the disciples as a missional community is the same process as that of shaping and equipping them to be true disciples. Jesus' encounters with the Law-centred Jews and his interactions with individuals in this part reveals to the accompanying disciples, the contemporary readers of the Gospel and the church today the importance of being a true disciple, participating in the mission of God. As God is missional, the discipleship community is also missional. This conclusion naturally opens the next part, Jesus' intimate interaction with his disciples, 'the Twelve' in particular. The narrative in the

---

[52] Jesus says, 'one of you is a devil' (6:70) indicating Judas, the son of Simon Iscariot. Nevertheless, the Gospel keeps using the term 'the Twelve' even after Judas' betrayal.

third part of the Gospel will demonstrate the characteristics of a discipleship community, thus of a missional community.

5. Equipping the Discipleship Community (13:1–17:26)

Introduction

I have divided the Fourth Gospel into four parts. In the second part (2:13–12:50),[1] I have discussed how Jesus encountered the Jews mainly in Jerusalem and Judea, and also how he interacted with different individuals. Those encounters and interactions have been described in the setting of various Jewish feasts, and have fulfilled dual purposes. One was to point out to the Jews, the previous sent community of God into the world, how the missional identity of the community had been distorted, losing the meaning of the Law given to them from God. The other was to reveal that the new community he is building includes all people who believe and remain in him. Those ministries of Jesus serve to equip the new discipleship community before Jesus sends them into the world. The disciples have watched the ministry of Jesus, including the signs, encounters and discourses, and have thus learnt who Jesus was and what Jesus desired for them.

Now, Jesus starts his direct discourse to his disciples. The third part of the Gospel (13:1–17:26) focuses on Jesus' interactions with his close disciples on the evening before his arrest. The Evangelist divided the narrative at this point. In the previous part (2:13–12:50), the Evangelist introduced many different arguments between Jesus and the Jews using the word Ἰουδαῖος 44 times in that part alone. The word only appears once in the third part,[2] and then reappears in the last part of the Gospel. As the Evangelist comments at the beginning of the narrative, '[h]aving loved his own who were in the world, he loved them to the end' (13:1b), Jesus spares these last hours of his life before the passion for his beloved disciples. The fact that Jesus performs and talks to

[1] See Chapter 3.

[2] Even in this case, Jesus is just referring to the Jews when he talks to his disciples: 'just as I told the Jews, so I tell you [the disciples] now' (13:13).

his disciples exclusively[3] in the narrative signifies that Jesus' primary concern before he 'leave[s] this world and go[es] to the Father' (13:1) is for his discipleship community.

The Evangelist highlights the primary concern of Jesus by devoting five chapters (13–17) of the narrative to the disciples. Since the third part is located between Jesus' encounters with the Jews and the passion narrative in the Gospel, it naturally functions as a conclusion of the preceding public ministry of Jesus and at the same time reveals the purpose of Jesus' ministry on earth, in the sense that he speaks to his disciples just before his death on the cross. In other words, we can see why this discipleship community was created through this encounter. The narrative includes Jesus washing his disciples' feet, his discourse and also his prayer for the disciples.

This third part will show the characteristics of the discipleship community as a missional community. Since those characteristics reveal a Johannine perspective on the nature of God's mission and also on the equipping and comissioning of the discipleship community, they will provide important aspects toward a biblical understanding of mission.

Washing the Disciples' Feet

A 'Sign' for the Disciples to Follow

The setting for the new narrative is once again a Jewish feast: 'It was just before the Passover Festival' (13:1). This is the third Passover in the Gospel. The previous Passovers also began with a similar description that the Passover was ἐγγύς (near, 2:13; 6:4). In the first Passover narrative, Jesus cleansed the temple in Jerusalem, mainly encountering the Jews in the temple. In the second Passover narrative in Galilee, he fed a great crowd with five loaves and two fishes. The audience there was a crowd that includes the Jews. In the previous Passovers, Jesus identified himself first with 'temple', revealing his death and resurrection in the first Passover, and then with 'bread', presenting himself as the bread of life in the second Passover. This third Passover narrative follows the pattern the Evangelist uses in the Gospel in general and the previous Passover narratives in particular, as Jesus performs an action and then gives a related discourse. Coloe (2004, 402) notes the pattern as follows:

> The brevity of the description of the action is not unusual in this Gospel, in which Jesus' deeds are termed σημεῖα (2:11; 4:34) and a discourse follows the action to interpret the meaning of the σημεῖα. This pattern continues in chap. 13, where,

[3] The prayer of Jesus is not exclusive to the disciples but certainly wider, yet it extends from the disciples rather than apart from the disciples.

following the foot washing, the rest of the chapter is primarily discourse and dialogue showing a structure of reverse parallelism.

There are both similarities and differences between the actions in the previous ministry and the washing of the disciples' feet in the new narrative. The similarity connects the new action with the previous actions; the difference reveals the uniqueness of the washing of the disciples' feet. The similarity is that the disciples do not realize what the actions and discourses mean when they are presented by Jesus. In the first Passover narrative, the Evangelist comments that 'After he [Jesus] was raised from the dead, his disciples recalled what he had said. Then they believed the scripture and the words that Jesus had spoken' (2:22). He also records in the second Passover narrative, 'On hearing it, many of his disciples said, "This is a hard teaching. Who can accept it?"' (6:60). Likewise, it was hard for the disciples to accept what Jesus was striving to do in the third Passover narrative. In the middle of the performance, Jesus says to Peter, who refuses to have his feet washed by Jesus, 'You do not realize now what I am doing, but later you will understand (13:7). The similarity demonstrates that the third Passover narrative continues the pattern not only of the previous Passover narratives but also of the 'sign' narrative itself in the Gospel. Jesus' washing of his disciples' feet is one of the 'signs' Jesus performed 'in the presence of his disciples' (cf 20:30).

Despite this similarity, however, Jesus' action here is distinguished in several ways from the previous ones. First, the audience of the third Passover narrative is the inner group of the disciples,[4] if not 'the Twelve'; the foot-washing is the first action Jesus performed exclusively for these disciples. The audience for each of the previous actions was either 'the Jews' or several individuals, even though the action and the following discourse for the audience became indirect teachings for the disciples. However, the action of washing the disciples' feet is conducted for the disciples only. Secondly, the action for the disciples requires the disciples to follow the example. In the previous actions, Jesus did not ask the audience to do the same. The purpose of the previous actions included signs to testify to the fact that Jesus was the Messiah and came from the Father. For this reason, Jesus did not ask the audience to perform the same actions. However, the foot-washing is not simply a one-time act of watching, but a sign for them also to emulate him. Jesus clarifies the purpose, saying, 'I have set you an example that you should do as I have done for you' (13:15). Thirdly, the crucial difference between the current action and the following discourse is the outcome in the discipleship community. For the previous actions of Jesus before the Jews and the crowds, the Evangelist comments that '[e]ven after Jesus had performed so many signs

[4] The disciples mentioned in this narrative (Chs 13–17) are Simon Peter (13:6), the disciple whom Jesus loves (13:23), Judas, the son of Simon Iscariot (13:26), Thomas (14:5) and Philip (14:8).

in their presence, they still would not believe in him' (12:37). However, the exclusive action and the following discourse for the disciples leads them to believe (cf 16:30). Then, what does the action mean, and how does Jesus use the action?

Having a Part with Jesus through the Foot-washing

The foot-washing is an exclusive action for the disciples and one which they are told to emulate. The Evangelist's opening comment of the section is a guide to how the action should be interpreted: 'Jesus knew that the hour had come for him to leave this world and go to the Father. Having loved his own who were in the world, he loved them to the end' (13:1). The foot-washing is a part of the loving act of Jesus for his disciples first, and then a loving act for them to do for one another (cf 13:14). Then, in what sense is the action a loving act for his 'own'? To understand the loving aspect of the action, two related questions should be examined. The two questions are: 'how does the foot-washing cause the disciples to have a part (μέρος) with Jesus (cf 13:8)?' and 'how is following the example (ὑπόδειγμα) related to having a part with Jesus?'

First, the foot-washing is not just a loving act of Jesus toward the disciples but it allows the disciples have a part with Jesus. Jesus says to Peter, 'Unless I wash you, you have no part with me' (13:8b). The word μέρος appears four times within the Gospel,[5] but the current use of the word is the only one that employs a secondary meaning, while the other three usages simply express the primary meaning of the word, 'part'.[6] For this reason, the word is translated in various ways in different versions – 'part', 'share', 'common' and 'fellowship' – to signify 'participation in' Jesus.[7] Additionally there are four usages[8] of the word in Revelation.[9] Three of them[10] have a secondary meaning. For the three usages of the word in Revelation, Köstenberger (2004, 406) states that 'μέρος is used with reference to people being assigned a place in God's eternal kingdom, either in fellowship with God (Rev 20:6; 21:8; 22:19) or separated from him (Matt. 24:51; Luke 12:46)'. Beasley-Murray (1999, 233–4) adds that 'μέρος is used among Jews in reference to having a part in an inheritance,

---

[5] 13:8; 19:23 (2x); 21:6.

[6] Parts or shares of the clothes (19:23); right side or part (21:6).

[7] Newman and Nida (1980, 432) introduce different translations of the verse such as NEB 'fellowship', JB 'common' and NAB 'share'. They say that 'NAB assumes that the background of the Greek word "part" is to be found in the Hebrew term that describes the God-given heritage of Israel', so translates 'you will have no share in my heritage'.

[8] Rev 16:19; 20:6; 21:8; 22:19.

[9] The word also appears in other books in the New Testament, but I just refer to the usages within the Gospel and in other Johannine letters.

[10] In Rev 16:19, the word is used with a primary meaning: 'three parts', but the other three (20:6; 21:8; 22:19) with a secondary meaning.

notably in the promised land, and eschatologically in the kingdom of God'. If I put together the interpretations of the commentaries and the different Bible translations, the word is understood to contain two meanings. One is to inherit or share in the kingdom of God and the other is to participate with God or have fellowship with him. The former has a one-time and everlasting sense, while the latter has a continuous and repetitive sense. I propose that the word μέρος in the foot-washing narrative represents the latter rather than the former. Jesus says to Peter, 'Those who have had a bath need only to wash their feet; their whole body is clean. And you [plural] are clean, though not every one of you' (13:10). The insistence that the foot-washing has a participating and fellowship sense is supported by the following discourse where Jesus talks about mutual dwelling through the vine and the branches. Coloe (2004, 411–15) proposes an interpretation of the foot-washing called 'welcoming into God's household'. With the 'household' aspect, she (2004, 413) divides the five chapters (13–17) into five phases:

> *Phase 1*: 13:1–3. Jesus gathers "his own" for a final meal.
> *Phase 2*: 13:4–11. He washes their feet to welcome them into the household that his departure will form, namely, "my Father's house" (see 14:2).
> *Phase 3*: 13:12–38. The disciples, including Judas, share food, and Jesus gives these "little children" experience of the Father's household through the requirement to love.
> *Phase 4*: chaps. 14–16. As the meal progresses, Jesus offers final teaching and explains the meaning his death will have for the disciples.
> *Phase 5*: chap. 17. At the end of the meal, Jesus prays that the disciples may share in the union between Father and Son (17:21–23).

This welcoming into God's household opens a new relationship between the disciples and God. In this exclusive narrative for the disciples, Jesus addresses his disciples with a new term. He calls them φίλος (friend), giving the reason as follows: 'You are my friends if you do what I command. I no longer call you servants, because a servant does not know his master's business. Instead, I have called you friends, for everything that I learned from my Father I have made known to you' (15:14–15). The new term affirms the new relationship of the disciples with God. The word translated into 'servant' is δοῦλος. That word appears 11 times in the Fourth Gospel. The NIV translates it only twice as 'slave'[11] and the rest as 'servant'.[12] I propose that 'slave' is a better translation, at least in the current verse (15:15), because the word 'slave' is appropriate when it is used in comparison with the son (8:35) or the master (13:16; 15:20). In the current verse (15:15), the word δοῦλος is compared with the word φίλος. By calling them 'friend', Jesus is signalling a shift for his disciples from being

---

[11] 8:34, 35
[12] 4:51; 13:16; 15:15 (2x), 20; 18:10 (2x), 18, 26.

the possession of the master to being the friend and intimate companion of the master; from being property within the household to being close associates of the master within the household. In this new relationship, the disciples know the will of the Father's business and they do it. The foot-washing signifies that Jesus loves the disciples in the sense that he invites them into the household of God, shifting them from 'slave' to 'friend', and he opens a way for them to have a part with him in continuous intimate relationship.

Secondly, what is the correlation between following the example and 'having part with Jesus'? As mentioned above, the foot-washing was performed as part of a loving act of Jesus for his disciples, and the loving act was to have an intimate relationship with his disciples. Now, Jesus requires his disciples to continue the loving relationship among themselves. He says, 'you also should wash one another's feet. I have set you an example that you should do as I have done for you' (13:14–15). The foot-washing is an exclusive action for the disciples and also an action for them to emulate. The fact that the word ὑπόδειγμα (example) is used only once in the Gospel affirms that this action has a unique meaning for the disciples to have fellowship with Jesus and also to continue among themselves. Michaels (2010, 735) points out that 'the present subjunctive, "might do," in contrast to the aorist, "just as I did," implies that he is urging them to continue to do repeatedly what he has done for them once for all'.[13]

One who wants to see a missional aspect in this foot-washing narrative may expect Jesus to instruct his disciples to do the same in the world, saying something such as, 'Just as I did for you, you also should do for others in the world where I am sending you'. However, Jesus says ὑμεῖς... ἀλλήλων meaning 'you (pl)... one another'. This is a mandate given to express mutual love among the community members, not a so-called mission to the world. However, I argue that this is an essential characteristic of the mission of the Fourth Gospel. The Fourth Gospel describes it as if all the attention of Jesus is on the discipleship community alone. However, establishing the discipleship community alone is not the goal of what Jesus is doing. Rather, forming a mature discipleship community that is equipped to move on is the goal – maturity being expressed as knowing, loving, living in truth and so on. The Fourth Gospel does not deem mission as quick to skip the maturity of the disciples and go straight to the world to perform a task. Jesus' welcome of the

---

[13] After careful study on the subject, Thomas (2014, 189) concludes that 'footwashing was practised as a religious rite by the Johannine community' and 'signified the cleansing of believers from post-conversion sin'. However, Michaels (2010, 735) says that 'the Gospel writer is urging the practice of footwashing, not as an independent third sacrament alongside baptism and the Lord's supper, but simply as an aspect of the Eucharistic meal'. Schnackenburg (1982, 2 Latin 4) points out that 'it was only much later, in the fourth century Latin Church (outside Rome), that the washing of feet was given a kind of sacramental significance'.

disciples into God's household does not end with the inclusion of 'the Twelve' alone nor does it continue with Jesus himself washing the feet of future disciples. To understand the point, one needs to know how the action is related to the discourse that follows, particularly the missional characteristics in the discourse. This will be discussed in the following section.

Missional Implication of the Action

How can it be proven that foot-washing, which seems to require loving service *within* the discipleship community, denotes a missional nature? First, an immediate explanation of the action reveals its nature. In the explanation, Jesus said, 'Very truly I tell you, no servant is greater than his master, nor is a messenger greater than the one who sent him' (13:16). This explanation for the foot-washing plays a role in connecting the action to the subsequent discourse. In the discourse, Jesus asks the disciples to remember this first clause, 'no servant is greater than his master', and adds the following conclusion: 'If they persecuted me, they will persecute you also' (15:20). This statement shows that the love and service exhibited in the foot-washing are connected to the ministry of the disciples in the world. The second clause, 'nor is a messenger greater than the one who sent him', becomes more evident. In this context, 'messenger' refers to the disciples and 'the one who sent' refers to Jesus, since it is parallel to the preceding clause. The expression of Jesus sending the disciples into the world appears explicitly in Jesus' prayer (17:18) and then again in the post-resurrection encounter (20:21).

Secondly, the missional nature of the activity is proven by the discourse that followed. I already pointed out that the foot-washing action plays the role of a 'sign' in the Fourth Gospel, which is connected to the following discourse in the narrative. Therefore, the sign, namely the foot-washing, should be viewed through the following discourse. In the vine discourse, the disciples are likened to branches, and the emphasis is that they should be attached to the tree. Moreover, the branches are fruitful because they are well attached to the tree. Through the action and the discourse, Jesus addresses the disciples as the branches that should remain in him, the vine, to bear fruit (15:4–5). I already pointed out that the foot-washing sign and discourse drew the disciples into Jesus' life and work. They now have a part (μέρος) with Jesus in his ministry, and the 'having a part' comprises both a participating and a fellowship dimension. The discourse of the vine and the branches explains the missional nature that the foot-washing implies.

Thirdly, the missional nature of the foot-washing activity is also proven by the prayer of Jesus after the discourse. As I highlighted, the word 'messenger' in the foot-washing narrative is linked to the prayer. Furthermore, Jesus' prayer as a conclusion of the previous action and his discourse reveals the missional aspect of the action. In the prayer, Jesus prays that 'they [the disciples] may be one' (17:11), which is the purpose of his command to the disciples to 'wash one another's feet'. Then, Jesus extends his prayer. 'I pray also for those who will believe in me through their message, that all of them may be one' (17:20–21). In this exclusive encounter of Jesus with his disciples, the continuation of the 'love' and 'oneness' from the divine community to the world through the discipleship community is consistent. In other words, Jesus' welcoming people into God's household will be continued through the disciples in the world.

If it is accepted that the foot-washing has a missional implication, then one needs to examine the content of the mission that action implies. The foot-washing has been presented to the disciples as ὑπόδειγμα to emulate, and Jesus will bring his people in the world into his 'household' through the disciples' ministry as they follow his example. The ὑπόδειγμα of Jesus must not be construed as the performance of the foot-washing per se, but should be interpreted as including the whole symbolic meaning behind the action that he, 'the Lord and Teacher', washed the disciples' feet. This 'sign' stands in stark contrast to what the disciples have seen in the encounters between Jesus and the Jews. I pointed out that Jesus' encounters with the Jews and his performing of many 'signs' before them became lessons for the disciples. The Evangelist expresses the same view in his concluding statement, saying, 'Jesus performed many other signs in the presence of his disciples' (20:30). The overall assessment of the Evangelist for the first half of the Gospel is that 'even after Jesus had performed so many signs in their [the Jews] presence, they would not believe in him' (12:37). At the same time, the Evangelist proposes that the whole ministry, 'signs' in his terms, of Jesus has been performed for the disciples 'in the presence of them'. By introducing this new ministry of Jesus for the disciples right after giving his negative evaluation of the Jews' response to the 'signs' of Jesus, the Evangelist presents the new way of mission that the disciples will carry out.

The new way of mission that the disciples should carry out is 'love' because Jesus performed the foot-washing to demonstrate his love for his 'own'. Michaels (2010, 735) insists that '[t]he noun "example" and the repetition of "you too" make it clear that Jesus is calling on his disciples to do for each other exactly what he has done for them. The repetition of the verb "to do" – "just as I did" and "that you might do" – confirms that he is urging them to imitate not just his humble attitude, but the literal action of washing feet'. However, the repetition of 'to do' should not be limited to the action itself. What he sets as an example is not merely an action but a loving action. I propose two missional aspects in this loving action.

First, love is the channel through which God reaches the world. The repetition of the word ἀλλήλων in the narrative reveals that the action the disciples should do is love. Jesus' command, 'wash one another's (ἀλλήλων) feet' (13:14), is changed into 'love one another (ἀλλήλων)' and is repeated in the narrative (13:34 (2x), 35; 15:12). The love he showed to and commanded of the disciples through the foot-washing is not simply to love one another but to love *as* (καθώς) Jesus did (13:34; 15:12). Through the whole narrative of Jesus' exclusive encounters with his disciples, the three words, 'to wash', 'to love' and 'to be one', have a similar substance. The foot-washing action was performed as a sign to be discussed in the following narrative and also was given as an example for the disciples to emulate by 'washing one another's feet'. In the following discourse, the meaning of the action is revealed by the command 'love one another', and again, the meaning is fully revealed in Jesus' prayer that 'all of them may be one' and 'they may be one as we are one' (17:21–22). The Johannine love and being one are always based on, connected with and extended from the love and oneness of the Father and the Son. Through this love and oneness 'the world will know' (17:23). Bauckham (2015, 40–41) points out this aspect as follows:

> Love for one another (in the Greek *agapēn en allēlois*, literally: "love between one another") is the nearest that humans come, in the Gospel's terminology, to being "in" one another. It is the human community's correspondence to divine community. So the missional aspect is not just the obvious thought that people will see that they are Jesus's disciples because they are obeying his command, but the more profound dimension that emerges more clearly in chapter 17: the world will recognize God's love as it is at work and reflected in the Christian community.

Secondly, the love shown in the action is love that changes the subject from oneself to others. Jesus, 'the Lord and the Teacher', makes himself nothing by taking the role and attitude of a servant or, more precisely, of a slave.[14] The point is not to love more or not merely to have washed the disciples' feet, but to change the subject by taking on the role of a servant. His love shown in this action is not just about giving something, in this case washing feet, while keeping oneself as the subject in this situation. That is dispensation rather than love. The love shown in this action constitutes a willingness to take on the role of a servant and thereby make the object the subject. The foot-washing is not just a matter of the Lord washing the feet of his disciples but of the Lord taking on a servant's role and making the disciples the subject. Jesus points out to the disciples that their washing of one another's feet is not as paradoxical as what Jesus did since the disciples are neither the master nor the one who sent (13:16). Changing the lordship or subject from oneself to others is the love Jesus talks about and the new way of mission that the disciples are expected to carry out.

Through the foot-washing, Jesus reveals the nature of mission rather than merely an activity of mission. This nature of mission is having a part with Jesus or remaining in the vine as branches of it, in order to bear fruit. By following

---

[14] Paul says 'Christ Jesus: Who, being in very nature God, did not consider equality with God something to be used to his own advantage; rather, he made himself nothing by taking the very nature of a servant being made in human likeness' (Phil 2:5–7).

the example of serving one another, the disciples are having fellowship not only with Jesus but also with one another. This crucial missional nature should not be replaced or reduced to an action, washing. The Evangelist persistently focuses on this missional nature rather than on mission as a task. What the disciples should emulate is the attitude and nature shown in the action rather than the action itself.

The Discourse for the Disciples

Mutual Indwelling

At the end of Chapter 14 of the Gospel, Jesus says to his disciples: 'Come now; let us leave' (14:31b). However, the disciples do not move until 18:1 when they 'crossed the Kidron Valley'. It is not certain whether the discourse of Jesus (chs. 15–16) happens before they depart (14:31) or on the way, after departing the place but before crossing the valley. However, it is clear that the Evangelist treats the discourse as an independent unit even though the content is related to the previous and the following narratives. In the previous narrative (chs. 13–14), Jesus washes his disciples' feet and converses with his disciples, answering their questions. In contrast, Jesus speaks to the disciples on several themes in the present discourse. I will discuss the themes to understand what Jesus delivers to his disciples through the last discourse.

The first theme found in the discourse is *mutual indwelling*. Mutual indwelling is a repeated theme in the Gospel. The theme is expressed by the use of the verb μένω in the discourse. In the previous chapter (see 3.3.3), I pointed out that the Fourth Gospel could be described 'as an exposition of what it will mean to μένω with Jesus'. Newman and Nida (1980, 209) point out that '[t]he verb "to remain" [μένω] is one of John's most important terms, and he uses it of the relationship between the Father and the Son (14:10), as well as of the believer's relationship with the Son (6:56; 15:4)'. The use of the verb μένω is concentrated in Chapter 15 of the Gospel, appearing 11 times[15] in that chapter alone out of 40 times in the entire Gospel. The usages are as follows (my emphasis underlined and in bold):

> 15:4 **<u>Remain</u> in me**, as I [also <u>remain</u>] (verb ellipsis) **in you** (μείνατε ἐν ἐμοί, κἀγὼ ἐν ὑμῖν). No branch can bear fruit by itself; it must **<u>remain</u>** in the vine. Neither can you bear fruit unless you **<u>remain</u> in me**.
> 15:5 I am the vine; you are the branches. If you [one] **<u>remain</u> in me** and I <u>[remain]</u> (verb ellipsis) **in you [him]** (ὁ μένων ἐν ἐμοὶ κἀγὼ ἐν αὐτῷ), you will bear much fruit; apart from me you can do nothing.

---

[15] 13 times if the verb ellipsis is included in two places (15:4, 5).

15:6 If you do not **<u>remain</u> in me**, you are like a branch that is thrown away and withers.
15:7 If you **<u>remain</u> in me** and my words **<u>remain</u> in you** (μείνητε ἐν ἐμοὶ καὶ τὰ ῥήματά μου ἐν ὑμῖν μείνῃ), ask whatever you wish, and it will be done for you.
15:9 As the Father has loved me, so have I loved you. Now **<u>remain</u> in my love** (μείνατε ἐν τῇ ἀγάπῃ τῇ ἐμῇ).
15:10 If you keep my commands, you will **<u>remain</u> in my love**, just as I have kept my Father's commands and **<u>remain</u> in his love**.
15:16 You did not choose me, but I chose you and appointed you so that you might go and bear fruit – fruit that will **<u>last</u>** – and so that whatever you ask in my name the Father will give you.

There are a few points to be observed. First, the verb μένω emphasizes the intimacy of the relationship. Out of 11 usages of the verb in the chapter (13 times including the ellipsis cases in 15:4 and 5), nine of them (11 times including the ellipsis) are followed by a spatial preposition ἐν plus personal pronouns showing that the verb means *uniting with someone or something of a person* (15:9, 10). The literal spatial meaning that someone remains in another person can be better expressed as someone uniting with another person. The relationship expressed in the discourse is a mutual relationship according to the Evangelist, introduced throughout the Gospel (1:1; 6:56; 10:38; 14:10; 14:20; 17:21). The mutual indwelling relationship appears through the pair of clauses in 15:4, 5 and also in 7 in some sense: 'Remain in me, as I also remain in you' (15:4), 'If you [one] remain in me and I in you [him]' (15:5) and 'If you remain in me and my words remain in you' (15:7).

Secondly, the relationship between Jesus and the disciples always follows and reflects the relationship between Jesus and the Father. At the beginning of the discourse, Jesus introduces himself as an interconnector of the relationship, saying, 'I am the true vine, and my Father is the gardener… I am the vine; you are the branches' (15:1, 5a). The relationship between the Father and the Son before the world was created has been described at the beginning of the Gospel (1:1), and has been revealed by Jesus on many different occasions, making himself equal to the Father (cf 5:18). Jesus proclaims that he and the Father are one (10:30). Now, the relationship in the divine community is expanding its scope to include the discipleship community through Jesus. In the Fourth Gospel, the expansion of the relationship is described as an essential purpose of Jesus, that is to say, the purpose of God through Jesus.

Thirdly, the relationship is sustained by love. The intimate relationship is a loving relationship. In the divine community, Jesus keeps the Father's commands and abides in the Father's love. Likewise, the discipleship community is required to keep Jesus' commands and abide in his love. Interestingly, the command of Jesus itself is to love each other (15:17). The discipleship community keeps the command of Jesus by loving each other, and by keeping the command, they remain in Jesus' love.

Fourthly, the loving relationship includes the ministry of the community. The ministry of the community is expressed in the discourse as 'going and bearing fruit'. Through the loving relationship, the discipleship community can bear fruit. Jesus implies that the discipleship community will be sent into the world to bear fruit. Carson (1991, 523) points out that 'the fruit primarily in view in this verse [15:16] is the fruit that emerges from mission, from specific ministry to which the disciples have been sent. The fruit, in short, is new converts'. I agree with Carson and other commentators who point out the missional implication of 'going and bearing fruit' in the discourse because the loving relationship includes the ministry of 'going and bearing fruit'.

At the same time, I argue that two things need to be considered to correctly understand the fruit-bearing that Jesus is talking about here. The two things are related to two verbs in the verse (15:16). The first verb is ὑπάγω (to depart). The verb ὑπάγω does not mean that the disciples depart from Jesus and do their ministry. The verb does not emphasize the departing aspect; instead it strengthens the bearing aspect. The verb is not equivalent to the verb πορεύομαι in Matt 28:19 where the participle form of the verb has its meaning of 'going'. Rather than using the direct verb 'to go', the Fourth Gospel uses the verb 'to send' with either ἀποστέλλω or πέμπω to express the mission of the discipleship community. Torrey (1936, 40) proposes that the translation should be 'to bear more and more fruit' rather than 'to go and bear fruit'.[16] Michaels (2010, 815–16) also points out that '[t]he accent is not on "going away" as Jesus will "go away" (13:33; 14:28), but on "bearing fruit" in the sense of making disciples or winning new converts'. Therefore, the sentence explains the foundation of the fruit-bearing of the disciples rather than expresses Jesus' command for the disciples to go and bear fruit.

The other verb is μένω (to remain). This verb has been used in the discourse for expressing the relationship either between the Father and Jesus or between Jesus and the disciples. This is the only instance (15:16) that the verb is used for the fruit. By adding the verb to the fruit (ὁ καρπὸς ὑμῶν μένῃ), Jesus emphasizes neither the bearing of fruit itself nor the sustainability of the fruit itself, but the same indwelling and uniting of the fruit to the vine. (See 17:20–21, 'I pray also for those who will believe in me through their message, that all of them may be one'.) The emphasis of 'going and bearing fruit' in mission without noticing Jesus' emphasis on the indwelling aspect may distort what the Fourth Gospel intends regarding mission. The emphasis of Jesus is not only on

---

[16] Torrey (1936, 30) suggests that '[t]he Fourth Gospel has two examples of this idiom ['*going and*' doing, or experiencing, this or that, is a way of expressing *constant increase* of the action or experience], both mistranslated: 12:11, "many of the Jews *went and* believed on Jesus," instead of, "many of the Jews, *in increasing number*, believed." 15:16, "I appoint you to *go and* bear fruit," instead of, "I appoint you to bear *more and more* fruit"'.

'bearing fruit' but also on unity – the unity of both the disciples and the 'fruit' with him, and the unity of all of them in the divine community through him.

The Community Hated by the World

The missional nature of the discipleship community has been explained as a loving relationship. By abiding in the Father, Jesus remains in the Father's love and bears the branches, the discipleship community. Likewise, the disciples are invited to abide in the divine community through Jesus, to remain in his love and bear fruit. The loving relationship of the Father and Jesus is extended through Jesus to the discipleship community and to the new believers through the disciples. This is a continuation of the loving relationship, and abiding is the critical element in this process.

In contrast, Jesus starts to explain the nature of the discipleship community from another angle, the angle of the world. The loving relationship in the previous discourse reveals the ultimate purpose of the community beyond the ministry expected, while the angle of the world shows what the community will experience in the world because of its identity. The verb μισέω (to hate) has been used in the latter in contrast to the word ἀγαπάω (to love) in the former.[17] The verb μισέω appears 12 times throughout the Gospel, and the subject of the verb in 11 usages out of the 12[18] is 'the world',[19] expressing that the world hates the Father, Jesus or the discipleship community. In particular, seven of them are concentrated in the discourse (15:18-25). Another verb διώκω (to persecute) is also used in the discourse almost as a synonym of μισέω. The usages of the two verbs in the discourse are as follows (my emphasis underlined and in bold):

> 15:18 If the world **<u>hates</u>** (μισέω) you, keep in mind that it **<u>hated</u>** (μισέω) me first.
> 15:19 If you belonged to the world, it would love you as its own. As it is, you do not belong to the world, but I have chosen you out of the world. That is why the world **<u>hates</u>** (μισέω) you.
> 15:20b If they **<u>persecuted</u>** (διώκω) me, they will **<u>persecute</u>** (διώκω) you also.
> 15:23 Whoever **<u>hates</u>** (μισέω) me **<u>hates</u>** (μισέω) my Father as well.
> 15:24b As it is, they have seen, and yet they have **<u>hated</u>** (μισέω) both me and my Father.
> 15:25 But this is to fulfil what is written in their Law: 'They **<u>hated</u>** (μισέω) me without reason'.

---

[17] The verb ἀγαπάω appears five times in the former paragraph (15:9–17).

[18] In 12:25, the verb has a positive sense in faith that 'anyone who hates [μισέω] their life in this world will keep it for eternal life'.

[19] 'Everyone' (3:20) and 'They' (15:25) are also used, but they are equivalent to 'the world'.

Jesus warns the disciples that the world will hate them. The world will hate and even persecute the discipleship community as the world hated and persecuted Jesus first. The above usages of the verb μισέω explain why the world hates the community. The hatred and persecution by the world against the community are primarily caused by the *belonging* of the community. Jesus clarifies that the world hates the disciples because the disciples do not belong to the world since Jesus has chosen them out of the world (15:19). The world hated the Father and Jesus (15:24), and the discipleship community belongs to the divine community, thus the world hates the community. Then, why does the world hate the discipleship community because of its belonging?

The world hated Jesus first and then hates the discipleship community because they belong to Jesus. So it needs to be clarified why the world hated Jesus first. The previous usages of the verb μισέω reveal the reason why the world hates Jesus (my emphasis underlined and in bold):

> 3:19–20 Light has come into the world, but people loved darkness instead of light because their deeds were evil. Everyone who does evil **<u>hates</u>** (μισέω) the light, and will not come into the light for fear that their deeds will be exposed.
> 7:7 The world cannot **<u>hate</u>** (μισέω) you [Jesus' brothers], but it **<u>hates</u>** (μισέω) me because I testify that its works are evil.

According to the Gospel, the Father loved the world and sent his Son to save the world through him (3:16), but the world hated the Son because their deeds were evil, and also because he testified that its works were evil. The above two statements are interrelated not merely because of the usage of the same verb, μισέω, but also because both verses are talking about the evil of the world.[20] Based on the first description about the light and evil relations (3:19–20), I argue that the testifying of Jesus in the second statement is more about testifying by the nature of the subject rather than by the action of the subject. Newman and Nida (1980, 223) point out that '[i]n this sentence [I testify that its works are evil], *I* is emphatic, while the verb tense denotes continuous or progressive action'. The emphatic subject ἐγώ (I) followed by the continuous verb tense expresses the continuous manifestation by the nature or existence of the subject as if the light shines by its nature rather than by its continuous action. Of course, the continuous manifestation does not exclude the verbal expression of Jesus (cf 8:31–59), but his existence as the light in the world keeps revealing the evil of the world. In this sense, the belonging and testifying are inseparable in the Fourth Gospel. Moreover, the nature of the testifier, whether it is Jesus or the discipleship community, flows from their belonging, and their testifying comes from their nature.

[20] The word πονηρός (evil) appears only three times in the Gospel (3:19; 7:7; 17:15), and all of them indicate the evil of the world.

The nature of the Father and Jesus introduced in the Gospel is love. The love of the Father for the world was the basis for sending his Son into the world (3:16), and Jesus remains in the Father's love. He asked his discipleship community to remain in his love. Loving one another was his new command to the community (13:34; 15:17). By this loving nature and the action that came from his nature, the world knows that they are the disciples of Jesus (13:35). The missional nature of the discipleship community should be understood by this. The community belongs to Jesus and will be sent into the world as an extended expression of God's community. The community is expected to manifest the loving nature of God as they abide in his love, and then the community will experience both bearing fruit and hatred in the world.

Παράκλητος

One of the significant teachings in Jesus' encounter with his disciples is the explicit references to the Holy Spirit. The references are found in the preceding chapter (14) and also in the present discourse (15–16). Jesus uses the term παράκλητος (advocate in NIV) when referring to the Spirit. Turner (1996, 77) explains the Greek word as follows:

> In Greek, the word is formally a passive verbal adjective, 'one called alongside', especially to offer counsel, support or assistance in a court, or in some other potentially adversarial setting. Typically *paraklētoi* intercede on someone's behalf, e.g. to a higher authority, or support their case in juridical or other proceedings, acting as intercessors, mediators, or supporting witnesses. 'Advocate' may thus regularly provide the best translation, providing it is taken in a sufficiently general sense rather than merely to denote a professional legal representative.

The Spirit has been mentioned in other narratives of the Gospel, but the term παράκλητος, referring to him, appears only in the present narrative for the disciples.[21] The passages mentioning the Spirit and his role are much longer in this narrative, but I list below just the verses that contain the term παράκλητος to better understand the meaning (my emphasis underlined and in bold):

> 14:16–17 And I will ask the Father, and he will give you another **advocate** (παράκλητος) to help you and be with you forever – the Spirit of truth. The world cannot accept him, because it neither sees him nor knows him. But you know him, for he lives (μένω) with you and will be in you.
> 14:26 But the **Advocate** (παράκλητος), the Holy Spirit, whom the Father will send in my name, will teach you all things and remind you of everything I have said to you.

[21] 14:16, 26; 15:26; 16:7.

> 15:26–27 When the **Advocate** (παράκλητος) comes, whom I will send to you from the Father – the Spirit of truth who goes out from the Father – he will testify about me. And you also must testify, for you have been with me from the beginning.
> 16:7 But very truly I tell you, it is for your good that I am going away. Unless I go away, the **Advocate** (παράκλητος) will not come to you; but if I go, I will send him to you.

Jesus' promise for sending the Holy Spirit to the disciples is given in the context that Jesus is leaving them but they will remain in the world to testify about him. The disciples will face and experience hatred and persecution in the world as they carry on their mission in the world. In other words, the Holy Spirit will be sent by the Father and the Son for the mission of the discipleship community in the world. Therefore, the above passages show how the Fourth Gospel describes the role of the Holy Spirit in relation to mission.

First of all, the position of the Holy Spirit in mission needs to be clarified. The clause that 'he [Holy Spirit] will testify about me [Jesus] (15:26)' raises several questions about the role of the Holy Spirit in mission, such as: Who would be the recipient of the testifying of the Holy Spirit – the world or the disciples or both? If the recipient is the world, does that mean that the Holy Spirit testifies about Jesus to the world apart from the disciples? If the recipient is the disciples, then is the testifying ministry of the Holy Spirit limited to the disciples?

First, I argue that the passage should not read the witness of the Holy Spirit as being introduced separately from the disciples' mission in the world. Jesus says that he will send the παράκλητος to 'you' [the disciples]. The Holy Spirit will be sent to the disciples, so the statement that the Holy Spirit will testify about Jesus should be interpreted in the scope of the ministry of the disciples in the world. The ministry of the Holy Spirit does not exclude the ministry of the disciples in the world. Billington (1995, 109) points out that '[t]he Paraclete's work is not independent of their witness; John does not teach a witness by the Spirit that is not also a witness through the believing community'. In view of the Fourth Gospel, the claim that the Holy Spirit bears witness in the world without the church is just as inappropriate as the church claiming to do mission in the world without the Holy Spirit.

Secondly, the statement that the Holy Spirit was sent to the disciples is not to say that the recipient of the witness of the Spirit is limited to the disciples alone. La Potterie (1963, 75) insists that 'the witness of the Holy Spirit must be distinct from that of the disciples: the Spirit will bear an *inner* witness in their hearts, so that they in their turn may be able to witness to him before men'. By the word *inner*, he (1963, 75) means that '[t]he role of the Spirit of truth will be to protect the disciples effectively in this trial, that is to prevent them from being shaken in their faith'. I do not agree that the witness of the Spirit is limited to the disciples in scope and effect. As the scope of Jesus' ministry always includes 'other sheep that are not of this sheep pen' (10:16) who will believe in me [Jesus] through their [the disciples] message' (17:20), the witness of the Spirit is also not limited to the disciples' heart but, ultimately, is towards the people in the world who will receive testimony about Jesus from the disciples. As Michaels (2010, 833) points out, 'Even though the Advocate will come *to* the disciples [16:7], his activity is directed *through* them to "the world" [16:8]'. He (2010, 825) stresses that '[t]hese twin testimonies, in fact, are not two but one, for the Advocate will testify solely in and through the lives and lips of the disciples'.

Then, how does the Holy Spirit relate to the disciples for the mission that the disciples will carry on in the world? Turner (1996, 77) points out that 'the functions actually attributed to "the Paraclete" in John are primarily teaching, revealing and interpreting Jesus to the disciples'. Based on those functions, I argue the role of the Spirit/Advocate in relation to the mission of the disciples as follows:

First, the Holy Spirit is a companion of the disciples in their missional journey in the world. According to the above passages, the Holy Spirit will be sent by both the Father ('the Father will send in my name', 14:26) and Jesus ('I will send to you from the Father', 15:26) to the disciples, so the Spirit is not a sender but a companion with them. The Father sent Jesus into the world, and Jesus formed a believing discipleship community in the world. Now, through the exclusive encounter with his discipleship community (chs. 13–17), Jesus is commissioning the discipleship community for the world. As Jesus says, he will send the discipleship community into the world just as the Father sent him into the world (17:18; 20:21). Since Jesus' sending of his disciples into the world is neither just sending them off nor simply following an example of the Father's sending of Jesus but rather encompasses the living participation of the community in the mission of God for the world, the Holy Spirit is sent to the discipleship community.

Secondly, the Holy Spirit lives with the disciples and will be in them. The verb μένω is used to express the intimate relationship that the Holy Spirit will have with the discipleship community. It shows that the Holy Spirit has the same relational characteristic that Jesus has in the discipleship community (see 5.3.1). Through the presence of the Holy Spirit, the discipleship community is connected with the triune God's community, clarifying that the mission of the discipleship community is always conducted in relationship with the triune God.

Thirdly, the Holy Spirit is an advocate. The word παράκλητος is translated as 'helper'[22], 'advocate' or 'comforter'[23] in various versions of the Bible.

---

[22] English Standard Version, New American Standard Bible, International Standard Bible.

[23] King James Bible, English Revised Version, Darby Bible Translation, Tyndale.

However, 'advocate' is favoured by more Bible versions (NIV, NRSV, NEB, REB, NAB, TNIV, NLT). Michaels (2010, 783) says that it is 'possibly because of the legal connotations of the term, and because of its appropriateness in 1 John 2:1'. Jesus says that he will send 'another παράκλητος' (14:16). It is not certain whether Jesus identifies himself as an advocate by the expression[24] or simply means that he will send another one who is an advocate.[25] I argue that the accent is on the role of the Holy Spirit rather than revealing Jesus' own identity as an advocate. In either case, however, the term should be viewed in relation to the discipleship community – an advocate for the discipleship community. The Holy Spirit will advocate the discipleship community through teaching, reminding and testifying about Jesus so that the community can carry out the mission in the world. Turner (1996, 87) confirms that 'the Spirit will convict the world of sin, righteousness and judgement *precisely by revealing the truth, and teaching its significance, to and through the disciples*'.

Fourthly, the Holy Spirit is introduced as the Spirit of truth. This characteristic of the Spirit defines to what extent the Spirit will be an 'Advocate' for the disciples. The Spirit is not sent to advocate the discipleship community do anything beyond its own purpose but as a companion and an advocate for teaching the community to become a community of truth (16:13) and to perform the ministry of truth in the world. The ministry that the Spirit will do through the discipleship community is introduced as follows (16:8–11):

> When he comes, he will prove the world to be in the wrong about sin and righteousness and judgement: about sin, because people do not believe in me; about righteousness, because I am going to the Father, where you can see me no longer; and about judgement, because the prince of this world now stands condemned.

Right after the above passage, Jesus says to his disciples: 'I have much more to say to you, more than you can now bear. But when he, the Spirit of truth, comes, he will guide you into all the truth' (16:12–13). This additional explanation provides two guidelines for interpreting the three themes (sin, righteousness and judgement) about which the Spirit will reprove the world. First, those three themes are just examples of what the Spirit will do to convict

---

[24] Jesus is described as παράκλητος in 1 John 2:1. Turner (1996, 79) supports this view saying, 'the Greek *allos* regularly (not always) means "another (of the *same* kind)", in contrast to *heteros* "another (different)". (see 5:43, the Evangelist himself uses *allos* with the meaning of 'different').

[25] Jesus' meaning depends on whether the word 'another' modifies the following noun or relates directly to the verb 'send'. Michaels (2010, 783) says that 'the alternative of reading "advocate" in a kind of predicate relationship to "another" – that is, "he will give you another [ἄλλον], as an advocate [παράκλητον]," without implying that Jesus was himself an "advocate" – is very unlikely'.

the world, so the reason the Spirit will convict the world is as important as understanding the theme itself. The second guideline is that the overall aim for the Spirit to do that is to guide the disciples into truth. In other words, the aim is to equip the disciples with the truth for their mission in the world. With those guidelines in place, I will now argue how those themes are related to the ministry of the disciples in the world.

An important question to consider when interpreting the passage is how the ὅτι clauses that explain the themes should be viewed. The word ὅτι has the meaning of both 'that' and 'because'. The former does not make sense in the passage, since 'I am going to the Father, where you can see me no longer' (16:10) cannot be the content of 'righteousness'. Thus, I interpret the word ὅτι as 'because' which explains the reason. The next question to consider would be the subject of the ὅτι clause, not within the clause but the subject to which the clause is connected. Abbott (1906, 158) suggests that Jesus is the subject, meaning '[*I say this*] *because*'. He insists that Jesus provides the reason why he mentions those three themes in particular with the ὅτι clauses.[26] However, I contend that the subject of the clause is the Spirit as it is in the sentence. Then, the full interpretation would be as follows:

> [The Spirit will convict the world] about sin, because people do not believe in me; [the Spirit will convict the world] about righteousness, because I am going to the Father, where you can see me no longer; and [the Spirit will convict the world] about judgement, because the prince of this world now stands condemned. (16:9–11)

By knowing these themes about which the Spirit will convict the world, along with other truth that he will reveal, the discipleship community will be equipped as a community of truth to testify about Jesus in the world. For this purpose, the Holy Spirit teaches the disciples all things and reminds them of everything Jesus has said to them (14:26).

This discourse of Jesus for his close disciples condenses the missional characteristics of the discipleship community. The connection between the Father as the gardener, Jesus as the vine and the disciples as the branches reveals that the relationship between God and the Word is connected to the discipleship community. It highlights *relationship* or *oneness* as the key characteristic of the mission of God and the mission of the church. The discourse envisions the growing of this relationship through those branches as they bear fruit. Since this whole process will be continued in the dynamic relationship between the Father, the Son and the discipleship community, the Holy Spirit, sent by the Father and the Son, will be with the disciples, enabling

---

[26] He (1906, 158) explains the reason as follows: 'the statement "I will judge the world about these three things" suggests to the reader "Why about these three in particular?" so as to prepare the way for a threefold "because" – "I say about sin, *because* it will..."'.

them to remain in Jesus and his word. This relationship aspect is one of the crucial contributions of the Fourth Gospel to a biblical understanding of mission.

Jesus' Prayer for His Discipleship Community

The Position of the Prayer

When he finishes the discourse to his disciples, Jesus starts his prayer to the Father for his disciples. In this section, I will discuss the characteristics of the prayer and the themes of the prayer as revealed in those characteristics. To understand the characteristics of the prayer correctly, I will examine the position of the prayer first, then clarify two matters: those for whom Jesus offered the prayer and the content of the prayer itself.

The introductory clause in the chapter, ταῦτα ἐλάλησεν Ἰησοῦς (After Jesus said this, 17:1), indicates that the prayer is offered right after his previous discourse with his disciples. In this line of reasoning, the prayer functions as a conclusion to the previous discourse. The conversation between the disciples and Jesus in the previous discourse offers further support for such a claim. In the discourse, the disciples confessed that they believed that Jesus came from God to which Jesus replies, 'Do you now believe?' (16:31).[27] Even though the response of Jesus in this verse does not confirm for the readers whether or not Jesus accepts the confession of the disciples as a sign that they believe, it signifies at least that he has been waiting for a confession like this from the disciples. Readers will know that the confession has been accepted by Jesus through Jesus' prayer to the Father in 17:8. Michaels (2010, 853) points out that '[t]he disciples' confession of what they "know" and "believe" (v. 30) will form the basis of Jesus' long prayer in the following chapter'.

It is clear that the prayer of Jesus for the disciples appears right after their confession. However, the prayer functions as a conclusion not only for the previous discourse but also for the whole ministry of Jesus. It is true that Jesus starts his prayer responsively after the confession of the disciples, but the confession of the disciples did not happen suddenly as shown in the response of Jesus to the confession. Instead, it is an outcome of Jesus' whole ministry with the disciples. A wider view of the structure of the Gospel reveals the prayer as located between the whole public ministry of Jesus and the upcoming passion narrative. Even though the prayer is offered right after the so-called 'farewell discourse', it is not just an attachment to the discourse in preparation for the upcoming situation. Instead, it is a conclusion and a summary of the whole

---

[27] ἄρτι πιστεύετε: This can be interpreted either as a question (most Bible versions) or as a statement (NEV, the previous version of NIV, interpreted the sentence as 'You believe at last').

previous ministry of Jesus[28] and his work in building a discipleship community in particular.

It shows that Jesus has completed something he has been waiting for and is now ready to move on to the next step. In this sense, the Johannine prayer is characterized more as the accomplishment of the previous ministry, whereas the prayer of Jesus in Gethsemane in the Synoptic Gospels (Matt 26:36–46; Mark 14:32–42; Luke 22:39–46) functions more as a preparation for the upcoming passion narrative. Carson (1991, 551) notes that '[i]n some respects the prayer is a summary of the entire Fourth Gospel to this point'. Of course, the ensuing passion and resurrection narrative is the climax of the Gospel. However, the prayer of Jesus in the Gospel functions as a conclusion for the previous narratives. Then, what is the 'something' for which he has been waiting? That something will reveal the character of the prayer.

In his prayer to the Father, Jesus himself confesses that he has completed the work God gave him to do (cf 17:4). What is the work God gave him to do, which he has completed to this point in time? The view that this 'completion' always means Jesus' achievement on the cross and his resurrection encourages some scholars to insist that the location of the prayer in the Gospel should come after Jesus' resurrection. Boyd is one who advocates this view. He (1967, 208) insists that 'the whole of 17 [Chapter 17 of the Fourth Gospel] is not pre-passion but post-resurrection' claiming that '[t]he passion and resurrection are undoubtedly Christ's greatest work. It is hardly conceivable that Jesus could be represented as saying that he had accomplished his fore-ordained work before his passion with reference to his death'. J. Hammer[29] also supports this view saying that the prayer in the Fourth Gospel 'was spoken in Jesus' final appearance just before he ascended into heaven'. I do not agree with those attempts to move the location of the prayer within the Gospel based on the fixed view that 'accomplishment' in the Gospel always means his accomplishment on the cross. Therefore, I suggest an alternative understanding of what Jesus means by the completion or accomplishment in his prayer, a position that leads to a better understanding of the character of the prayer itself.

The Accomplishment in the Prayer

What does Jesus mean by the 'completion' or 'accomplishment' of the work given him, which he mentions in his prayer (17:4)? To answer the question, one needs to know how the Evangelist uses the verb τελειόω and a similar verb τελέω in the Gospel. The former occurs five times throughout the Gospel, while the latter occurs twice, being limited to the passion narrative. Here is the

---

[28] There are scholars who consider the prayer in the Fourth Gospel 'as a summary of the Fourth Evangelist's theology' (Barrett, Merlier, et al.) [cited in Agourides, 1968, 138].

[29] J. Hammer (*Bibel und Kirche* 14, 1959, 33–40, cited in R. E. Brown, 1970, 584).

list of the usages of the two verbs in the Gospel (my emphasis underlined and in bold):

1. τελειόω
4:34 My food, said Jesus, is to do the will of him who sent me and to **<u>finish</u>** his work (τελειώσω αὐτοῦ τὸ ἔργον).
5:36b For the works that the Father has given me to **<u>finish</u>** – the very works that I am doing – testify that the Father has sent me (τελειώσω αὐτά, αὐτὰ τὰ ἔργα ἃ ποιῶ).
17:4 I have brought you glory on earth by **<u>finishing</u>** the work you gave me to do (τὸ ἔργον τελειώσας ὃ δέδωκάς μοι ἵνα ποιήσω).
17:23 … so that they be brought to **<u>complete</u>** unity (ἵνα ὦσιν τετελειωμένοι εἰς ἕν.
19:28 Later, knowing that everything had now been finished, and so that the Scripture would be **<u>fulfilled</u>**, Jesus said, "I am thirsty" (ἵνα τελειωθῇ ἡ γραφή).

2. τελέω
19:28 Later, knowing that everything had now been **<u>completed</u>**, and so that the Scripture would be fulfilled, Jesus said, "I am thirsty" (τετέλεσται).
19:30 When he had received the drink, Jesus said, "It is **<u>finished</u>**." With that, he bowed his head and gave up his spirit (τετέλεσται).

Generally speaking, the two verbs have the same meaning[30] indicating the completion of something, yet their meanings within the Gospel are distinguishable.[31] As seen above, the verb τελέω is used only in the passion narrative in the Gospel. It indicates that something reaches an end. The verb τελέω has that meaning in the passion narrative when Jesus reaches the end of his ministry, including the cross. In other words, it emphasizes the status of the completion, that something is finished. On the other hand, the verb τελειόω focuses on the accomplishment or fulfilment of something; the first three usages of the verb, in particular, reflect this idea.

The first three usages of τελειόω occur together with the word ἔργον (work) in the Gospel indicating the accomplishment of the work God has given to Jesus.[32] In the first usage of τελειόω (4:34), Jesus is aware that his encounter with the Samaritan woman is part[33] of doing the will of God who sent him and that encounter accomplishes the work of God. Jesus, through his ministry, is

---

[30] BDAG, 2000, 996-97. τελειόω: to complete an activity, complete, bring to an end, finish, accomplish. τελέω: to complete an activity or process, bring to an end, finish, complete. EDNT, 1993, vol.3, 344. τελειόω as a causative vb. (with virtually the same meaning as τελέω) is used for complete, bring to an end, place in a certain (final) condition and thus make complete/perfect, but also fulfil (Scripture).

[31] Dodd distinguishes the two verbs, emphasizing the sacrificial sense of τελέω (1963b, 437–438).

[32] The other two (the fourth and fifth) are used in a passive form meaning being perfect.

[33] ἔργον in this verse occurs as a singular form, whereas it occurs in a plural form in 5:36.

doing the mission given him by the one who sent him. Köstenberger (2004, 101) insists that '[i]n the present passage [4:34], Jesus affirms his commitment to complete the task that God has given him to do, that is, his redemptive work at the cross'. The significance of the whole process of Jesus' ministry will be missed if τελειόω is connected only to the cross. All of his ministries, including his encounter with the Samaritan woman in the present passage and also the cross later, are an accomplishment of God's will. In the second usage of the verb (5:36), Jesus says to the Jews that he is doing the works (plural) God has given him to accomplish. By using the present tense in the main verb,[34] Jesus affirms that what he is doing in his public ministry are the works he is expected to accomplish. The third usage of the verb occurs in his prayer (17:4). In the prayer, Jesus says that he has accomplished the work God has given him. Unlike the subjunctive form of the previous two usages, τελειόω in 17:4 occurs as an indicative form,[35] meaning that he *has accomplished* the work given him.

If a reader removes the assertion that the accomplishment of Jesus always indicates his work on the cross, the reader will discover what Jesus means by τελειόω in 17:4. In the same paragraph, Jesus says, 'I have revealed you [God] to those whom you gave me out of the world' (17:6a), and also 'I gave them the words you gave me and they accepted them. They knew with certainty that I came from you, and they believed that you sent me' (17:8). Based on the three usages of τελειόω with the word ἔργον, I argue that the accomplishment Jesus is referencing in his prayer (17:4) is what he has accomplished throughout his whole ministry, including his encounter with the Samaritans, with the Jews and with his disciples. Dodd (1963, 437) supports this claim, saying, '[i]n xvii. 4, τελειοῦν is used for the completion of Christ's task, which is defined as the disclosure of the "name" of God (6) and the deliverance of His ῥήματα (7) to men'.

In particular, the accomplished work he emphasizes in his prayer is that he has revealed the words God gave him to the discipleship community, both through his ministries in front of them and through his discourses with them, so that they would believe in him. Jesus' whole ministry includes his encounters with the Jews and Gentiles, but the focus of his ministry has been the discipleship community. Jesus has been waiting for the *following* or *accompanying* discipleship community to be a *believing* discipleship community. The confession that the disciples make at last affirms for Jesus that he has accomplished the work, thus the 'hour' for the cross has come. This accomplishment is a prerequisite to the cross. Unless the following discipleship community becomes a believing discipleship community, Jesus cannot go to the cross because the disciples are the ones whom Jesus will send into the

---

[34] The verb ποιῶ in this verse is present active indicative.

[35] The verb itself is a participle in the phrase but the main verb in the previous phrase is an indicative, so it also has an indicative sense.

world to testify about him. In other words, the discipleship community is the anticipation of a missional discipleship community in the world. Therefore, the 'believing' of the disciples is what Jesus has been waiting for before he takes the cross and then sends them into the world. As the apostle Paul writes (Rom 10:14–15), no one can believe in Jesus without the sent community. Jesus has accomplished the formation of the believing discipleship community which will be a missional community. Therefore, he is ready to take the cross.

The Connectivity of the Petitions

The claim that the accomplished work is the formation of the believing discipleship community is further supported by the fact that Jesus' petitions in the prayer are actually for the discipleship community. Jesus' prayer contains three petitions. First, Jesus prays for himself (17:1–5). Secondly, he prays for the discipleship community (17:6–19). Thirdly, he includes in his prayer those who will come to him through the discipleship community (17:20–26). However, the point is not how many petitions appear in the prayer, but rather that the prayer is one prayer – a prayer for the discipleship community. In this section, I will discuss the connectivity of the three petitions, and the reason for the connections between them.

The petitions are three in form but one in reality. Agourides (1968, 141) states that 'the so-called High Priestly Prayer will not have three subjects (viz. first, a prayer of Jesus for Himself; secondly, a prayer for His disciples; and thirdly, a prayer for the Church), but one main subject, the petition to the Father for the "twelve"'. Those three petitions are all connected within the prayer, focusing on the discipleship community rather than existing as three separate prayers for individual constituencies. The connectivity among those petitions is expressed by the use of the adverb καθώς (as) in the prayer. Among all the New Testament books, the Fourth Gospel is the book in which the adverb καθώς[36] appears most frequently. It appears eight times[37] within the prayer alone, one in the first part, four in the second part, and three in the third part of the prayer. The list is as follows (my emphasis underlined and in bold):

> 1. The first petition (prayer for Jesus himself)
> 17:1b–2 Father, the hour has come. Glorify your Son, that your Son may glorify you. **<u>For</u>** (or just as, καθώς) you granted him authority over all people that he might give eternal life to all those you have given him.
>
> 2. The second petition (prayer for the discipleship community)
> 17:11 … so that they may be one **<u>as</u>** (καθώς) we are one.

[36] The use of the adverb καθώς in the Fourth Gospel (31 times) is more than the sum of use of it in the Synoptic Gospels combined (3 in Matt; 7 in Mark; 16 in Luke).
[37] 17:2, 11, 14, 16, 18, 21, 22, 23.

17:14 … for they are not of the world **any more than** (or just as not, καθὼς οὐκ) I am of the world.
17:16 They are not of the world, **even as** (καθώς) I am not of it.
17:18 **As** (καθώς) you sent me into the world, I have sent them into the world.

3. The third petition (prayer for the future discipleship community)
17:21 Father, **just as** (καθώς) you are in me and I am in you. May they also be in us so that the world may believe that you have sent me.
17:22 … they may be one **as** (καθώς) we are one.
17:23b Then, the world will know that you sent me and have loved them **even as** (καθώς) you have loved me.

As seen in the above usages of καθώς, those three different groups reveal the development of the prayer based on the connection of the three different petitions. In the first petition, the subordinate sentence (17:2) led by καθώς provides a basis for the request of Jesus to the Father, 'Glorify your Son, that your Son may glorify you' (17:1b). Carson (1991, 554) points out that 'v. 2 establishes the ground for the petition of v. 1b'. Even though the prayer of Jesus in this petition is for himself in form, the expected outcome of the prayer, in reality, is for the disciples to have eternal life. In the second petition, the content of the petition is extended to the discipleship community. All of the subordinate clauses led by καθώς introduce the divine relationship and ministry and provide the main clauses with the goal or criteria on how the discipleship community is to be and what the discipleship community is to do. The discipleship community is supposed to be one καθώς the Father and Jesus are one (17:11), not to be of the world καθώς Jesus is not of the world (17:14, 16) and be sent to the world καθώς the Father sent Jesus into the world (17:18). What the discipleship community is supposed to be or to do – and even not to be – is based on either Jesus himself or Jesus in relationship with the Father. There is nothing the community should be or do apart from what Jesus has already revealed to them. The identity and ministry of the discipleship community is the reflection of the divine relationship and ministry. Again, the focus of the prayer is on the discipleship community. In the third petition, the content of the petition is expanded to preview the expected outcome of the presence of the discipleship community in the world. The discipleship community's reflection on the divine relationship is the basis for the outcome that the world knows and believes in Jesus. The usages of καθώς in the petitions provide a pattern for the connection of the three petitions.

To sum up, the foundation of the prayer is what the Father and Jesus reveal through their relationship and ministry, the focus of the prayer is on the discipleship community and the scale of the prayer includes the world. Jesus hopes for the world to know and believe that God sent him into the world and loved the world (17:21, 23). This is a repeated claim of Jesus in the Gospel, such as 'God so loved the world' (3:16), '[God sent his Son] to save the world through him' (3:17), and '[Jesus came] to save the world' (12:47). Since he defines eternal life in his prayer as knowing the only true God, and Jesus Christ whom God sent, the anticipation of Jesus is for the world to have eternal life.

The Missional Aspect of the Prayer

In the previous section, I have argued that the three petitions comprise one prayer for the discipleship community, and the prayer for them includes what will happen through them in the world. The inclusion of the world in the prayer provides the readers the possibility of a missional aspect of the prayer. I am not proposing a missional aspect of the prayer based on its direct evangelistic character. Jesus clarifies that he is not praying for the world but for the discipleship community (17:9). If someone associates the word *missional* with evangelism, the prayer might not be understood as missional since Jesus says that his prayer is not for the world. However, the missional aspect of the prayer does not depend on its direct evangelistic character. Instead, the prayer reveals the missional identity of the discipleship community in the world. Jesus makes clear what he is praying for by using the word ἐρωτάω (I ask) in his prayer. This word appears four times in three verses in the prayer, as follows (my emphasis underlined and in bold):

> 17:9 I **<u>pray</u>** [ἐρωτάω] for them. I am not **<u>praying</u>** [ἐρωτάω] for the world, but for those you have given me, for they are yours.
> 17:15 My **<u>prayer</u>** [ἐρωτάω] is not that you take them out of the world but that you protect them from the evil one.
> 17:20 My **<u>prayer</u>** [ἐρωτάω] is not for them alone. I pray also for those who will believe in me through their message.

As seen above, the usages of ἐρωτάω reveal what Jesus prays for. Jesus clarifies that he is not praying for the world but for the discipleship community (17:9). The statement affirms that the prayer is specific, explicitly intended for the discipleship community. However, this prayer is not intended just for the discipleship community alone. He continues that his prayer is not for the community to be taken out of the world but for God to protect the community from the evil one in the world (17:15). The discipleship community needs God's protection because they will be in the world. The purpose of being in the world is not to be separated from the world. Jesus' prayer for their protection is not merely for their preservation in the world, but because they will be a sent community to the world. The purpose for which they will be sent to the world becomes clear in the last usage of ἐρωτάω. Jesus says that his prayer is not for the discipleship community alone. By saying this, Jesus clarifies that the prayer is not exclusive to the contemporary discipleship community, 'the Twelve'. His prayer is extended to include those who believe in him through the message of the disciples. The inclusiveness of the prayer further supports the position that the prayer functions as a summary or conclusion for the whole ministry of Jesus. The prayer parallels the earlier statement of Jesus: 'I have other sheep that are not of this sheep pen. I must bring them also' (10:16). The missional aspect is revealed in this prayer (17:20b). The believers in this verse are related to the missional aspect of the disciples. Even though the use of the present tense with a future meaning in the word (τῶν πιστευόντων) 'is not unnatural' (Newman and Nida, 1980, 541), futurity is not the point of the verse. As Michaels (2010, 874) points out, the emphasis is 'simply on the fact that the "word" reaches them not directly from Jesus, but indirectly through his disciples'. According to the prayer, the 'other sheep' will come to believe through the word of the disciples (διὰ τοῦ λόγου αὐτῶν). It manifests the missional aspect of the disciples.

However, the missional aspect of Jesus' prayer is not limited to the ministry of the disciples alone. Moreover, the ministry aspect is not even the primary focus of the missional aspect of the prayer. The emphasis of the prayer is on the discipleship community itself. Jesus prays not for the ministry of the disciples but for the community of both the immediate disciples and the believers to come. The purpose of his prayer for the communities is explained in the following verses, and I propose that that purpose is the highlight of the prayer and the central theme of the missional aspect of the prayer. In the next section, I will discuss the purpose of the prayer for the communities and its missional implications.

Unity as a Missional Aspect of the Prayer

I have argued that what Jesus has accomplished before the passion narrative is the formation of the believing discipleship community, and Jesus' prayer is for that community since that community will be a sent community in the world. I also have argued that what the discipleship community is sent to be and do is to reflect the divine being and doing expressed by καθώς. In the previous section I pointed out that the missional aspect of Jesus' prayer is not limited to the ministry of the disciples; rather the missional aspect is revealed through the purpose of Jesus' prayer for the communities. Then what is the purpose of his prayer for the communities? In 17:21, the conjunction ἵνα is used three times expressing the purpose of the previous statements as follows (bolded by the author):

> 17:21 … **ἵνα** πάντες ἓν ὦσιν, καθὼς σύ, πάτερ, ἐν ἐμοὶ κἀγὼ ἐν σοί, **ἵνα** καὶ αὐτοὶ ἐν ἡμῖν ὦσιν, **ἵνα** ὁ κόσμος πιστεύῃ ὅτι σύ με ἀπέστειλας (… that all of them may be one, Father, just as you are in me and I am in you. May they also be in us so that the world may believe that you have sent me).

Since verse 21 is a continuation of the previous sentence, the main verb of the sentence is still ἐρωτάω (I pray). In the sentence structure, the three clauses led by ἵνα describe the sequential purposes of Jesus' prayer for the communities. First, the purpose of Jesus' prayer for the communities is for them to be one (πάντες ἓν ὦσιν). This recalls the earlier comment of the

Evangelist regarding what the high priest had said (11:49–50): 'Jesus would die for the Jewish nation, and not only for that nation but also for the scattered children of God, to bring them together and make them one' (11:51b–52). The unity of the discipleship communities is the goal of Jesus' prayer and his death. Jesus presents the divine relationship as an example of unity: '... just as you [the Father] are in me [Jesus] and I am in you'. Secondly, Jesus prays for the participation of the discipleship communities in the divine relationship. The divine relationship is not simply an example for the discipleship communities but a reality for them to join. As mentioned above, the prayer of Jesus in the Fourth Gospel functions as a conclusion and summary of the whole ministry of Jesus in the Gospel, leaving the passion narrative and the post-resurrection narrative alone. The emphasis on the unity of the discipleship community and the community of God in the conclusion recalls for the readers the foundation statement at the beginning of the Gospel. The ἀρχή (beginning) in the foundation statement (1:1) reappears in the prayer as πρὸ τοῦ τὸν κόσμον εἶναι (before the world began, 17:5) and πρὸ καταβολῆς κόσμου (before the creation of the world, 17:24). It reveals that the Evangelist uses the foundation statement not only as the point of departure but also as the goal of Jesus' incarnation and ministry. The divine relationship introduced in the foundation statement is now extended for the discipleship community to join. Thirdly, the prayer encompasses the world, in order that the world may believe. However, Jesus does not pray directly for the world to believe nor does he pray for the ministry of the communities so that the world may believe. Rather, Jesus prays for the unity of the discipleship communities, and even the participation of them in the divine unity, so that the world may believe God has sent him. This does not necessarily mean that unity is the prerequisite for the mission, but, as Michaels (2010, 875) proposes, Jesus 'views the unity of the disciples and their mission to the world as inseparable'.

To sum it up, since he has accomplished what he has been desiring and working for, Jesus begins his prayer. That 'accomplishment' is the formation of the believing discipleship community. Since the formation of the community has been the focus throughout his whole ministry, his prayer for them then functions as a conclusion or summary of his whole ministry rather than as a reference to the previous discourse with his disciples. The prayer includes the ministry of the discipleship community in the world, but the missional aspect of the prayer is not limited to their ministry in the world. Instead, the missional aspect is proposed as an integration of the unity and ministry of the communities, focusing more on the unity of the communities being invited to participate in the divine unity.

Chapter Summary

The third part of the Gospel (chs. 13–17) chronicles the intimate interaction of Jesus with his disciples. This part consists of three sub-parts: first, Jesus takes action to wash his disciples' feet, followed by a final discourse to his disciples before the passion narrative and finally, Jesus' prayer to his Father. The narrative follows the 'sign' discourses of the Gospel, which begin with an action followed by a discourse explaining the meaning of the action. Salier (2004, 172) defines the 'sign' of the Fourth Gospel as follows: 'The σημεῖα are actions, performed by Jesus, that attest his identity as the divine Messiah, who is sent by the Father to bring life to the world', so it 'is intended to prompt a response of faith in Jesus by the reader'. The foot-washing is not one of the many actions of Jesus but, rather, a unique act in the sense that he performed it only for the disciples. Unlike the other signs of Jesus, the foot-washing is not merely to reveal his identity as the sent one from the Father; instead, its aim is for the disciples to follow as a loving and missional community in the world. Through the foot-washing, Jesus showed his love for the disciples, a love that includes a new relationship with them and the invitation for them to follow his example. By following his example, the disciples will form a new loving relationship among themselves and also with the people who will believe in Jesus through their message.

The discourse of Jesus following the action highlights the relationship aspect once again. It clarifies that the essence of the foot-washing is not the action itself but the serving and loving relationship demonstrated through the action. Through the vine illustration in particular, Jesus emphasizes the mutual dwelling between the Father, Jesus and the disciples, and that mutual dwelling includes the fruit-bearing of the disciples. However, the focus of the fruit-bearing is not solely on the 'bearing' but the 'remaining', the remaining of the disciples and the fruit through them in Jesus, the vine. I pointed out that this is one of crucial contributions of the Gospel to a biblical understanding of mission.

Jesus' prayer to his Father functions as a conclusion not only for the narrative for the disciples but more extensively for the whole of his previous ministry. In the prayer, Jesus reports to the Father that he has accomplished the work given him, and the work is to form a believing community. The prayer reveals clearly that the ministry focus of Jesus is to form a believing discipleship community, to have an intimate relationship through a mutual dwelling, just as he has the relationship with the Father, and to send the community into the world to testify about him. Jesus is ready to take the cross because the community is ready to be sent into the world.

Through this third part of the Gospel, the Gospel reveals the essential nature of the mission that Jesus has been doing and that the disciples are expected to do. It has to do with the loving and mutual indwelling of the communities involved in God's mission. Mission expressed in this part can be defined as the expansion of the loving indwelling of the communities, from the divine community to the discipleship community through Jesus and from Jesus to the world through the discipleship community with the Holy Spirit. It starts with the loving relationship of the Father and the Son. The Son has been sent by the

Father in the midst of the loving relationship. The Son invites his disciples to join the loving divine community through him and also to follow the example of the divine loving by loving each other. The loving relationship ultimately includes the joining of the 'other sheep' to the divine community through the disciples. Bauckham (2015, 41) summarizes the loving continuation as follows:

> By the end of chapter 17 we know that this love of God for the world comprises the movement of God's love that begins in the mutual loving communion of the Father and the Son, entails the Son's mission to include humans in that divine love, creates the loving community of disciples of Jesus, and thereby reaches the world'.

6. The Accomplishment of Jesus and the Commissioning of the Discipleship Community (18:1–21:25)

Introduction

I have divided the Fourth Gospel into four parts. In the previous chapter, I have examined how the third part of the Gospel, Jesus' intimate interaction with his disciples, reveals a shaping and equipping aspect for the community to participate in the relationship of God, which includes the commissioning of them. In this last part (chs. 18–21), the Gospel contains the passion, resurrection and also the post-resurrection narrative. I will examine how the findings in the previous parts are affirmed in this climatic part of the Gospel. The main argument in the chapter will encompass three issues.

First, I will examine what the completion of Jesus' work on the cross means. Jesus says 'It is finished' (19:30) on the cross. How does the completion of his mission on the cross reflect his previous ministry, and to what extent does the completion open a new chapter for the disciples in the world? The answer will be explored not only within the passion narrative but also in the post-resurrection narrative – Jesus' encounter with the disciples after the resurrection, in particular.

Secondly, I will examine the purpose of the Gospel writing. The Evangelist reveals explicitly the purpose of the Gospel record: 'These are written that you may believe that Jesus is the Messiah, the Son of God, and that by believing you may have life in his name' (20:31). Since the purpose statement is given at the ending part of the Gospel, after readers have read the whole Gospel, the statement needs to be viewed and interpreted in the light of the entire Gospel.

Thirdly, I will argue how the last chapter of the Gospel plays a vital role as a reconfirmation of the theme that the previous parts have revealed. I do not agree that the Gospel ends, in reality, with the purpose statement in 20:31. I will examine the two disciples who appear in the final narrative, and seek to discover what messages are revealed through the episodes of the disciples regarding the missional characteristics of the community.

Jesus and the Disciples in the Passion and Resurrection Narrative

What Jesus Has Completed on the Cross

Jesus declares the completion of his mission on earth on the cross saying, 'It is finished (τετέλεσται)'[1] (19:30). The word τελέω is used only twice in the Gospel, and both usages appear in the passion narrative, meaning 'everything is finished' (cf 19:28, 30). The word τελέω is related to and is compared with its synonym τελειόω within the Gospel.[2] The Evangelist uses the verb τελειόω to describe both the achievement of Jesus' work which is the forming of the discipleship community[3] and the fulfilment of Scripture as a whole (19:28).[4] Therefore, the verb τελέω in the final statement of Jesus on the cross expresses the completion of both τελειόω, the achievement and the fulfilment. I see that those two aspects of the completion explain the redemptive and the missional characteristics of Jesus, which are explained by the references to the sacrificial lamb of Passover and the king of his kingdom respectively in the passion narrative.

First, Jesus is identified as the redemptive Christ. The Gospel already described Jesus as 'the Lamb of God, who takes away the sin of the world' (1:29) through the mouth of John the Baptist. Jesus' ministry has been introduced within the Passover narratives as well, unfolding the meaning of the feast (cf 2:13; 6:4; 13:1). In this last Passover narrative, Jesus is the 'Lamb of God', who is killed on the cross. The Evangelist connects Jesus with the sacrificial lamb as much as possible in the passion narrative. First, the connection is expressed by the quotation from the Old Testament: 'Not one of his bones will be broken' (19:36).[5] The quotation from the Passover regulations in Exodus identifies Jesus on the cross as the sacrificial lamb of the Passover. Besides the direct quotation, the word ὕσσωπος (hyssop, 19:29) also recalls the same word in the Passover regulations (cf Exod 12:22). Secondly, the Evangelist emphasizes repeatedly that the day Jesus is killed on the cross is παρασκευή (the day of preparation, 19:14, 31, 42). By this word, he connects Jesus' death with the slaughter of the Passover lamb. Michaels (2010, 941) points out that '[t]he "preparation" normally meant Friday, the day before the Sabbath (see Mark 15:42), but in connection with "the Passover" it refers to the day before Passover, when lambs were slaughtered in "preparation" for the

---

[1] Perfect passive indicative-third person singular of the verb τελέω.

[2] For the difference between τελειόω and τελέω within the Fourth Gospel, see 4.4.2.

[3] For the argument, see 4.4.2.

[4] The Evangelist uses the word πληρόω when the fulfilment refers to a specific Scripture verse or theme (12:38; 13:18; 15:25; 17:12; 18:9, 32; 19:24, 36).

[5] In the regulations for the Passover, God said to the Israelites: 'Do not break any of the bones' (Ex 12:46).

Passover meal'.[6] Through those connections, the Evangelist affirms that Jesus is the one prophesied in the Old Testament, and Scripture is fulfilled (τελειόω). Jesus has completed his mission as the redemptive Christ, fulfilling what was prophesied in the Scripture.

Secondly, what Jesus has completed on the cross includes the forming of the discipleship community. Jesus on the cross has completed his mission of both fulfilling what was prophesied in the Old Testament and forming the believing discipleship community for the mission to be continued. The achievement (τελειόω) part of the completion (τελέω) is related to the second description about Jesus in the passion narrative, the missional Christ. I observe that the missional Christ is expressed by the word βασιλεύς (king) and another word βασιλεία (kingdom) in the narrative. The word βασιλεύς (king) appears 12 times[7] and the word βασιλεία (kingdom) three times[8] in the passion narrative alone, out of 16 times and five times respectively in total in the Gospel. It shows that the two words are used intensively in the passion narrative. Unlike the Synoptics[9], the Fourth Gospel describes Jesus revealing himself as a king in a more pronounced way. The conversation between Jesus and Pilate is as follows:

> 18:33b "Are you the king of the Jews?"
> 18:34 "Is that your own idea," Jesus asked, "or did others talk to you about me?"
> 18:35 "Am I a Jew?" Pilate replied. "Your own people and chief priests handed you over to me. What is it you have done?"
> 18:36 Jesus said, "My kingdom is not of this world. If it were, my servants would fight to prevent my arrest by the Jewish leaders. But my kingdom is from another place."
> 18:37 "You are a king, then!" said Pilate. Jesus answered, "You say that I am a king. In fact, the reason I was born and came into the world is to testify to the truth. Everyone on the side of truth listens to me."

The expression 'my kingdom' (ἡ βασιλεία ἡ ἐμή, 18:36) reveals that Jesus has a kingdom. Based on what Jesus says, Pilate confirms what he had asked Jesus about his kingship: οὐκοῦν[10] βασιλεὺς εἶ σύ (You are a king, then!). Then, the following statement of Jesus reveals the purpose of the king's birth

---

[6] Michaels (2010, 942) proposes that 'it was the "preparation" in *both* senses, for it seems to have been a year in which the Passover also fell on a Sabbath'.
[7] 18:33, 37 (2x), 39; 19:3, 12, 14, 15 (2x), 19, 21 (2x).
[8] 18:37 (3x).
[9] To the question of Pilate asking if Jesus is the king of the Jews, Jesus simply answers Σὺ λέγεις (You have said so) in the Synoptics (Matt 27:11; Mark 15:2; Luke 23:3).
[10] The adverb οὐκοῦν is used only once in the Gospel. It has an inferential sense (BDAG, 736). The accented οὐκοῦν drops the negative and interrogative force, so that it can be used, in the sense "well then," even with an imperative (Abbott, 192).

and coming to this world. By using the phrase εἰς τοῦτο (for this) twice,[11] Jesus emphasizes the purpose, which is to testify to the truth. Jesus is about to die, yet his statement shows the expectancy of the kingdom: 'Everyone on the side of truth listens[12] to me' (18:37). I submit that this expectancy of Jesus for the expansion of his kingdom, testifying to the truth in the world, is based on his accomplishment of establishing the believing community and their upcoming mission in the world. Jesus is the king of the kingdom not of the world but 'from another place', and the kingdom will be expanded through the discipleship community and their ministry. As mentioned above, the declaration of the completion (τελέω) in the final statement of Jesus includes the accomplishment (τελειόω) of the forming of the believing discipleship community. Therefore, the completion on the cross implies that the preparation has been completed for the upcoming ministry that will be continued by the discipleship community.

In this section, I have claimed that the Evangelist demonstrates Jesus is both the redemptive Christ and also the missional Christ. The former is demonstrated by the fulfilment of the related verses in the Old Testament while the latter is demonstrated by the kingdom expectation based on the accomplishment of forming the believing community. In other words, the former is based on the Old Testament and the latter on the new, believing community. In this sense, I claim that the Evangelist reveals Jesus throughout the Gospel as both the sacrificial lamb for the sin of the world and the king of his kingdom, to which the discipleship community belongs, and its expansion, in which the discipleship community is supposed to participate.

Completion of the Creation Process of the New Community

I have argued that the Fourth Gospel could be summarized as the establishment of a new missional community (cf 3.5). The discipleship community has been called to be a new missional community. Therefore, the ministry of Jesus in the Gospel could be seen as a process of creating that community. The new creation process had begun with the incarnation of Jesus, the incarnate Word, through whom the new community would be created. The new creation process then proceeds throughout the whole Gospel. The disciples are introduced to Jesus, have an intimate relationship with him and learn from him through both his encounters with the Jews and his interactions with individuals and also his direct encounters with themselves. Through the passion and resurrection, Jesus finishes what he is supposed to achieve before he goes back to his Father. The narrative after the resurrection shows the completion of the new creation process for the discipleship community and their commissioning into the world.

---

[11] εἰς τοῦτο γεγέννημαι καὶ εἰς τοῦτο ἐλήλυθα.

[12] ἀκούει – the present tense of the verb ἀκούω is used in the sentence.

First of all, the Evangelist starts the post-resurrection narrative with a new expression τῇ δὲ μιᾷ τῶν σαββάτων (the first day of the week, 20:1). Since all four Gospels (cf Matt 28:1; Mark 16:2; Luke 24:1) use the same phrase to begin the post-resurrection narrative, the Gospel writers reveal a common theme by the phrase, as opposed to the Evangelist alone using it to express something unique. Carson (1991, 635) notes that 'it may have to do with the desire to present the resurrection of Jesus as the beginning of something new'. However, the use of the phrase by the Evangelist seems unique in two ways. First, it is special because it runs contrary to his pattern. It is important to the Evangelist to show that what Jesus said in his previous ministry he achieved through his passion and resurrection. In the first Passover narrative, the Evangelist commented on what Jesus said about how he would raise the destroyed temple in three days: 'But the temple he had spoken of was his body. After he was raised from the dead, his disciples recalled what he had said. Then they believed the Scripture and the words that Jesus had spoken' (2:21–22). For this reason, it might be more appropriate for the Evangelist to use τῇ ἡμέρᾳ τῇ τρίτῃ (on the third day) than the phrase τῇ δὲ μιᾷ τῶν σαββάτων in the Gospel, as the apostle Paul did in one of his letters (cf 1 Cor 15:4). The fact that the Evangelist used the phrase nonetheless tells us that this was something of consequence beyond the achievement of the prophesied.

Secondly, it is special because he uses it to connect with a new narrative. He repeats the phrase once again[13] to introduce the first encounter of Jesus with the disciples as a whole after his resurrection. The encounter demonstrates the completion of the creation process for the discipleship community. I propose that the reason why the Evangelist uses the phrase τῇ δὲ μιᾷ τῶν σαββάτων and repeats it to introduce the first post-resurrection encounter with the discipleship community is to highlight the encounter, the completion of the creation of the discipleship community. Köstenberger (2004, 561) observes that '[t]he expression "on the first day of the week" reads more literally, "on one of the Sabbath [week]" and may allude to the week of creation'. N. T. Wright (2002b, 140) makes a case for creation typology as follows:

> In the beginning was the **Word**… and the Word became flesh. The flesh has spoken, breathed, brought life and light. New creation has spilled out around him wherever he has gone. 'Here's the man!' The sixth day. Creation is complete. God saw all he had made, and it was very good. Flesh dies. Chaos comes again. Darkness descends on the little weeping group at the cross. Two men in the fading light do what has to be done. Then the long Sabbath, the rest in the cold tomb. And now, still in the darkness, the first day of the week. The new week. The new creation. The eighth day.

---

[13] 20:19, ὀψίας τῇ ἡμέρᾳ ἐκείνῃ τῇ μιᾷ σαββάτων (the evening of that first day of the week).

The completion of the creation of the discipleship community is signified by Jesus breathing over the community. On the evening of the day of resurrection, the first day of the week, Jesus breathes on the disciples and says, 'Receive the Holy Spirit (πνεῦμα ἅγιον)' (20:22). The Evangelist uses a very special verb ἐμφυσάω (to breathe) in the narrative. The word appears only once (*hapax legomenon*), not only in the Gospel but also throughout the whole New Testament. The breathing of Jesus on the disciples recalls the creation of man in Genesis (2:7) and the recreation out of the dry bones in Ezekiel 37:9. These usages 'narrate the divine creation or re-creation of human beings through the act of ἐμφυσᾶν' (Bennema, 2012, 94). The Lord God breathed (ἐμφυσάω, LXX)[14] when he created the man, Adam, and also when he recreated human beings (Ezek 37:9). In the Gospel, it is not unusual that the Evangelist uses special words or expressions to connect with the Old Testament story. There are a few other examples in the Gospel, such as σκηνόω (to tabernacle, 1:14), ἀναβαίνω καὶ καταβαίνω (to ascend and descend, 1:51),[15] δάκτυλος (finger, 8:5) and so on, which correspond to 'tabernacle' (Exod 25:8–9), 'Jacob's ladder' (Gen 28:12) and 'the tablets of stone' (Exod 31:18) respectively in the Old Testament. As God formed the first man from the dust of the ground in the first creation and he recreated human beings out of the dry bones, Jesus, that is to say, God through the incarnate Word, formed the discipleship community through his whole ministry. Then, Jesus breathed on the disciples as God breathed on Adam and on the dry bones. As seen earlier (see 5.3.3), Jesus has promised his disciples that he would send the παράκλητος (advocate), referring to the Holy Spirit. For this reason, it is strange that Jesus uses πνεῦμα rather than παράκλητος in this scene. Michaels (2010, 1011) summarized the point as follows:

> In the Gospel itself, a variety of expressions have been used for the Advocate's coming: "I will ask the Father, and he will give you…" (14:16); "the Father will send in my name" (14:26); "whom I will send to you from the Father" (15:26); "if I go, I will send him to you" (16:7). None of these quite match the present scene in which "Holy Spirit" comes on the disciples as breath from Jesus' mouth.

---

[14] Gen 2:7b ἐνεφύσησεν εἰς τὸ πρόσωπον αὐτοῦ πνοὴν ζωῆς, καὶ ἐγένετο ὁ ἄνθρωπος εἰς ψυχὴν ζῶσαν ([the Lord God] breathed into his nostrils the breath of life, and the man became a living being). This word also appears in Ezekiel 37:9 τάδε λέγει κύριος ἐκ τῶν τεσσάρων πνευμάτων ἐλθὲ καὶ ἐμφύσησον εἰς τοὺς νεκροὺς τούτους καὶ ζησάτωσαν (This is what the Sovereign Lord says: Come, breath, from the four winds and breathe into these slain, that they may live).

[15] Compare καὶ οἱ ἄγγελοι τοῦ θεοῦ ἀνέβαινον καὶ κατέβαινον ἐπ' αὐτῆς (Gen 28:12, LXX) and καὶ τοὺς ἀγγέλους τοῦ θεοῦ ἀναβαίνοντας καὶ καταβαίνοντας ἐπὶ τὸν υἱὸν τοῦ ἀνθρώπου (John 1:51).

The πνεῦμα ἅγιον in the narrative refers to the Holy Spirit even though no definite article appears in the phrase.[16] The modifier ἅγιος (holy) appears five times in the Gospel and always with either the Father, Son or Holy Spirit.[17] Therefore, it is difficult to interpret πνεῦμα ἅγιον other than the Holy Spirit. How, then, should the Spirit-πνεῦμα and the Spirit-παράκλητος be seen in the Gospel? There are different views on the giving of the Spirit comparing the Holy Spirit in John and in Acts 2.[18] However, I will examine how those two different terms need to be seen within the Fourth Gospel.

I argue that the Spirit-παράκλητος is one of the aspects of the Spirit-πνεῦμα in the Gospel relating to the disciples' mission in particular. The word πνεῦμα in the Gospel appears twenty-four times.[19] Four of them (14:17, 26; 15:26; 16:13) relate to the Spirit-παράκλητος. They appear in the narrative when Jesus interacts with 'the Twelve'. The Spirit-παράκλητος is introduced to the disciples for their mission after Jesus' 'glorification'. There are two other verses (three usages) where the Spirit-πνεῦμα relates to the disciples. In 7:39, it is written 'But this He spoke of the Spirit [πνεῦμα], whom those who believed in Him were to receive; for the Spirit [πνεῦμα] was not yet given, because Jesus was not yet glorified'. In the present verse, it is written 'Receive the Holy Spirit' (20:22). The other seventeen usages of the word relate to Jesus (1:32, 33; 3:34, 11:33; 13:21; 19:30), baptizing (1:33), birth 3:5, 6, 8), worshipping (4:24, 24), and life (6:63). Based on the above observation, I argue that the Spirit-πνεῦμα is generally used referring to the Holy Spirit in the Gospel, even when it refers to whom the disciples will receive without specifying the role of him. The Spirit-παράκλητος is mentioned only when Jesus interacts with the disciples explaining the role of the Holy Spirit, referring to their mission after his glorification. Therefore, the action of breathing of Jesus and giving of the Holy Spirit in 20:22 signifies that the creation of the initial discipleship community, if not 'the Twelve', is completed and at the same time their mission is started. The Spirit-πνεῦμα in the verse emphasizes the new birth or new creation of the discipleship community but does not exclude the aspect of the Spirit-παράκλητος since they have learned that the Spirit-πνεῦμα they will receive is the Spirit-παράκλητος. Jesus says, 'But the Helper [παράκλητος], the

---

[16] The existence of the definite article cannot be a standard for whether the word represents the Spirit or just a spirit. Evidence can be found elsewhere in the Gospel where the Evangelist uses either case to refer to both the Spirit and a spirit. For instance, πνεῦμά without any definite article in 7:39 refers to the Sprit while πνεῦμά with a definite article in 13:21 and 19:30 refers to a spirit.

[17] Holy Spirit (1:33); Holy One [Jesus] of God (6:69); Holy Spirit (14:26); Holy Father (17:11); Holy Spirit (20:22).

[18] For the different views on the comparison between the Johannine giving of the Spirit and the Acts Pentecost, see Bennema's *The Giving of the Spirit in John 19–20: Another Round* (2012, 104).

[19] 1:32, 33 (2x); 3:5, 6 (2x), 8 (2x), 34; 4:23, 24 (2x); 6:63 (2x); 7:39 (2x); 11:33; 13:21; 14:17, 25; 15:26; 16:13; 19:30; 20:22.

Holy Spirit [πνεῦμα], whom the Father will send in My name, He will teach you all things, and bring to your remembrance all that I said to you' (14:26, also refer to 14:16–17 and 15:26). For the functions of the two terms, Turner (1996, 100–101) points out that, the Spirit- πνεῦμα 'brings the disciples to the new creation life of the resurrected Israel' and the Spirit-παράκλητος replaces Jesus '(a) as the means of his continued presence with the disciples', '(b) as the one who teaches about and who illumines the Christ-event', and '(c) as the one who uses (b) as the basis and means of witness to the world'.

If the above argument that the Spirit-πνεῦμα in 20:22 includes the aspect of the Spirit-παράκλητος is accepted, then how could the relationship between this Johannine event and the Pentecost in Acts 2 be explained? Turner (1996, 100) suggests that it is 'one theological "gift" in 'two chronological stages'.[20] On the other hand, Burge (1987, 133) argues that 'although John is aware of the separate historical events of "the hour," he conceives of them theologically as a unified whole'. Carson (1991, 649–55) views the Johannine event as a 'symbolic' one saying 'there is no intrinsic reason for thinking that the imperative of 20:22, *Receive the Holy Spirit*, must be experienced immediately'.

I argue that those two events are two different events but not as a progress of the giving of the Spirit. It is progressive not because of the giving of the different aspects of the Spirit each time but because of the progressive expansion of the discipleship community by the Holy Spirit. Michaels (2010, 1011–12) observes that 'this "Life [πνεῦμά]," this empowerment, becomes "the Advocate [παράκλητος]" in a personal sense only later, in the course of their mission and its accompanying persecutions'. I agree with the above view not as two different events of the giving of the Spirit but as a progressive understanding of the disciples. Based on my argument that the Fourth Gospel is a feast-centred narrative (see 4.3), I view that the Johannine event in 20:22 occurs during the First-fruits Festival and the event in Acts 2 occurs in the Pentecost Festival.[21] The former relates to 'the Twelve' and the latter to the wider community, including them. The Father created the discipleship community as the new creation through the incarnate Word, Jesus Christ, and being one with them, sending them to the world in the Spirit-πνεῦμα/ παράκλητος) and the disciples will be one with others in the same Spirit-πνεῦμα/ παράκλητος.

[20] Bennema (2012, 104) suggests a three-stage process (19:30; 20:22; Acts 2).

[21] Thus, the term *Johannine Pentecost* is chronologically correct and I do not agree that John 20 and Acts 2 reflect the same event.

The Purpose of the Creation of the Discipleship Community

In relation to the new creation narrative, that is to say, the completion of the discipleship community, there are a few themes that need to be noted regarding the missional aspects.

First, Jesus manifests the purpose of the new creation of the discipleship community. In the narrative, he says 'As the Father has sent [ἀποστέλλω] me, I am sending [πέμπω][22] you' (20:21). Even though Jesus said the same statement in his prayer to the Father, 'As you sent [ἀποστέλλω] me into the world, I have sent [ἀποστέλλω] them into the world' (17:18), this is the first time for him to say to the disciples explicitly that he is sending them as the Father has sent him. Jesus has created the discipleship community to send them into the world as he himself has been sent by the Father. As discussed above (see 5.4.3), the subordinate clause led by καθώς (just as) represents the divine relationship and ministry and provides the main clause with the goal or criteria on how the discipleship community is to be and what it is to do. The adverb καθώς in the statement does not mean that he is sending them simply *because* the Father has sent him, but it means that he is sending them *in the same way* the Father has sent him. Throughout the whole creation process of the discipleship community, Jesus let them know the meaning of the Father's sending of himself, first through his encounters with the Jews, then through his direct encounter with the disciples themselves.

Secondly, the creation narrative shows the missional role of the newly created community. Jesus says to them, 'If you forgive [ἀφίημι] anyone's sins [ἁμαρτία], their sins are forgiven; if you do not forgive them, they are not forgiven' (20:23). The word ἀφίημι (to leave) appears 15 times[23] in the Gospel but is never used with ἁμαρτία (sin) being interpreted as 'to forgive' except for the present verse (20:23).[24] In a sense, this is a very intentional and specific description for the ministry that the newly created discipleship community will carry on. The Fourth Gospel has mentioned that the disciples would testify about Jesus but never specifically expressed any ministry like the above statement. Therefore, Jesus' saying that the authority to forgive sins is given to the disciples is a distinctive statement. According to the Synoptics, the Jews understood that God alone can forgive sins (cf Matt 9:3; Mark 2:7; Luke 5:21), and Jesus insisted that he had the authority on earth to forgive sins (cf Matt 9:6; Mark 2:10; Luke 5:24). None of the Synoptic Gospels assert that the authority to forgive sins is given to the disciples. The distinctive statement in the Fourth Gospel reveals how the Evangelist views the missional role of the discipleship

---

[22] Michaels (2010, 1009) points out that 'the two verbs [ἀποστέλλω and πέμπω] for "send" are used interchangeably'.

[23] 4:3, 28, 52; 8:29; 10:12; 11:44, 48; 12:7; 14:18, 27; 16:28, 32; 18:8; 20:23 (2x).

[24] The verb κρατέω (to hold) is used only in the verse meaning the opposite of the verb ἀφίημι.

community. In the Gospel, the disciples anticipated the great works Jesus would perform (cf 1:50), and Jesus performed many 'signs' in the presence of the disciples (cf 20:30). As a result, the disciples became a believing discipleship community (cf 17:8). In his direct encounter with the disciples, Jesus told the believing discipleship community, 'Very truly I tell you, whoever believes in me will do the works I have been doing, and they will do even greater things than these, because I am going to the Father' (14:12). In the new creation narrative, Jesus declares that the newly created discipleship community will have the authority to forgive sins in the world, and the forgiveness of sins in the world is the work that the discipleship community will continue in the new chapter of the salvation history unfolding before them. Schnackenburg (1982, 324) points out that 'John is concerned with the supreme passing on of Jesus' authority and commission; the fellowship of the disciples is to make him present in the world and to continue his ministry of salvation'. It is important to recognize that the Fourth Gospel describes the missional aspect of the discipleship community, not as a separate ministry but as a part of their relationship with the triune God. The disciples are called to the discipleship community of Jesus, and they learn from him that they become a believing community, belonging to the triune God. They receive the right to become the children of God (cf 1:12) and, as such, they are given the authority to forgive sins in the world, to continue the works Jesus had been doing. The missional aspect of the discipleship community in the Fourth Gospel is always understood by the relationship they have with the triune God.

Missional Purpose of the Gospel

The Evangelist's Purpose for the Gospel

Once he has finished the passion and resurrection narrative, the Evangelist provides the purpose of the Gospel writing, explicitly saying, 'Jesus performed many other signs in the presence of his disciples which are not recorded in this book. But these are written that you may believe that Jesus is the Messiah, the Son of God, and that by believing you may have life in his name' (20:30–31). According to this statement, the Gospel is for the readers to believe and have life in the name of Jesus. The consequent questions the statement raises to understand the purpose of the Gospel are: Who are the readers – believers or non-believers or both? and, What is the meaning of 'believing'? There have been several attempts to answer these questions. First, there is an attempt to answer by examining the tense of the verb πιστεύω (to believe) in the statement. However, it is a controversial one because the tense of the verb appears in two different variants in manuscripts, one in the present tense and the other in the aorist tense. In his commentary, Metzger (1994c, 219) explains the two variants of the verb and their succeeding interpretations:

> Both πιστεύητε [present] and πιστεύσητε [aorist] have notable early support. The aorist tense, strictly interpreted, suggests that the Fourth Gospel was addressed to non-Christians so that they might come to believe that Jesus is the Messiah; the present tense suggests that the aim of the writer was to strengthen the faith of those who already believe ("that you may continue to believe").

It is not the aim of the study to determine which tense is the original; instead, I argue that the entire purpose of the Gospel cannot and should not be decided by the tense of a single verb. Some scholars already addressed the limitation of the view. Beasley-Murray (1999, 386) states that '[i]t is increasingly recognized, however, that a decision like this can hardly rest on a fine point of Greek grammar, not least in view of the fact that the Evangelist does not always keep the rules in his use of tenses'. Carson (1991, 662) also points out that 'it can easily be shown that John elsewhere in his Gospel can use *either* tense to refer to *both* coming to faith and continuing in the faith'. Secondly, there is an attempt to answer by considering the wider context of the verb. Both the syntactical analysis of the statement and the syntactical comparison of the ἵνα clause[25] belong to the attempt. Carson (1991, 662) suggests that the interpretation of the clause ἵνα πιστεύ[σ]ητε ὅτι Ἰησοῦς ἐστιν ὁ Χριστὸς ὁ υἱὸς τοῦ θεοῦ might be: 'you may believe that the Christ, the Son of God, is Jesus', rather than 'you may believe that Jesus is the Messiah, the Son of God'. The new translation of the statement presumes that the readers already know about the concept of 'Messiah' and are looking for who the Messiah could be. Therefore, the readers would be 'unconverted Jews, along with proselytes and God-fearers'.

However, the statement cannot be taken out of the Gospel and be interpreted independently of it. The statement is part of the whole Gospel, and provides the reason why the Evangelist selected the stories he included in the Gospel. The analysis based on the single verb, clause or syntax has its value, but the value can be justified only when the whole Gospel supports the analysis. The fact that the Evangelist selects what the readers read in the Gospel, apart from 'many other signs' to make the readers believe and have life in the name of Jesus, signifies that the selected stories, that is to say, the written Gospel as a whole, decides who the readers are and what the character of 'believing' in the Gospel is. No matter what the tense of the verb πιστεύω may be, what tense the ἵνα clauses contain most and what the syntactical analysis would mean, the readers of the Gospel and the meaning of 'believing' in the purpose statement have to be interpreted in light of the Gospel narrative as a whole. In this sense,

---

[25] Carson (1991, 662) writes, 'H. Riesenfeld [*Studia Theologica* 19, 1965, 213–20.] has argued that John commonly uses the present tense after *hina* ('in order that')', thus 'the Fourth Gospel was composed with believers in mind'. Carson critiques this position, saying, 'most of his examples are drawn from 1 John, where demonstrably readers *are* Christians'.

Santram's[26] approach is worthy of attention. Since the Evangelist hints that he chose several stories to include in his Gospel out of many signs Jesus performed, Santram takes note of the relation between 'sign' and 'believing' in the Gospel. Unlike the above two views, his argument includes all the 'signs' of Jesus in the Gospel. He (1975, 114) insists that '[h]ere *pisteuein* is inseparably bound up with semeia (signs)'. He continues that '[a] study of John's use of *sēmeion* in relation to *pisteuein* will, therefore, provide us with a reasonably determinative criterion for a choice between *pisteuēte* and *pisteusēte*'. His argument on the relation of 'sign' and 'believing' is as follows (114):

> The word *sēmeion* is used 17 times in John's Gospel including 20:30f. Since 20:30f involves the very problem we are trying to solve we should consider only the remaining 16 references to see how John uses *sēmeion* in relation to *pisteuein.* In 9 out of these 16 passages believing is directly related to signs. In each of these reference is made to signs as events designed to lead people to believe in Jesus. The signs are meant to *create* faith in those who do not as yet believe. They have a *missionary* purpose.
>
> It is to be noted that out of these 9 instances 7 have a reference to believing and in each of these the inceptive aorist of *pisteuein* has been used. This tense indicates the beginning of the believing-response to the signs, implying that those who now respond or are expected to respond in faith are not as yet believers.

The reason why I quote his lengthy explanation is that my argument on the issue is based on similar points but in a different way. I will discuss the 'sign', 'disciples' and ἵνα clause, including 'believing' in the purpose statement, from the whole story's point of view.

Σημεῖα ἐποίησεν ὁ Ἰησοῦς ἐνώπιον τῶν μαθητῶν

There are two parts in the statement of purpose as seen above. One is that Jesus performed many signs in the presence of his disciples, and the other is that the Evangelist selected what is written in the Gospel among those signs for the readers to believe. I will examine the first part of the statement, and then discuss the primary purpose in 20:31, based on the findings of the examination of the first part.

The Evangelist uses a unique expression in the first part of the statement (20:30): σημεῖα ἐποίησεν ὁ Ἰησοῦς ἐνώπιον τῶν μαθητῶν (Jesus performed… signs in the presence of his disciples, 20:30). It is noteworthy that the Evangelist expresses Jesus doing the signs in the presence of the disciples. Because the 'signs' were performed by Jesus mainly in front of the crowds or

---

[26] P. B. Santram is an Indian scholar, and the paper on the purpose of the Fourth Gospel was presented at a conference held in Pune, India in Feb. 1974 and published in the following year (Santram, 1975 in Bibliography).

the Jews (cf chs. 2–12) in the Gospel, it would be more appropriate to say, 'in the presence of the crowd or the Jews', though the disciples were there as well. To understand the purpose statement, it needs to be observed what the Evangelist means by 'sign' in the statement, what the phrase 'in the presence of the disciples' signifies, and how the unique expression relates with 'believing'.

The word σημεῖον (sign) appears 17 times in the Gospel,[27] and all of them except the last one in the statement of purpose are used in the first half of the Gospel (chs. 2–12). For this reason, the 'signs' in the statement can be seen as referring only to the stories considered as signs in the first half of the Gospel. The above analysis of Santram is also based on that assumption. However, the assumption that the reference of the 'sign' in the statement is only for the events in the first half of the Gospel does not explain why the Evangelist uses the word again in the conclusion after the second half of the Gospel, which includes Jesus' exclusive encounter with his disciples and the passion and resurrection narratives. The Evangelist has already provided a conclusion for the first half of the Gospel: 'Even after Jesus had performed so many signs in their [the crowds or the Jews] presence, they still would not believe in him' (12:37). It is unnatural to interpret that the Evangelist uses the word 'sign' in 20:30, after almost eight chapters' absence, to refer only to the same signs expressed in 12:37. To solve the unnatural appearance of the word, some suggest that the statement of purpose has been taken originally from what is called 'signs source'. However, the source criticism approach is not under consideration in this study, since the study reads the Gospel as it is in the present text. As Bittner[28] points out, 'a preoccupation with such theories had displaced the important question of the meaning and function of the term σημεῖον'.

The use of the same word, σημεῖον after the lengthy absence surely is a comparison of the two concluding statements (12:37 and 20:30-31), referencing the two different communities in particular. The first concluding statement in 12:37 confirms that the Jews 'still would not believe in' Jesus even after Jesus' encounters with the them in the first half of the Gospel. The second concluding statement in 20:30–31 implies that the disciples believe in him, and the readers of the Gospel are expected to do the same. The statement echoes the confession of the disciples and Jesus' reply in the earlier discourse (cf 16:29–31). The disciples' confession did not come right after the first half of the Gospel but in the midst of Jesus' exclusive encounter with them, which includes Jesus' washing of the disciples' feet and his discourse. The disciples' belief is achieved not based on the 'signs' as events alone but on the entire ministry of Jesus. Likewise, the statement of purpose does not mean that the readers read

---

[27] 2:11, 18, 23; 3:2; 4:48, 54; 6:2, 14, 26, 30; 7:31; 9:16; 10:41; 11:47; 12:18, 37; 20:31.

[28] W. Bittner *(Jesu Zeichen im Johannesevangelium*, 1987, 14–16, cited in W. H. Salier, 2004, 3).

the 'signs' only as events in the first half of the Gospel to believe in Jesus. Rather, the statement of purpose implies that, out of many 'signs', what is included in the Gospel represents the written Gospel as a whole. Thus the word 'signs' in 20:30 'embraces the whole activity of Jesus' as Bultmann (1971, 698) points out. Lincoln (2000, 176) supports the view stating '[i]t is more likely that, in this summary statement of purpose about the book as a whole, σημεῖον, *sign*, has the further connotation of being able to represent Jesus' mission as a whole'.

The change of the phrase from 'signs in front of them' [the crowds and the Jews] in 12:37 to 'signs *in the presence of* the disciples' in the statement, provides another view on the 'signs' – the whole ministry of Jesus. In the structural analysis in this missional reading, I proposed that the Gospel introduced Jesus' encounters with the Jews and his interactions with individuals (chs. 2–12) and his encounter with the discipleship community (chs. 13–17). If it is accepted that the 'signs' in the statement of purpose signifies the whole ministry of Jesus, then, by implication, the 'signs' in front of the crowds or the Jews in the first half of the Gospel are part of the 'signs' in the presence of the disciples. Even though two different encounters are shown in the first and the second part of the Gospel, the concluding statement reveals that Jesus' ministry has always been geared toward the discipleship community, beginning with their initial following and culminating in the declaration of their believing and their commissioning. The phrase, 'signs *in the presence of*[29] the disciples' and the following implication of the selection out of many 'signs', reveals the whole ministry of Jesus for the discipleship community and the overall progress of the community. Therefore, the second part of the statement on 'believing' in 20:31 implies the full believing process of the discipleship community, so it should be interpreted with this understanding. The believing process will be discussed in the next section to understand 'believing' in the statement of purpose.

Johannine 'Believing' Including Mission

The verb πιστεύω (to believe) is one of the key words to understanding the purpose of the Fourth Gospel. It appears in almost every chapter[30] of the Gospel, 98 times in this Gospel alone.[31] The word appears only in the verb form πιστεύω, and no noun form πίστις is found in the Gospel. Since I divided

---

[29] Unlike the preposition ἔμπροσθέν (in front), which is used in 12:37 and other places in the Gospel (1:15, 30; 3:38; 10:4), the Evangelist uses an adverb, ἐνώπιον (in the eyes of), only in this purpose statement in the Gospel. Barrett (1978, 575) says that it 'is a common Hellenistic word, common in Luke-Acts', but it is significant enough, meaning more than just a spatial translation, at least within the Fourth Gospel.

[30] There are only three chapters where the word does not appear (15, 18 and 21).

[31] 11 times in Matt, 14 times in Mark and 9 times in Luke.

the Gospel into four different parts, I will look at how the verb πιστεύω is used in each of those parts.

The verb πιστεύω appears twice in the pre-incarnation narrative (1:7, 12) as follows: ἵνα πάντες πιστεύσωσιν δι' αὐτοῦ (so that through him [John the Baptist] all might believe [the light], 1:7) and ἔδωκεν αὐτοῖς ἐξουσίαν τέκνα θεοῦ γενέσθαι, τοῖς πιστεύουσιν εἰς τὸ ὄνομα αὐτοῦ (to those who believed in his name, he gave the right to become children of God, 1:12). The declaration is that God desires that everyone believe in Jesus [the light], and he will take those who believe as his children. In the process of believing, a testifier is needed. I already suggested that John the Baptist in the above sentence signifies a forerunner, whom God sent to prepare for Jesus to come to Israel. In the prayer of Jesus, which I view as the conclusion of his whole ministry before the passion narrative, some changes are found regarding 'believing'. The verb πιστεύω appears three times in the prayer as follows: καὶ ἐπίστευσαν ὅτι σύ με ἀπέστειλας (and they [the disciples] believed that you sent me, 17:8b), περὶ τῶν πιστευόντων διὰ τοῦ λόγου αὐτῶν εἰς ἐμέ (for those who will believe in me through their message, 17:20) and ἵνα ὁ κόσμος πιστεύῃ ὅτι σύ με ἀπέστειλας (so that the world may believe that you have sent me, 17:21). Through the comparison of the introductory and the concluding sentences, it is observed that the 'all' has been replaced by 'the world', 'through John the Baptist' by 'through the disciples' message', and 'in his name' by 'you have sent me'. The significant change is the testifier. The world may believe in Jesus whom God has sent into the world, through the testimony of the disciples rather than that of John the Baptist. Therefore, the usages of the verb πιστεύω throughout the Gospel show the forming of the believing discipleship community who will be the testifier.

In the second part of the Gospel (2:13–12:50), the verb πιστεύω is used in the narrative as Jesus encounters individuals, the Jews, and the crowd, including the accompanying disciples. The reward of the 'believing' is introduced as 'having eternal life'.[32] Even though in many cases[33] the audience believes in Jesus or in what he performed, the overall conclusion of the Evangelist in the second part is, 'Even after Jesus had performed so many signs in their presence, they still would not believe in him' (12:37). In the third part of the Gospel (chs. 13–17) during which Jesus encounters his disciples exclusively, the verb πιστεύω is used more specifically. As mentioned above, the previous testifier for Jesus has been replaced by the disciples. Therefore, the usages of the verb in this exclusive encounter for the disciples show the characteristics of the 'believing' in the Gospel. The usages of the verb in the third part are as follows (my emphasis underlined and in bold):

---

[32] 3:15, 16, 36; 5:24; 6:40; 6:47.

[33] 2:23; 4:41, 50; 6:69; 7:31; 8:30; 9:38; 10:42; 11:27; 11:45; 12:11; 12:42.

13:19 ἵνα πιστεύσητε ὅταν γένηται **<u>ὅτι ἐγώ εἰμι</u>** (so that when it does happen you will believe **<u>that I am who I am</u>**).
14:1 μὴ ταρασσέσθω ὑμῶν ἡ καρδία πιστεύετε εἰς τὸν θεόν, καὶ εἰς ἐμὲ πιστεύετε (Do not let your hearts be troubled. You believe in God; believe also in me).
14:10–11 οὐ πιστεύεις ὅτι ἐγὼ ἐν τῷ πατρὶ καὶ ὁ πατὴρ ἐν ἐμοί ἐστιν… πιστεύετέ μοι ὅτι ἐγὼ ἐν τῷ πατρὶ καὶ ὁ πατὴρ ἐν ἐμοί εἰ δὲ μή, διὰ τὰ ἔργα αὐτὰ πιστεύετε (Don't you believe that I am in the Father, and that the Father is in me?… Believe me when I say that I am in the Father and the Father is in me; or at least believe on the evidence of the works themselves).
14:12 ὁ πιστεύων εἰς ἐμὲ τὰ ἔργα ἃ ἐγὼ ποιῶ κἀκεῖνος ποιήσει, καὶ μείζονα τούτων ποιήσει (whoever believes in me will do the works I have been doing, and they will do even greater things than these).
14:29 ἵνα ὅταν γένηται πιστεύσητε (so that when it does happen you will believe).
16:9 περὶ ἁμαρτίας μέν, ὅτι οὐ πιστεύουσιν εἰς ἐμέ (about sin, because people do not believe in me).
16:27 αὐτὸς γὰρ ὁ πατὴρ φιλεῖ ὑμᾶς, ὅτι ὑμεῖς ἐμὲ πεφιλήκατε καὶ πεπιστεύκατε **<u>ὅτι ἐγὼ παρὰ [τοῦ] θεοῦ ἐξῆλθον</u>** (No, the Father himself loves you because you have loved me and have believed **<u>that I came from God</u>**).
16:30–31 ἐν τούτῳ πιστεύομεν **<u>ὅτι ἀπὸ θεοῦ ἐξῆλθες</u>** ἀπεκρίθη αὐτοῖς Ἰησοῦς, Ἄρτι πιστεύετε (This makes us believe **<u>that you came from God</u>**. 'Do you now believe?' Jesus replied).
17:8, 20–21 mentioned above.

I highlight two points in the above usages. First, the content of what to believe has been specified for the disciples. It is preceded by the ὅτι clauses and calls for them to believe who Jesus is (13:19), the relationship between the Father and himself (14:10–11) and where he came from (16:30). The disciples have watched as Jesus communicates similar discourses to the Jews (8:28; 10:38).[34] The difference is in the expected outcomes: that the Jews will know (γινώσκω) ὅτι ἐγώ εἰμι (8:28) while the disciples will believe (πιστεύω) ὅτι ἐγώ εἰμι (13:19), and that the Jews may know (γινώσκω) and understand (γινώσκω) that the Father is in Jesus and Jesus is in the Father, but the disciples are required to believe (πιστεύω) the same thing. The disciples' 'believing' does not come from any isolated event.[35] Rather, it comes from an intimate relationship with Jesus, reaching to the level of believing his identity and his relationship with the Father, and from the disciples themselves enjoying a

[34] 8:28 ὅταν ὑψώσητε τὸν υἱὸν τοῦ ἀνθρώπου, τότε γνώσεσθε ὅτι ἐγώ εἰμι (When you [the Jews] lifted up the Son of Man, then you will know that I am he); 10:38 εἰ δὲ ποιῶ, κἂν ἐμοὶ μὴ πιστεύητε, τοῖς ἔργοις πιστεύετε, ἵνα γνῶτε καὶ γινώσκητε ὅτι ἐν ἐμοὶ ὁ πατὴρ κἀγὼ ἐν τῷ πατρί (But if I do them [the works of the Father], even though you [the Jews] do not believe me, believe the works, that you may know and understand that the Father is in me, and I in the Father).
[35] As mentioned, there are many examples that the audience believes after seeing what Jesus performed, but the overall evaluation of the Evangelist for the first half of the Gospel is that they still would not believe in Jesus (12:37).

loving relationship with the Father because of their 'believing' (16:27). Secondly, the 'believing' of the disciples is also related to the ministry in which they will participate. The believing discipleship community is anticipated to continue the works of Jesus and even to do greater things. The disciples' believing is not merely for their own benefit but includes expansion into the world. In conclusion, the Evangelist focuses on how Jesus Christ is making the discipleship community a believing discipleship community through the Gospel, and the believing community is sent into the world and continues to remain in the triune God through the Holy Spirit. Therefore, 'believing' in the statement of purpose as given in the conclusion is believing that includes relationship and ministry. Determining whether the Gospel is written for Christians to keep their faith or for non-Christians to come to believe is not the point. What is important is understanding the depth (remaining in the triune God) and the extent (expected ministry) of believing in the Gospel, whether the reader already believes or not. Believing in Jesus means belonging to the triune God's community and, at the same time, belonging to the missional discipleship community.

Beginning of the Missional Community

The Role of the Final Chapter

I have observed that the Fourth Gospel focuses on the discipleship community. The Evangelist tracks how Jesus has placed an emphasis on creating the believing discipleship community. He views the 'signs' Jesus performed throughout his public ministry to be performed in the presence of his disciples. He also devotes much space in the Gospel to Jesus' exclusive encounter with the disciples. The post-resurrection narrative also focuses solely on Jesus' encounter with his disciples. Considering this concentration of Jesus toward his disciples, the last chapter of the Gospel contains an indispensable story. Without the story in the last chapter, the narrative on the discipleship community very likely would have been incomplete. Nevertheless, this last chapter has been suspected of not being part of the Fourth Gospel for various reasons. As a basis for such doubts, the appearance of 26 new words in the chapter is often cited.[36] There are 62 and 17 new words in Chapter 19 and

[36] Ζεβεδαῖος (Zebedee, v2), ἁλιεύω (to fish, v3), πρωΐα (early morning, v4), αἰγιαλός (beach, v4), προσφάγιον (fish, v5), δίκτυον (a net, v6), ἰσχύω (to be strong, v6), ἰχθύς (a fish, v6), ἐπενδύτης (outer garment, v7), γυμνός (bare, v7), μακρὰν (far off, v8), πῆχυς (a cubit, v8), σύρω (to draw, v8), ἀποβαίνω (to come out of, v9), ἀριστάω (to eat breakfast, v12), τολμάω (to dare, v12), ἐξετάζω (to search out, v12), βόσκω (to feed, v15), ἀρνίον (a little lamb, v15), ποιμαίνω (to keep sheep, v16), νέος (young, v18), ζώννυμι (to fasten, v18), γηράσκω (to be old, v18), ἐκτείνω (to stretch out, v18),

Chapter 20 respectively. Therefore, it is not strange to have 26 new words for the new story about fishing and the conversation between Jesus and Peter in the final chapter. Regarding the vocabulary, there are many examples that could be used to show that the last chapter is consistent with the previous chapters. Smalley (1978, 96) points out as follows:

> Nevertheless, there is no textual evidence to show that John's Gospel ever existed without John 21; and despite some admittedly untypical features in the chapter, this section of John is markedly Johannine in many respects. Notice, for example, the distinctive use of 'Tiberias' in verse 1; the occurrence in verse 2 of the characteristic names Simon Peter, Thomas the Twin and Nathanael of Cana; the appearance of the beloved disciple at verses 7 and 20ff.; and the double ἀμήν in verse 18 introducing a saying of Jesus.

Barrett (1978, 577) acknowledges the fact that the 'linguistic and stylistic considerations' are not sufficient evidence for the claim that 'ch. 21 was written by a different author'. Nevertheless, he (1978, 577) calls attention to the content problems of the final chapter as support for his claim that the final chapter was not written by the same author as the rest of the Gospel:

> Moreover, it is difficult to think that an author would wish to spoil the effect of the apostolic mission charge of 20.21–3 by representing the disciples, in a later narrative, as having returned to their former employment and as unable at first to recognize the Lord when he appeared.

However, it is hard to agree with the above positions. As Köstenberger (2004, 588) points out, the disciples 'probably had returned to Galilee in obedience to Jesus' command (Matt. 26:32; 28:7, 10 par), and 'Peter, the commissioning in 20:21–23 notwithstanding, temporarily returns to his old occupation'. As for the disciples' not recognizing Jesus, Köstenberger (2004, 589–90) suggests that 'the early morning hour (cf 20:1) or the distance from the shore [or both] may have made it difficult for the disciples to see Jesus clearly'. Michaels (2010, 1006) warns that '[t]he job of a commentary is not to interpret what the Gospel might have been "at some point," but what it was by the time it was released into the world'.

I contend that the narrative in the final chapter reveals the Evangelist's style of conveying themes through the detailed narratives. Even though the declaration of commissioning the discipleship community has been made in the previous chapter, the Evangelist does not end the Gospel with the declaration. Instead, he reveals the character of the mission that has been addressed once again by showing how the declaration is applied to the disciples who have

---

ἐπιστρέφω (to turn, v20), οἴομαι (to think, v25). cf Barrett (1978, 576) counts 28 including τρίτος and πρόβατον, but those two words appear in the previous chapters.

experienced the recent frustrating events. The Evangelist focuses on two disciples, in particular, from the passion to the post-resurrection narrative including the final chapter. He focuses on the two of them, sometimes together and sometimes individually. Since one of the essential aspects of the completion of Jesus' work through the passion and resurrection narrative is the achievement of the forming of the believing discipleship community, the way that the Evangelist describes the disciples in the narrative – and the two disciples in particular – exposes the characteristics of the discipleship community as a sent community.[37] This will be discussed in the next section.

Peter's Appearances

The Evangelist highlights two disciples in the narrative – Peter and the beloved disciple. The two of them appear together before the crucifixion in the high priest's courtyard (18:15–16), at the empty tomb after the resurrection of Jesus (20:3–10) and by the Sea of Galilee (21:20). Additionally, each of them appears in other scenes of the narrative (cf 18:10; 19:26–27). The narratives about the two disciples reveal the characteristics of the discipleship community as a missional community.

First, the story of Peter in the narrative highlights the difference between human passion and passion based on a loving relationship with God. Peter is portrayed as an ardent disciple of Jesus. In the foot-washing narrative, Peter showed both his humble attitude by denying to be washed and his aspiration to be related to his master, asking him to wash his whole body. His words prove his commitment to Jesus, 'I will lay down my life for you' (13:37). His behaviours, striking the high priest's servant with his sword (18:10) and following Jesus even into the high priest's courtyard (18:16), also prove his commitment. Despite this eagerness of Peter, Jesus seems not to accept his commitment. Jesus responds to Peter's words, saying, 'Will you really lay down your life for me? Very truly I tell you, before the rooster crows, you will disown me three times!' (13:38) and 'Put your sword away! Shall I not drink the cup the Father has given me?' (18:11). As Jesus said, Peter denies Jesus three times in the high priest's courtyard.

The post-resurrection narrative shows that at least Peter's commitment to Jesus is genuine. He and the beloved disciple run to the tomb (20:4), and Peter jumps into the water to come to Jesus in Galilee (21:7). The narrative in the final chapter shows what the commissioning in the previous chapter really means, regardless of such personal sincerity. The Evangelist points out the similar setting of Peter's denials and the narrative on the shore of Galilee, using

---

[37] Cullmann (1962, 31) says that 'the Risen One assigns a unique position to each of them for the future, but gives each of them a different role'. Hartin (1990, 58) also says that 'as friends each has a distinctive function to perform which is not lessened by the function that is given to the other'.

several common words. The word ἀνθρακιά (charcoal fire)[38] appears only in the Fourth Gospel and is used only twice, one in the courtyard of the high priest where Peter denies the Lord (18:18) and the other on the shore of Galilee where Jesus meets Peter (21:9). The word πρωΐ in 18:28 and πρωΐα in 21:4 indicate that the two events occur at a similar time of day. Three denials and three confessions of love also appear in contrast in the two events. The similar settings highlight the antithetical nature of the two events that took place. The former signifies the disciple's own endeavour that can only result in failure, as Jesus pointed out in his previous vine discourse for the disciples. 'No branch can bear fruit by itself; it must remain in the vine' (15:4). By contrast, the final encounter of Jesus with Peter in the last chapter reconfirms that a loving relationship, that is to say, remaining in the vine, is the basis for the ministry the disciples are expected to carry on and also clarifies that the ministry of the disciples is to feed and care for Jesus' sheep, not their own. In comparing the two events, I observe that Jesus' encounter with Peter does not focus on what kind of job Jesus is giving to Peter, whether it is pastoral or evangelistic.[39] Instead, it stresses the identity of the ministry, that the ownership belongs to Jesus and the disciples are commissioned to be a shepherd for him. What Jesus says to Peter in 21:18 summarizes the contrast: 'Very truly I tell you, when you were younger you dressed yourself and went where you wanted; but when you are old you will stretch out your hands, and someone else will dress you and lead you where you do not want to go'.

Through the narrative of the final chapter, the meaning of the commissioning in the previous chapter is reaffirmed: the mission of the discipleship community is based on their loving relationship with the Lord rather than on their own passion, and the ministry is owned by the Lord rather than by themselves. Jesus compressed all this into one phrase: 'Ἀκολούθει μοι' (Follow me, 21:19). The phrase ἀκολούθει μοι appears twice in the Gospel, one in the first chapter (1:43) and the other in the last chapter (21:19). It is not clear whether Jesus uses the same word with two different meanings, but I argue that it is understood as having two different meanings by the disciples involved. The former is understood as a physical following while the latter as a lifelong following of a true disciple. Therefore, the Fourth Gospel shows the process of discovering the true meaning of what the disciples follow, beginning with their literal following of Jesus. The following includes the commissioning into the world. Newbigin (1982, 19) points out that 'One could, in fact, describe the whole book as an exposition of what it will mean to "follow Jesus"'. Bauckham (2015, 145) suggests that 'if we look carefully at John's use of the verb "to follow" (*akolouthein*) throughout the Gospel, we gain the strong impression

---

[38] cf θερμαίνω (Mark 14:67); πῦρ (Luke 22:55).

[39] cf Carson (1991, 677–78): '[t]he emphasis is now on the pastoral rather than the evangelistic'.

that, for John, to truly follow Jesus was something that became possible for the disciples only after Jesus' death and resurrection'.

Considering all this, the true following or launching of the discipleship community begins after the passion and resurrection of Jesus and after the completion of the creation process of the discipleship community. In this sense, the final chapter is not just an addition to the main body or an epilogue of the story. Instead, it is the start of the commissioned discipleship community in a real sense. The Evangelist does not end the Gospel with the declaration of the commissioning of the discipleship community in Chapter 20. Instead, he finishes the Gospel with Jesus' preparation of a meal with his disciples, the emphasis of the loving relationship to Peter, the relationship characteristic of the discipleship community and Jesus' correction of the comparison.

The Beloved Disciple

The story of the beloved disciple in the pre- and post-resurrection narrative also reveals the characteristics of the discipleship community and, in particular, the relationship aspect. If the statement in 21:24 – that the beloved disciple is the Evangelist himself, author of the Gospel – is accepted, then the Evangelist's emphasis on relationship throughout the Gospel is based on his own experiences through his journey with Jesus. Not only the expression 'the disciple ὃν ἠγάπα [ὁ Ἰησοῦς] (whom [Jesus] loved)' (13:23; 19:26; 21:7, 20) but also his closeness with Jesus in the Gospel (cf 13:23) confirms the relationship he has with Jesus. The expression 'the disciple ὃν ἠγάπα [ὁ Ἰησοῦς] (whom [Jesus] loved)' appears four times in the Gospel as follows (my emphasis in bold):

> 13:23 ἦν ἀνακείμενος εἷς ἐκ **τῶν μαθητῶν** αὐτοῦ ἐν τῷ κόλπῳ τοῦ Ἰησοῦ, **ὃν ἠγάπα ὁ Ἰησοῦς** (One of them, **the disciple whom Jesus loved**, was reclining next to him).
> 19:26–27 Ἰησοῦς οὖν ἰδὼν τὴν μητέρα καὶ **τὸν μαθητὴν** παρεστῶτα **ὃν ἠγάπα**, λέγει τῇ μητρί, Γύναι, ἴδε ὁ υἱός σου. ἶτα λέγει τῷ μαθητῇ, Ἴδε ἡ μήτηρ σου. καὶ ἀπ' ἐκείνης τῆς ὥρας ἔλαβεν αὐτὴν ὁ μαθητὴς εἰς τὰ ἴδια (When Jesus saw his mother there, and **the disciple whom he loved** standing nearby, he said to her, "Woman, here is your son," and to the disciple, "Here is your mother." From that time on, this disciple took her into his home).
> 21:7 λέγει οὖν **ὁ μαθητὴς** ἐκεῖνος **ὃν ἠγάπα ὁ Ἰησοῦς** τῷ Πέτρῳ, Ὁ κύριός ἐστιν (Then **the disciple whom Jesus loved** said to Peter, "It is the Lord!").
> 21:20 Ἐπιστραφεὶς ὁ Πέτρος βλέπει **τὸν μαθητὴν ὃν ἠγάπα ὁ Ἰησοῦς** ἀκολουθοῦντα (Peter turned and saw that **the disciple whom Jesus loved** was following them).

The above stories highlight that relationship is one of the essential characteristics of the discipleship community in the Gospel, whether it is a relationship with the Lord or a relationship among themselves. These stories reveal the depth of the relationship the beloved disciple has had with Jesus, and furthermore, that the relationship is an essential characteristic of the community rather than just a personal experience of the beloved disciple. First, the Evangelist shows that his own experience with Jesus became a frame of reference to understand the divine relationship between the Father and the Son. The Evangelist uses the word κόλπος (bosom) twice (1:18; 13:23) in the Gospel. He himself was reclining ἐν τῷ κόλπῳ τοῦ Ἰησοῦ (in the bosom of Jesus, 13:23). The scene recalls what the Evangelist depicted about the one and only Son as ὁ ὢν εἰς τὸν κόλπον τοῦ πατρὸς (literal translation by the author: who is in the bosom of the Father, 1:18). The one and only Son in the κόλπος of the Father and the beloved disciple in the κόλπος of the Son shows an example of what Jesus prayed: 'Father, just as you are in me and I am in you. May they also be in us' (17:21).

Secondly, the episode at the cross confirms that intimate relationship is not just a personal experience of the beloved disciple but it is to be his mission ever afterwards. At the climax of his earthly life, Jesus united his mother and his beloved disciple into a new mother–son relationship.[40] Considering the situation right before his death on the cross, the episode describes not just a devoted son who made the disciple merely a son to replace himself for his mother, but shows how essential and identical the relationship is to the mission of the discipleship community in the world.

Thirdly, the beloved disciple's recognition of Jesus matches what Jesus mentioned about his own sheep. Jesus was standing on the shore of Galilee, but the disciples on the boat did not know that it was him, probably because it was early morning (21:4). The beloved disciple recognized him first (21:7). It is not noted whether the similar situation he experienced in that same place[41] or the previous encounter with the resurrected Jesus triggers his recognition of Jesus. Of course, it is not because his sight was better than others or because he was closer to the shore than others. The relationship he had with Jesus throughout the whole ministry of Jesus made it possible. Jesus said 'his sheep follow him because they know his voice' (10:4) and 'I am the good shepherd; I know my sheep and my sheep know me – just as the Father knows me and I know the Father' (10:14). The appearance of the disciple in the second half of the

---

[40] Bennema (2009a, 75) claims that 'this incident illustrates how the community of believers that Jesus had already constituted during his lifetime (namely those who adequately responded to him and followed him) should function – with practical care for one another's needs'. As I mentioned, the incident shows one of the important characteristics of the new community – intimate relationship. Since Jesus already called his disciples before he began his public ministry, this incident cannot be seen as the beginning of the new community. The forming of the new community is not a singular event but a process realized through being with Jesus. As Bauckham (2015, 145) mentions, 'for John, to truly follow Jesus was something that was possible for the disciples only after Jesus' death and resurrection'.

[41] cf Luke 5:4, 7–10.

Gospel, the post-resurrection narrative in particular, and the designation as 'the disciple ὃν ἠγάπα [ὁ Ἰησοῦς] (whom [Jesus] loved) reaffirms how crucial relationship is in the discipleship community.

Chapter Summary

I have demonstrated that this fourth part of the Gospel reveals two aspects of the completion of Jesus' mission on earth. The completion (τελέω) of Jesus' mission on earth (19:30) was expressed by the synonymous verb τελειόω with two different meanings in the narrative. One is the fulfilment (τελειόω) of that which was prophesied in the Old Testament, which I called the redemptive role of Jesus. The Evangelist presents Jesus as the one who was prophesied in the Hebrew Bible, the sacrificial one for the salvation of the world, in particular. The Evangelist points out that 'the Scripture would be fulfilled (τελειόω)' (19:28). The other is the accomplishment (τελειόω) of the forming of the believing discipleship community, which I viewed as the missional role of Jesus.

In a sense, this climax of the Gospel functions as a transition from one role to the next. A new phase of salvation history will be opened by the newly formed discipleship community. The post-resurrection narrative focuses on this latter aspect. The new creation process, started with the incarnation of the Word, culminates in the completion of the discipleship community and will be continued by the community in the world. This argument is supported by the creation typology in the narrative: 'On the evening of that first day of the week.... And with that he breathed on them and said "Receive the Holy Spirit' (20:19–22). This creation aspect of the formation of the discipleship community provides a lens for reading the previous narratives, both the second part and the third part of the Gospel, as the creation *process* of the discipleship community. The 'signs' and teachings of Jesus and, more importantly, dwelling with the disciples, all together became the materials for the formation of the community. Then, he breathed on them after the resurrection, declaring the birth of the community and its identity as a sent community.

This whole picture contributes toward understanding the purpose statement of the Gospel. I have suggested two arguments based on this reading. First, the purpose of the Gospel writing is related to the shaping and equipping of the discipleship community. Regardless of whether the reader of the Gospel is already a Christian or not, the Evangelist points out that 'believing' in Jesus includes both belonging to or remaining in the triune God by belonging to or remaining in the discipleship community and being commissioned to the world to testify about Jesus in the world. The Evangelist desires that whoever reads the Gospel would reach that level of 'believing', that is, to be a part of the discipleship community. Secondly, the final chapter of the Gospel is not just an addition to the main body of the Gospel. The post-resurrection narrative, including the final chapter, reveals the nature of the mission that the commissioned discipleship community must carry on. Without this narrative, the mission of the discipleship community would end with just a declaration by Jesus. The narrative in the final chapter, the narrative regarding the two disciples in particular, reconfirms the loving relationship that is characteristic of the mission.

N. T Wright (2002a, x–xi) states, ‘It [the Fourth Gospel] is, in fact, one of the great books in the literature of the world; and part of its greatness is the way it reveals its secrets not just to high-flown learning, but to those who come to it with humility and hope. So here it is: John for everyone!’ I agree with him that the Gospel is for everyone, but with a slightly different perspective. It is for everyone, both for the one who already believes and for non-believers. However, what I found through a missional reading of the Gospel is that the Gospel emphasizes that everyone should belong to the discipleship community. In this sense, the Fourth Gospel is for everyone to be a disciple and for their participation in the mission of God.

Part III

Findings and Conclusion

7. Findings and Implications

Introduction

I have read the given text from a missional point of view. In this chapter, I will discuss what I have found in my missional reading of the Gospel, the new insights gleaned from it. I will also revisit *missio Dei* taking into consideration the findings as an application of the reading. Finally, I will demonstrate a few contributions of the reading to a biblical understanding of mission based on the findings.

I will address three main findings of the reading. First, I will demonstrate the extent to which the Gospel is associated with the creation aspect in 7.2. The Gospel reveals a Johannine creation narrative, from Creation to New Creation by presenting the discipleship community as a new creation. I will examine what the Johannine grand narrative implies. Secondly, I will address the extent to which the discipleship community comes into focus in the Gospel in section 7.3. This includes how Jesus shapes and equips the disciples. Thirdly, I will demonstrate how the Gospel shows a progression between God and the new community through Jesus in the Holy Spirit in section 7.4.

In section 7.5, I will revisit *missio Dei* as an application, considering what I have found in a missional reading of the Gospel. Since the concept is heavily based on the Fourth Gospel, the extent to which the Fourth Gospel accommodates the concept needs to be examined. After the discussion, I will demonstrate a few contributions of the findings to a biblical understanding of mission in section 7.6.

The Gospel as a New Creation Process

One of the important dimensions of a missional hermeneutic I applied to the reading of the Gospel is a grand narrative view, reading the given text as a grand narrative. From that angle, I view the Gospel as a creation-centred narrative, a story from Creation to the new community as a new creation, and Jesus is the agent of the creation process. There are three places where the Gospel narrative corresponds closely to the creation narrative of Genesis.

Those places appear at the beginning of the Gospel, then at the beginning of Jesus' ministry and again at the post-resurrection narrative.

First, the opening of the Gospel, 'in the beginning' recalls the opening of Genesis. Myers (2015, 128) points out that '[t]he flowing cadence of the prologue continues to imitate the opening chapter of Genesis bringing in images of light, life, "becoming" (γίνομαι), and "begetting" (γεννάω)'. The Gospel is connected to Genesis not only by the opening but also by mentioning directly the creation event of Genesis. In particular, the Gospel highlights the position of ὁ λόγος in Creation. 'Through him [ὁ λόγος] all things were made; without him nothing was made that has been made' (1:3). By starting with the relationship between ὁ λόγος and ὁ θεός in the previous verses (1:1–2), the Gospel reveals that the creation of all things through ὁ λόγος is based on that relationship. Then, the Evangelist states that the agent of Creation becomes a man, Jesus. Therefore, the incarnation of ὁ λόγος and his ministry on earth can be seen from the creation point of view. Myers (2015, 129) affirms that 'the incarnation of the Word in the person of Jesus makes another creation moment for the believing community and cosmos'. In short, the relationship between God and the Word is the foundation for the creation of all things through the Word. The Evangelist introduces Jesus as the incarnate Word, the agent of Creation, implying that his life and ministry could be viewed as a creation process for a new creation.

Secondly, Jesus' first week in his ministry also relates to Creation. Jesus gathers various disciples during this week, just as God creates the world in the first week of Genesis. Bauckham (2015, 133) points out as follows:

> If the argument that the events of 1:40–42 take place on a distinct day is accepted, then the whole narrative (1:19–2:11) covers precisely a week. Given the biblical and Jewish significance of the week as a period of time, established by the Creator at the beginning (Gen. 1:1–2:4), there is an obvious appropriateness in beginning of the Gospel's narrative of new creation with a week.

In this narrative, the Evangelist describes daily events using 'the next day' (1:29, 35, 43), 'that day' (1:39) and 'the third day' (2:1). The narrative reveals that Jesus gathers his first disciples in this week.[1] By using the word 'disciples' of Jesus for the first time in the Cana story (2:2, 11, 12), the Gospel signifies that the initial gathering of the disciples is completed before Jesus starts his journey to Jerusalem with them. The Evangelist records that the disciples believe in Jesus (2:11). After that, the act of calling someone to become a disciple, as with 'the Twelve', never again appears in the Gospel. The Evangelist uses the term 'disciple' broader than 'the Twelve' in some cases (cf 6:66), but it mainly refers to the inner group of the disciples, if not 'the

---

[1] The Evangelist indicates that at least five disciples have gathered in 1:35–51. They are Andrew, an unnamed, Peter, Philip, and Nathanael.

Twelve'. Jesus himself makes a distinction between 'the Twelve' and others by saying, 'Have I not chosen you, the Twelve?' (6:70). Bennema (2009a, 119) notes that 'the phrase "his disciples" occurs frequently and mostly refers to Jesus' twelve disciples, or at least includes them'.

Even though the narrative of the first week of Jesus functions as a summary of the creation aspect of the Gospel, it should not be understood to mean that the process of the formation of the new community is finished. Instead, the character and scope of the new community will be revealed to the disciples through Jesus' encounters with the Jews and his interactions with different individuals throughout the Gospel. These interactions show the inclusion of all ethnicities and all social classes in the community. The gathering of disciples in the first week is not the completion but the start of the creation process Jesus will accomplish through his life and ministry.

Thirdly, the creation theme reappears in the post-resurrection narrative of the Gospel. Bauckham (2015, 133) points out that 'there is one other week whose seven days are carefully enumerated by the writer of the Gospel, a week that is almost (though not quite) at the end of the narrative'. He continues, saying, '[c]areful comparison can show that these two momentous weeks in the Gospel's narrative correspond to each other in some key respect' (133). Jesus appears to his disciples on the very same evening that he was resurrected, the last day of Bauckham's second week. The Evangelist describes the day as 'that first day of the week' (20:19), signifying that something new begins now. In this meeting with the disciples, Jesus breathes on the disciples, saying, 'Receive the Holy Spirit' (20:22). The Evangelist uses ἐμφυσάω (to breathe) in the narrative, the verb that appears only once in the entire New Testament. Jesus' breathing on the disciples recalls the breathing of God in Creation. The Greek Old Testament (LXX) uses the same verb, ἐμφυσάω (to breathe) in Genesis 2:7. N.T. Wright (2002b, 150) observes that 'in the new creation, the restoring life of God is breathed out through Jesus, making new people of the disciples and, through them, offering this new life to the world'.

To summarise the discussion to this point, a missional reading of the Gospel, particularly a grand narrative view, reveals that the Gospel has a creation motif, which provides the basic structure. It demonstrates the divine relationship as the foundation of Creation, Jesus as the agent of Creation and new creation and the discipleship community as a new creation, which continues the creation process in the world in the Holy Spirit. I will discuss how this finding contributes to a biblical understanding of mission later.

The Gospel as a Development of the Discipleship Community

The second significant dimension to arise out of a missional reading of the Fourth Gospel is an understanding of how Jesus shapes and equips the discipleship community for mission. It begins with gathering them (the first part), continues with the disciples accompanying Jesus in his ministry (the second part), culminates in Jesus' intimate time with them before his crucifixion (the third part) and ends with their reconfirmation after his resurrection (the last part). Indeed, the creation process of the discipleship community in a sense is the process of shaping and equipping the disciples to participate in the mission of God. The shaping and equipping dimension is not merely one of many ministries of Jesus. I observe that the Fourth Gospel treats the development of the discipleship community as the highlight of Jesus' ministry in many ways.

First, the Fourth Gospel prioritizes the development of the discipleship community. It presents Jesus carrying out his ministry with the discipleship community first, last and through all the time. Kanagaraj (2002, 83) points out as follows:

> Though the term ekklêsia does not occur in the Gospel of John, its author paints an important picture of the Christian community, a community which is far different from what is found in other parts of the NT. The Church which John envisages is the community of disciples who were called by Jesus. The word "disciple" (mathêtês) occurs in John 78 times, whereas in Mark 46 times and in Luke 37 times only. One can understand the importance John gives to the community of disciples.

The disciples are the ones whom Jesus chose (6:70), who remain in the word of Jesus (8:31) and whom Jesus sent into the world (20:21). The Gospel begins its description of Jesus' ministry by showing how he gathers his disciples and ends it with his interaction with two of his disciples. Even though Jesus performs many signs in front of the crowd, his disciples are the primary audience. The Evangelist notes that Jesus performed various signs *in the presence of* the disciples (20:30). This signifies that the signs mentioned in the Gospel, and also many other signs not recorded in the Gospel, are meant to educate the disciples. The Gospel reveals that Jesus devotes his life and death to the development of the community. 'I [Jesus] am the good shepherd. The good shepherd lays down his life for the sheep' (10:11); 'I lay down my life for the sheep' (10:15); 'Greater love has no one than this: to lay down one's life for one's friends. You are my friends if you do what I command' (15:13–14). In a word, the development of the discipleship community is a priority of Jesus' ministry, according to the Gospel.

Secondly, the Gospel presents the discipleship community as one of two achievements that Jesus has accomplished in the world. Jesus proclaims 'it is finished (τελέω)' on the cross. In the Gospel, Jesus' completion (τελέω) is expressed by two different fulfilments (τελειόω). On the one hand, the meaning of completion (τελέω) is the fulfilment (τελειόω) through him of what was prophesied in the Hebrew Bible and, on the other hand, the achievement (τελειόω) is that the discipleship community is ready to be sent to the world. The former reveals from the past to the present that Jesus is the one who has been sent by the Father, as prophesied in the Bible. The latter reveals from the present to the future that the community will continue the mission of God in the world. Jesus reports this achievement to the Father: 'I [Jesus] have revealed you [the Father] to those whom you gave me out of the world. They [the disciples] were yours; you gave them to me and they have obeyed your word' (17:6). Therefore, the formation of the discipleship community is a highlight of Jesus' ministry and of the Gospel.

Thirdly, the sending of the Holy Spirit by the Father and the Son is for the discipleship community. The Gospel introduces the Holy Spirit as παράκλητος (14:16, 26; 15:26; 16:7), signifying that he is sent to help the disciples in the ministry that they will continue, as Jesus has commissioned. Jesus says that the Holy Spirit will be sent to 'help you [the disciples] and be with you forever' (14:16). The Holy Spirit as an Advocate will testify about Jesus. However, the Fourth Gospel clarifies that the Advocate is sent to the disciples to be with them and also to lead them into all truth. N. T. Wright (2016, 187) points out:

> …when the Spirit comes, the Spirit will do these things through Jesus's followers. The convicting work of the Spirit is not solitary activity; we do not stand by and watch while the Spirit does this work. An important part of the New Testament's missional theology is the call to respond to John 16 in this way: if we pray for the Spirit, we should expect that the Spirit will be teaching us how to hold the world to account.

Based on those observations, I submit that Jesus, in the Fourth Gospel, pours everything into the discipleship community, as though they themselves are the goal. Then, in what sense does Jesus shape and equip the disciples? The Gospel reports that many people believe in Jesus and follow him. There are 'disciples' who do not sustain discipleship among them (cf 6:66). Even though they are all called by the term 'disciples', it is difficult to determine whether or not the disciples whom Jesus shapes and equips are represented by them. Instead, the disciples whom Jesus shapes and equips are represented by 'the Twelve', though not necessarily limited to that number. Bennema (2009a, 125) writes, '[a]s a collective character, 'the Twelve' represents Johannine discipleship'.

If it is accepted that the discipleship community Jesus equips is represented by 'the Twelve', the meaning of equipping should be examined in light of Jesus' interactions with them. Jesus gathers the disciples before he starts his public ministry, signifying that his life and ministry from that point onward function to shape and equip them. The Evangelist's comment that 'Jesus performed many other signs in the presence of his disciples' (20:30) supports this position. Through his ministries, Jesus shows the scope and quality of the discipleship community God desires to restore. It includes all ethnicities and all social classes. The shaping and equipping of the disciples are not merely about what they should do but, more importantly, about who they should be. The final interaction of Jesus with them (chs. 13–17) before the passion highlights their 'oneness' with God through Jesus, among themselves and with the ones who will come to the community through their message. Again, I will discuss how this second finding contributes to a biblical understanding of mission later.

The Gospel as a Progression: the Father, the Son and the Discipleship Community in the Holy Spirit

Two dimensions of a missional hermeneutic I applied to this study were a grand narrative view and an equipping view. The third finding of a missional reading of the Gospel comes from an integral view of those two dimensions. The former relates to God or to the mission of God, while the latter relates to the discipleship community. The Gospel, however, shows a progression between God and the community. I will demonstrate the ways in which the Gospel reveals the progression.

The Gospel reveals the progression as a *bi-directional transitive relationship* between God and the new community through Jesus in the Holy Spirit. One direction of the progression can be defined by the term *missio* (sending) and the other direction by the word *theosis* (union with God). The former relates to the progression from God toward humans, and the latter from humans toward God. The *missio* direction starts from the divine relationship between God and the Word (cf 1:1). Their inner or 'immanent' relationship was first expressed through the creation of all things (cf 1:3) then through the sending of the Son by the Father into the world (cf 1:14; 3:16). The Son does the will of the Father (cf 4:34; 5:30; 6:38), so he forms the discipleship community and builds a relationship with them. Based on the relationship he has with them, the Son sends the community into the world (20:21). In other words, the inner relationship of Jesus and his disciples is expressed by the sending of the discipleship community into the world for people to join the community through their message (cf 17:20). The disciples are given the authority to forgive sins in the world (cf 20:23). In a sense, the *missio* direction is descending since the Father's love reaches to the world first through the Son and then through the disciples of the Son in the Holy Spirit.

On the other hand, the *theosis*[2] direction is ascending, going back to God. By *theosis*, I simply mean that the community participates in the divine relationship of the Father and the Son in the Holy Spirit. Byers (2017, 183) clarifies that 'Johannine theosis, therefore, does not envision the divinization of human beings in such a way that they are merged with the identity of the one

---

[2] This is an Eastern Orthodox theological term, which can be interpreted as 'deification' or 'union with God'. In this paper, I am not referring to the doctrine of the church but using it as a thematic term. In other words, I use it as 'participation in the divine relationship' rather than as 'participation in the divine nature'. See Hallonsten (2007, 283–84) for the distinction between the theme and the doctrine of *theosis*.

God of Jewish scriptural traditions'. Jesus says, 'Whoever believes in me does not believe in me only, but in the one who sent me. The one who looks at me is seeing the one who sent me' (12:44–45). Jesus tells the disciples that they have seen the Father by seeing the Son, since the Son is in the Father and the Father is in him (cf 14:9–10). The disciples participate in the divine relationship through Jesus. Jesus' prayer in John 17 expresses this *theosis*: 'they may be one as we are one – I in them and you in me – so that they may be brought to complete unity.

This 'bi-directional transitive relationship' is interrelated. The Father's sending of the Son comes out of their union, and the disciples' union with God comes out of the sending. Again, Jesus' sending of the disciples comes out of the disciples' union with God through Jesus, anticipating their union with those who will also join by their message. As the Son was able to achieve what he has achieved based on his union with the Father, so the disciples are able to bear fruit because of their union with God. If we emphasize *missio* only, there will be plenty of fruit that falls to the ground and dries up. Likewise, if we emphasize only the *theosis*, there will be rotten branches that are protruding here and there. The *missio* should be based on the *theosis*, and the *theosis* must be confirmed by the *missio*.

In short, union with God (*theosis*) and bearing fruit (*missio*) are not twofold but interrelated. In that sense, the Johannine *theosis* is a 'missional *theosis*' and the Johannine *missio* is a '*missio* based on union'. Bearing fruit comes out of the union, not vice versa. Therefore, union with God or oneness with God is a priority.

Revisiting *Missio Dei* as an Application of the Findings

Reasons for Revisiting Missio Dei

I have demonstrated three findings from my missional reading of the Fourth Gospel. In this section, I will examine a well-known mission concept, *missio Dei*, with the insights from the findings. I have both a missiological and a practical reason for doing this.

First, the missiological reason is that the Fourth Gospel bears a close relationship to the doctrinal development of *missio Dei*, a Latin term for the mission of God. The modern understanding of the term *missio Dei* draws heavily from Bosch' definition. He (1991, 390) states that '[t]he classical doctrine on the *missio Dei* as God the Father sending the Son, and God the Father and the Son sending the Spirit was expanded to include yet another "movement": Father, Son, and Holy Spirit sending the church into the world'. As seen above, the *missio Dei* statement is related with many scriptural verses in the Fourth Gospel, such as 'I have not come on my own: God sent me' (8:44), 'the Holy Spirit, whom the Father will send in my name' (14:26),

'When the Advocate comes, whom I will send to you from the Father – the Spirit of truth who goes out from the Father' (15:26) and 'As the Father has sent me, I am sending you' (20:21). Guder (1999, 3) affirms this connection:

> The word *mission* is the Latinized version of the central theme of John's Gospel: *sending*. "As the Father has sent me, so I send you" (John 20:21). As the Father sends the Son, as the Father and the Son send the Spirit, so the triune God sends the church to carry out its mandate of witness.

Since the missiological concept, *missio Dei*, heavily depends on its foundation from the Fourth Gospel, it is necessary to examine the Fourth Gospel to determine whether or not it supports the concept. That is the missiological reason why I revisit the concept.

Secondly, I have a practical reason for this discussion. In the middle of the 20th century, this concept emerged as a way of reflecting on mission practices from earlier times. Bosch (1991, 389) explains the background as follows:

> During the preceding centuries mission was understood in a variety of ways. Sometimes it was interpreted primarily in soteriological terms: as saving individuals from eternal damnation. Or it was understood in cultural terms: as introducing people from the East and the South to the blessings and privileges of the Christian West. Often it was perceived in ecclesiastical categories: as the expansion of the church (or a specific denomination). Sometimes it was defined salvation-historically: as the process by which the world – evolutionary or by means of a cataclysmic event – would be transformed into the kingdom of God.

Those understandings for mission provided the motive for the church, and mission agencies in particular, to carry forward select ministries on the mission field. However, the excessive emphasis on the actions of the church in mission led to the fundamental question of whose mission it is, and a new concept of mission developed, claiming that, primarily, mission is not the mission of the church but of God, *missio Dei*. Although the concept has been developed theologically and missiologically through several global mission conferences, these did not significantly affect the actual mission practices of the church or of mission agencies in particular. The *missio Dei* was a 'seminary theology or missiology' for me when, as a seminary student, I was introduced to the concept during a debate about what comes after God in both mission and church. When I joined a mission agency, I never heard the term again. I found that various mission movements, advocated by American missiologists and mission practitioners in the 1980s, had stifled the development of *missio Dei* and its application to the mission field. However, the term reappeared and gained attention in the 21st century with a reflection on task-oriented mission. Dowsett (2007, 36) points out the problem of the modern mission as follows:

> … in many evangelical mission circles the behavioural sciences increasingly took over as the shapers of policy and praxis: anthropology, methods and strategies, a focus on measurable results, business management theory of leadership. These rather than theology became dominant. Useful though some of these things are as tools, they are very dubious masters, especially when they, rather than biblical missiology, determine what we do and how we do it. They also produce an endless (and wearying) stream of fashions – Unreached People Groups, 10/40 Window, AD 2000, Homogeneous Unit Principle, and many more. All bring helpful insights, but their proponents tend to overstate their case and see everything through their particular grid.

The reappearance of *missio Dei* in recent years[3] is the reason why I revisit the concept myself. If we were to go back to the previous discussion of *missio Dei* without evaluation and reflection, the discussion of the church on mission would continue to oscillate between the mission of God and the mission of the church in the future.

The Origin of the Modern Concept of Missio Dei

As seen above, the *missio Dei* statement of Bosch has its root in the Fourth Gospel. Despite such close relations between the Fourth Gospel and the *missio Dei* statement, I have a question as to whether the statement correctly conveys the mission as read in the Fourth Gospel. To understand where Bosch got his statement, it is necessary to know the origin of it. It is found in the following sentences (Bosch, 1991, 390):

> Indeed, Barth may be called the first clear exponent of a new theological paradigm which broke radically with an Enlightenment approach to theology. His influence on missionary thinking reached a peak at the Willingen Conference of the IMC (1952). It was here that the idea (not the exact term) *missio Dei* first surfaced clearly. Mission was understood as being derived from the very nature of God. It was thus put in the context of the doctrine of the Trinity, not of ecclesiology or soteriology.

As Bosch stated above, the modern concept of *missio Dei*, that is to say, the Trinitarian basis for mission, is traced to the theology of Barth, and the Willingen Conference of the IMC (1952) is recognized as the place where it was introduced. Aagaard (1965, 252) supports this. 'The Willingen conference in 1952 as a whole meant that the approach advocated by Barth already in 1932 was now generally acknowledged. The ground for mission was found in the

---

[3] Kirk Franklin (2017, 22), the Executive Director of Wycliffe Global Alliance, says that '[w]e lead in mission without an awareness of the significance of the *missio Dei*'. The concept reappears as a theme of reflection among mission practitioners around the time when Chris Wright's book, *The Mission of God* (2006), was published.

triune God and His mission'. Aagaard (1965, 244) observes the contribution that this, the new missiological concept, brought to mission understanding:

> Definitions of the term mission always run into difficulties, because the term was defined phenomenologically in the 16th century and remained defined in that way throughout Baroque-theology including the neo-pietist movements. The burden of the Warneck-tradition was not least the fact that the phenomenological and pragmatic definition had become a consensus, which kept mission and theology apart. Here also Barth made change possible. In his 1932 lecture he gave the answer to this dilemma, an answer which still echoes in Protestant missiology. With a keen jump he escaped the phenomenological imprisonment and redefined mission on the basis of the Trinitarian theology of the ancient church. Mission is first of all Missio Dei, the missio of the Son and of the Spirit by the Father. What we call mission only has Christian reality in so far as it participates in the Missio Dei. The idea of participation has therefore come to the forefront. God himself is the subject of mission, the church only participates in this mission.

Despite the contribution that the new understanding of mission has made to mission discussion, I think that the *missio Dei* concept developed after Barth is partially right, or seems right on the surface, but in fact highlights only one aspect. It thus leads to a distorted mission concept in light of the mission understanding derived from the Fourth Gospel. According to Eberhard Busch (1975, 218), Barth pointed out at the Brandenburg Mission Conference in 1932 that '[t]he task of theology was not so much to provide the missionary "weapons" as to ask questions about his relationship with the basis and the object of his activity'.[4] Barth pointed out the danger of excessive focus on the activity of the church in mission and proposed that the key is her relationship with God, which provides the right direction for the mission of the church. As several scholars have argued, it seems clear that Barth contributed to the change of focus on mission from wielding 'weapons' to understanding the basis of it – the Trinitarian basis in particular. However, it is not clear if the Trinitarian basis Barth proposed is identical to the *missio Dei* concept developed after him. Flett (2010, 12) stresses that Barth is irrelevant to today's understanding of *missio Dei*:

> In reality, Barth never once used the term *missio Dei*, never wrote the phrase "God is a missionary God," and never articulated a Trinitarian position of the kind expressed at Willingen. No textual evidence indicates that Barth interacted with the missiological discussions that were engaged with his theology.

In reality, it is difficult to say that the concept of modern *missio Dei* is based on Barth's Trinitarian theology. Even if it is based on that, it does not

---

[4] The title of the lecture was 'Die Theologie und die Mission in der Gegenwart' (Theology and Mission in Modern Times).

automatically prove that the concept is right, especially in view of the Fourth Gospel. I see two significant problems in *missio Dei*, which have developed post-Barth.

Overemphasis on Sending

First of all, the modern *missio Dei* concept overemphasizes the action of sending compared to the other aspects of God's character. It is correct to say that Barth stressed the importance of the Trinity,[5] but he did not highlight the sending aspect of the Trinity. The following quotation[6] shows how he understood the relationship between the essence and the work of God:

> To the unity of Father, Son and Spirit among themselves corresponds their unity *ad extra*. God's essence and work are not twofold but one. God's work is His essence in its relation to the reality which is distinct from Him and which is to be created or is created by Him. The work of God is the essence of God as the essence of Him who (N.B. in a free decision grounded in His essence but not constrained by His essence) is revealer, revelation and being revealed, or Creator, Reconciler and Redeemer. In this work of His, God is revealed to us. All we can know of God according to the witness of Scripture are His acts. All we can say of God, all the attributes we can assign to God, relate to these acts of His; not, then, to His essence as such. Though the work of God is the essence of God, it is necessary and important to distinguish His essence as such from His work, remembering that this work is grace, a free divine decision, and also remembering that we can know about God only because and to the extent that He gives Himself to us to be known. God's work is, of course, the work of the whole essence of God. God gives Himself entirely to man in His revelation, but not in such a way as to make Himself man's prisoner. He remains free in His working, in giving Himself.

As seen above, Barth placed more weight on the essence of God than on the work of God, even though he insisted that the two aspects are one. In his letter to Thurneysen (Barth & Thurneysen, 1964, 176), Barth said, 'A Trinity of *being*, not just an economic Trinity! At all costs the doctrine of the Trinity! If I could get the right key in my hand there, then everything would come out right'. Therefore, taking a particular aspect of the doctrine of the Trinity, which is the sending aspect of it, and then insisting *missio Dei* is based on it, is another form of the 'proof-text' method. In other words, it is a 'proof-doctrine' or 'missionary-doctrine' approach to mission.

---

[5] He says '[t]he doctrine of the Trinity is what basically distinguishes the Christian doctrine of God as Christian, and therefore what already distinguishes the Christian concept of revelation as Christian, in contrast to all other possible doctrines of God or concepts of revelation. (Barth, *CD* I, 1, 301).

[6] Barth, *CD* I, 1, 371.

I am not saying that mission should not be based on Trinitarian theology. Instead, the opposite is true. I claim that mission should reflect the attributes of the triune God. However, there is a problem in that the 'proof-doctrine' approach itself does not fully reflect the triune God. There is also another problem: the approach causes a serious error in missiology and mission practices when they are developed based on that approach. The error is found in the *missio Dei* statement of Bosch himself. Based on the sending aspect of the Trinity, that of 'God the Father sending the Son, and God the Father and the Son sending the Spirit', Bosch (1991, 390) adds another clause: that of 'Father, Son, and Holy Spirit sending the church into the world'. However, the added clause is not supported in the Fourth Gospel. In the Gospel, *Jesus* sends the discipleship community into the world. 'As the Father has sent me, I am sending you [the disciples]' (20:21). Jesus also sends or asks the Father to send the Holy Spirit, the παράκλητος (advocate), *for his disciples*. The παράκλητος is not a sender but the one who is to be with the disciples in the world, according to the Fourth Gospel. The surprising fact is that Bosch knew what Barth had in mind about the sending Church. Bosch (1980, 165–66) summarizes it as follows:

> Barth then contrasted religion with *faith*. The Christian religion, he added, might *become* faith, because of divine creation, election, justification and sanctification. God's revelation-in-Christ was no new religion but the abolition of all religion. It was on this point that Barth's theology became relevant for mission, but then first and foremost for the Church on the *home* front, the sending Church, which believed that she "had" the gospel and might now impart it to "non-Christianity". But, said Barth, we never "have" the gospel; we perpetually "receive" it, ever anew. The dividing line thus does not run between "us" and "them"; it also runs right through the sending, Christian Church herself. More than that: it runs through the heart of every Christian. We are all "Christo-pagans". For this reason there is no fundamental difference between preaching "at home" and "on the mission field". The Church remains Church of pagans, sinners, tax-gatherers. The only difference is that, on the mission field, the Church ventures in the form of "beginnings" what she ventures at home in the form of "repetitions".

Barth was concerned with how the Church herself and her mission practice should be related to the essence of the triune God, but the *missio Dei* concept and statement, which are alleged to have originated from Barth's Trinitarian theology, merely claim the sending aspect. It is further distorted by putting the Holy Spirit in the sending subject. Therefore, the *missio Dei* discussion shifted to the question of who the subject of mission is, which again led to a dichotomy between God and his church. This causes another problem, that is, the ambiguity of the position of the church in mission.

Ambiguity for the Role of the Church in Mission

The modern *missio Dei* concept blurred the position of the church in mission. The concept does not provide a convincing explanation for the role of the church in mission. It provides what the mission is *not* about rather than what the mission *is* about with regard to the position of the church in mission. The quotations that Bosch took from various scholars to explain the concept of *missio Dei* negatively describe the role of the church in mission. He (1991, 390) writes:

> In attempting to flesh out the missio Dei concept, the following could be said: In the new image mission is not primarily an activity of the church, but an attribute of God. God is a missionary God (cf Aagaard 1973:11–15; Aagaard 1974:421). "It is not the church that has a mission of salvation to fulfil in the world; it is the mission of the Son and Spirit through the Father that includes the church" (Moltmann 1977:64). Mission is thereby seen as a movement from God to the world; the church is viewed as an instrument for that mission (Aagaard 1973:13). There is church because there is mission, not vice versa (Aagaard 1974:423).

Most of these negative manifestations of the mission of the church result from the concept of *missio Dei* being introduced and developed as a counter-reaction to the era when 'phenomenological and pragmatic' mission was the mainstream. Flett (2010, 36) reveals the reason for these negative descriptions as follows:

> *Missio Dei*'s genesis as a response to the prolonged interrogation of mission's motives, methods, and goals helps explain this deficient theological development. It is not, in the first instance, a constructive concept; rather, it serves a critical function. Grounding mission in the doctrine of the Trinity distances the Western missionary enterprise from every colonialist association.

So, unlike the original intention of finding and recovering the essence of the mission, the *missio Dei* discussion shifted its focus to a discussion of the subject of mission and, in particular, the owner of mission. Moreover, as the frame for the ownership of mission belonging to God has been constructed, the position of the church in mission has now become fluid, since the proposed frame insists that the *missio Dei* is bigger than the *missio ecclesiae*, the mission of the church. Bosch (1991, 391) describes the modified statement, saying, 'God's own mission is larger than the mission of the church (LWF 1988:8). The *missio Dei* is God's activity, which embraces both the church and the world, and in which the church may be privileged to participate'. Those who try to maintain the role of the church in mission insist that the *missio Dei* included the *missio ecclesiae*, but others excluded the involvement of the church in God's mission. Goheen (2000, 117–18) highlights the distinction between the two:

> We might label the two divergent views as Christocentric-Trinitarian and Cosmocentric-Trinitarian. This distinction points to the starting point and motivation for the development of a Trinitarian basis for mission. For the first, the Trinitarian perspective is an enlargement and development of the Christocentric mission theology that dominated the former decades. In this view, the centrality and indispensability of the church in God's mission is maintained. The second term points to a motivation to formulate a Trinitarian perspective that opens the way to acknowledge the providential work of the Father through the Spirit in culture and world history apart from Christ and the church.

The 'Christocentric-Trinitarian' view fails to deal legitimately with the role of the church in mission. It sees the church as an instrument for mission or, at best, a participant in it. Based on my reading of the Fourth Gospel, I argue that neither of these views provides a satisfactory opinion regarding the position or role of the church in mission. This distorted interpretation of the role of the church in mission is due to the 'Missiocentric-Trinitarian' view. By that term I mean that the *missio Dei* concept is overwhelmingly dependent on the sending of Trinitarian theology, as discussed in the previous section. The 'Missiocentric-Trinitarian' view inevitably led mission discussion into the subject of the sending, and the subject of the sending has been overextended to include the ownership and the scope of mission. However, the Fourth Gospel does not express such a separation in mission. Rather, the Gospel continues to stress the opposite. Although 'sending' is one of the essential themes of the Fourth Gospel, it is always introduced on the premise of a relationship, rather than being introduced as an isolated subject. What needs to be asked is not only who sends whom but also who relates to whom and how they relate to understanding mission in the Fourth Gospel.

I have examined a popular missiological concept, *missio Dei*, from a Johannine missional perspective, which is acquired from a missional reading of the Gospel. Despite the contribution of the concept that shifted the discussion on mission from the activities of the church to the attributes of God, the concept has created a problematic dichotomy between the mission of God and the mission of the church. The Fourth Gospel, which is considered to be a basis for the concept, does not support such a dichotomy if read missionally.

Back to the research question of this study: 'To what extent does the Fourth Gospel as a whole contribute to the biblical understanding of mission?' I will now suggest its contributions to a biblical understanding of mission.

Contributions to a Biblical Understanding of Mission

Shifting from Mission to God

In what ways does the Fourth Gospel as a whole contribute to a biblical understanding of mission? I have argued that a 'proof-doctrine' approach to mission is one of the causes for the *missio Dei* concept to fail to connect mission to the essence of God, even though the Trinitarian theology was taken as the basis for it. The term *missio Dei*, which uses the possessive form of God either as a modifier or as the owner for the nuclear part *mission* in the phrase, inevitably highlights mission rather than God. As a result, mission is trapped in the discussion of ownership and does not progress toward an understanding of God's missional attributes.

We have discovered that the Fourth Gospel speaks more of *God* [of mission] than of *mission* [of God], even though those two should not be separated. The former is an open-ended discussion while the latter is the opposite. In the latter case, the more mission is God's, the more limited the mission of the church becomes, because the term has been connected with the concept of ownership. In the former case, however, the more missional attributes of God are revealed, the more enriched becomes the mission of the church based on that, because the abundant missional attributes of God do not limit the mission of the church but rather provide those characteristics the church should possess for mission.

It is obvious that the Fourth Gospel posits that the Father sends the Son, and the Son sends his disciples into the world. The problem is not in the word 'sending' per se, but in overlooking the foundation and content that the word contains. 'Sending' is one of the most frequently used words in the Fourth Gospel. The word 'sending' is represented by two synonyms, ἀποστέλλω and πέμπω in the Gospel.[7] The former appears 28 times and the latter 32 times. Bosch (1980, 240) observes that '[f]orty-six times in the Gospel of John alone Jesus says that the Father has sent him, often adding that it is for the sake of the salvation of the world'. Furthermore, it is one of the characteristics of the Fourth Gospel that the words are used in their verb form, including the verb 'to send'. Therefore, actions and movements seem to be a key to the reading of the Gospel. Köstenberger (1998, 199), who studied the *modes of movement* in the Fourth Gospel, says:

> The Fourth Gospel portrays Jesus' mission according to three major emphases, each involving a certain *mode of movement*: Jesus as the Son *sent* from the Father, Jesus as the one who *came* into the world and *returned* to the Father, and Jesus as the eschatological shepherd-teacher who called others to *follow* him in order to help *gather* the eschatological harvest.

Based on his study, he (1998, 41) defines mission as 'the specific *task* or purpose which a person or group seeks to accomplish, *involving various modes of movement*, be it sending or being sent, coming and going, ascending and descending, gathering by calling others to follow, or following'. It might be

---

[7] Köstenberger (1998, 106) says that 'John's use of ἀποστέλλω and πέμπω is best explained by his preference for a word in a certain grammatical form or by stylistic variation'. For the study about the two words, see Köstenberger (1998, 97–106).

true on the surface, but the mission that the Fourth Gospel reveals goes beyond those movements.

The Johannine sending statement does not stand as an independent proposition within the Gospel. The sending statement is introduced to the disciples in the post-resurrection narrative, which is the end of the Gospel, and thus should be understood within the context of the whole Gospel. The Father's sending of his Son is based on the relationship between himself and the Son. What should be noted about mission in the Fourth Gospel is the content on which the sending is based. In this sense, the *missio Dei* insistence that 'Father, Son, and Holy Spirit send the church into the world' is neither the focus of the Fourth Gospel nor a correct statement in view of the Gospel. The statement I advocate from a missional reading of the Gospel is: 'As the Father sends the Son, the Son sends his disciples into the world, and the Father and the Son send the Holy Spirit to the disciples'. Bauckham (2015, 36) points out the following discrepancy between the doctrine of the Trinity and the Fourth Gospel:

> The Gospel of John has exercised a strong and appropriate influence on trinitarian theology down the centuries, and the passages that I have been discussing are among the most important in this regard. In at least one important respect the theological tradition has gone beyond the Gospel. Although this Gospel has much to say about the Holy Spirit or Paraclete and leaves us in no doubt that the Spirit in its own way belongs to the identity of the one God, the passages that we have examined [in the Fourth Gospel], those that use "oneness" and "in-one-another" language, are binitarian rather than trinitarian. The Gospel does not use that language to characterize the relation of the Holy Spirit to the Father and the Son… My point is not that the Gospel's comprehensive understanding of God is not trinitarian, but simply that the "oneness" and "in-one-another" language is used only in a binitarian way, to refer to the relationship of the Father and the Son.

The Gospel focuses on the foundation that enables the sending. The Father's sending of his Son takes place on the basis of the relationship between the Father and the Son. Similarly, the sending of the disciples takes place on the basis of what the Father has done through the Son and on the basis of the relationship of the Son with the disciples, that is, their remaining in him enables them to bear fruit, according to John 15. I submit that the foundation for the sending is the relationship and oneness between the Father and the Son and knowing the will of the Father in the relationship. This extends to the disciples' relationship with those who come to believe through them. Therefore, 'the relationship between the Father and the Son' and 'knowing the Father's will' are the points of departure for mission in the Fourth Gospel. I will examine those two aspects in following sections.

The Relationship between the Father and the Son, and Mission

I have demonstrated that the Fourth Gospel focuses on the foundation that enables movements, including sending. Jesus' sending of his disciples is not the point of departure for mission in the Fourth Gospel, nor is the Father's sending of the Son. It is the relationship between the Father and the Son, the unity or oneness of them. Starting mission with the Father–Son relationship rather than with the Father's sending of the Son or Jesus' sending of his disciples, provides a different emphasis of mission. Köstenberger (1998, 189) insists that 'love and unity are not in and of themselves the mission as if the revelation of the nature of God were merely an existential component of the believing community'. He (1998, 189) sees the 'love and unity' as the *foundation* for mission but not as the mission itself, and therefore claims, '[w]hile love and unity are to be the foundation, they must be accompanied by an actual "going" (cf 15:16) in order for fruit to be borne'.

According to my reading of the Gospel, however, the above insistence is incomplete; it only represents mission on the surface level, but does not represent the whole picture. More importantly, that view is in danger of distorting mission. The moment that the foundation (unity) and the action (sending) are viewed separately, the distortion surfaces. The distortion manifests itself as either an intolerant, selfish love that loses the action or activism that has lost its roots. The former is illustrated by Jesus' encounter with the Jews, who had an exclusive view of God's love and relationship with them, while the latter is seen in Jesus' encounters with his disciples. I already argued that the verb ὑπάγω (to go) in 15:16 is not equivalent to the verb πορεύομαι in Matt 28:19. The verb ὑπάγω carries the meaning of 'constant increase'[8] of the 'bearing' rather than 'actual going'. The more serious problem of the above claim is the dichotomous view that segregates the foundation from the action.

In my judgement, the Fourth Gospel does not separate these two aspects. These two are connected by the former enabling the latter. Jesus says to the disciples, 'Remain in me, as I also remain in you. No branch can bear fruit by itself; it must remain in the vine. Neither can you bear fruit unless you remain in me (15:4); If you remain in me and I in you, you will bear much fruit; apart from me you can do nothing' (15:5). Remaining and bearing are not two separate actions. It is not that the branch should remain in the vine and also should go and bear fruit. Wallace (1996, 720) points out, 'the *solemnity* and *urgency* of the action' in the aorist imperative in Greek, which should be interpreted 'as if the author says, "Make this your top priority"'. Thus, he (1996, 721) suggests the meaning of μείνατε (15:4), the aorist imperative of the verb μένω, as follows: '[o]bviously the command is not ingressive: "Begin to remain in me." Nor is it momentary and specific. This is a general precept, but

---

[8] Torrey (1936, 30).

the force of the aorist is on urgency and priority'. In other words, remaining in Christ is the urgent priority of the disciples in itself, and it is also essential for bearing fruit, as if remaining in the vine is the top priority of the branch for bearing fruit. Furthermore, the Gospel decribes 'disciple' of Jesus as the one who 'hold[s] to Jesus' teaching' (literally, remain in my words, 8:31).[9]

Therefore, the loving relationship or oneness between the Father and the Son is the point of departure for the loving relationship between Jesus and the disciples, thus for mission in the Gospel. Hastings (2012, 78) explains:

> It is a consequence of our union with the triune God in Christ (theosis) by the Spirit. It is something that arises from our *participation* in God's mission, participation of the *koinōnia*, persons-in-communion kind. In other words, we are given encouragement to engage in mission as a consequence of who we are in Christ, not by a command from outside ourselves. The indicatives precede the imperatives, and usually the commands are actually hortatory, not imperatives.

The relationship between the Father and the Son appears as first and foremost, or 'firstly', in the Gospel narrative. 'In the beginning was the Word, and the Word was with God, and the Word was God' (1:1). Jesus says 'I came from the Father and entered the world; now I am leaving the world and going back to the Father' (16:28). For Jesus, the Father, or oneness with him in particular, is the point of departure for his mission and, at the same time, is the point of arrival. In comparison, the Father's sending is 'secondly', and Jesus' sending of his disciples is 'lastly' in the narrative. Oneness begins with the unity of the Father and the Son, leading to the unity of the Son and his disciples, extending further to include the unity of the discipleship community and the community that will believe through the disciples. 'I [Jesus] and the Father are one' (10:30), 'not only for that nation [the Jewish nation] but also for the scattered children of God, to bring them together and make them one' (11:52), that 'they [the discipleship community and the community to believe through the disciples] may be one as we [the Father and the Son] are one' (17:22). Appold (1976, [261]) claims, 'it may be said that John's Gospel is conceived and developed from the standpoint of Jesus' oneness with the Father'. He (1976, 285) explains the connection between the oneness and the other themes that follow in the Gospel as follows:

> The resulting oneness relation with the Revealer is not just a spiritual or an internal relation invisible to others around. It has instead concrete, perceivable manifestations, central among which is the corresponding oneness among the believers. The picture here is not so much that of a vertical-horizontal dimension but rather that of an emanative sequence or a chain of action whereby oneness describes, as point of origin, the relational/revelational correspondence of Father

[9] The Greek sentence is μείνητε ἐν τῷ λόγῳ τῷ ἐμῷ.

and Son, and then successively but interconnectedly the relation of Revealer and believer, and also believer and believer. Thus, the line leads from Christology to soteriology to ecclesiology, and oneness serves as the theological abbreviation for the constitutive aspects of all three.

Knowing the Father and His Will and Mission

The relationship between the Father and the Son includes knowledge; knowing the will of the Father in particular. The dynamic interaction (εἰμί πρός) between the Father and the Son enables them not only to dwell in one another but also to know one another. In the study of the first verse of the Gospel,[10] I pointed out that the combination of the stative verb εἰμί and the transitive preposition πρός were oxymoronic. Based on the internal use of both εἰμί plus a preposition and a verb plus πρός in the Fourth Gospel, I claimed that the oxymoronic combination denoted both the perfect being together and the perfect communicating between them, as in with one another. Vincent (1889, 34) describes the meaning of the preposition πρός in the verse:

> The preposition πρός, which, with the accusative case, denotes motion towards, or direction, is also often used in the New Testament in the sense of *with*; and that not merely as *being near* or *beside*, but as a living union and communion; implying the active notion of intercourse.

Such an intimate relationship is expressed by the incarnate Son knowing the Father and knowing his will. Jesus describes it as follows: 'I know him [the Father] because I am from him and he sent me' (7:29); 'what I heard from him [the Father] I tell the world' (8:26); 'I am telling you what I have seen in the Father's presence' (8:38); 'the Father knows me and I know the Father' (10:15). As the relationship includes knowledge of one another, that knowledge includes knowing the will of one another. Therefore, knowing the Father and his will is the foundation of and, indeed, the all-encompassing substance of the ministry that Jesus achieves in the world. Jesus himself confirms this, saying, 'the Son can do nothing by himself; he can do only what he sees his Father doing, because whatever the Father does the Son also does' (5:19); 'For the works that the Father has given me to finish – the very works that I am doing – testify that the Father has sent me' (5:36); 'My teaching is not my own. It comes from the one who sent me' (7:16); 'I have brought you [the Father] glory on earth by finishing the work you gave me to do' (17:4).

Therefore, the Father's sending of the Son is not merely a movement but implies that the Father and the Son have an intimate relationship, dwelling in each other, and they have perfect knowledge of one another, particularly the Son's knowledge about the will of the Father. Jesus' declaration to his

---

[10] For the discussion about the phrase, see 2.2.2.

disciples, 'As (καθώς) the Father has sent me, I am sending you' (20:21), does not mean that he is sending the disciples just *because* the Father has sent him. Instead, it means that Jesus is sending his disciples in the same way the Father had sent him and, therefore, even as his sending emanated from his relationship and the knowledge he had with the Father, so the disciples also were sent on the premise of their relationship with and knowledge about him. Furthermore, Jesus' sending of his disciples is not limited to following the manner in which the Father sent himself, but such relationship and knowledge enable the discipleship community – and all communities that will come through them – to become one, just as the Father and the Son are one.

Co-mission

I propose that mission characterized by the Fourth Gospel is 'co-mission'. The Johannine commissioning statement, 'As the Father has sent me, I am sending you' (20:21), condenses the entire Gospel and implies this co-mission aspect of the Gospel. The adverb καθώς (as) implies what Jesus has revealed to the disciples about the Father throughout the whole Gospel. He is sending his disciples on the basis of his relationship with the Father and the Father's sending of him into the world. Hastings (2012, 82) points out that the Johannine commission is 'the Greatest Commission because it is a "co-mission"'. He (2012, 82) interprets the statement as follows:

> Just as Christ is sent as the Son in union with the Father, so now they were sent ones because of their union with Christ, by the Spirit he was about to breathe into them. The Spirit would mediate the presence of Christ in them so that they would be his body, his hands and feet on earth. This is the miracle of theosis, the union of Christ with his church.

I will demonstrate the ways in which the Gospel expresses the co-mission.

First, the Gospel emphasizes both the mission of God and the participation of the discipleship community in it. As Bosch (1980, 239) states, '[m]ission has its origin neither in the official Church nor in special groups within the Church. It has its origin in God… it is clear that it is the *Triune God* who is the subject of mission'. The Gospel not only unfolds the origin of mission but further extends its testimony to the participation of the discipleship community in the mission of God. Jesus' emphasis on the Father as the one who sent him is not only to reveal that the subject of mission is the Father but also to explain the significance of his sending of the disciples.

In that sense, the Father's sending of the Son should not be used as an argument for the ownership of mission. It is not the mission of God nor the mission of the disciples with regard to the ownership of mission. The ownership emphasis in the mission of God is an overreaction to the mission of the church. The more the ownership of God in mission is emphasized, the more the role of the church is reduced or disappears. The focus should be shifted to the missional characteristics of both God and the church. The more the missional attributes of God are found in co-mission, the more the missional attributes of the church become enriched, because they are not separated.

Secondly, the Gospel demonstrates the continuation of God's love for the world through the Son and the community in the Holy Spirit. God's love and concern are for the whole world (3:16), so the scope of his mission should include the whole world. The Fourth Gospel clarifies that God created the whole world through the Word: 'Through him all things were made; without him nothing was made that has been made' (1:3). Furthermore, the love of God for the world is expressed by the sending of his only Son Jesus, the incarnate Word (3:16). Jesus says, 'I and the Father are one' (10:30), and also 'All I have is yours [the Father's], and all you have is mine' (17:10). Then, the Father and the Son send the Holy Spirit to the discipleship community. This fact testifies that God works through the Son in the Spirit, and continues to work through the discipleship community in the Spirit. Therefore, the Gospel does not contrast between the size or scope of the mission of God and that of the church. As Goheen (2000, 117) points out, '[w]hile it was clear that the mission of God was primary and the mission of the church was derivative, it was not clear how the *missio Dei* was greater than the *missio ecclesiae*'. Bosch (1991, 391) explains how those two divergent views on the scope of the mission of God were started:

> After Willingen (and, already at Willingen, in the American report) the missio Dei concept gradually underwent a modification – a process traced in great detail by Rosin (1972). Since God's concern is for the entire world, this should also be the scope of the missio Dei. It affects all people in all aspects of their existence. Mission is God's turning to the world in respect of creation, care, redemption and consummation (Kramm 1979:210). It takes place in ordinary human history, not exclusively in and through the church. "God's own mission is larger than the mission of the church" (LWF 1988:8). The missio Dei is God's activity, which embraces both the church and the world, and in which the church may be privileged to participate.

I already insisted that Jesus' achievement is to form the discipleship community. In essence, human communities and their actions are incomparable to the holy community and its actions. However, based on the will of God, who determined to be one with all who come to him through the created community, the discipleship community will have a crucial position in mission.

Mission is what God begins by sending his Son into the world. In perfect relationship with the Father, Jesus proceeds with it by fulfilling what was prophesied and accomplishing the formation of the discipleship community. The discipleship community that has been given authority by Jesus continues through the guidance of the Holy Spirit, who is with the community.

Chapter Summary

I have demonstrated my findings from a missional reading of the Gospel. The Gospel contains a creation motif. God who created the world through the Word sent the incarnate Word to restore the world. Jesus, the agent of creation, forms a discipleship community, a new creation, to continue the creation process through them in the world. This creation motif emphasizes the new community as a new creation while at the same time not eliminating God as the subject of all processes. The narrative focuses on the development of the community. Jesus gathers the disciples before he inaugurates his public ministry to the Jews in Jerusalem and accompanies them in his encounters with the Jews and interactions with individuals to show the scope and quality of the new community to them. Before the passion, Jesus spends intimate time with the disciples explaining what it means to be disciples. There is a bi-directional transitive relationship between God and the community. On the one hand, the descending direction is *missio*, that God sends the Son and the Son sends the disciples in the Holy Spirit. On the other hand, the ascending direction is *theosis*, that the community participates in the divine relationship. The Gospel demonstrates that *missio* and *theosis* are interrelated since the divine relationship of the Father and the Son enabled the Father's sending of the Son, and Jesus' sending of the disciples is based on the relationship of Jesus and the disciples. The Gospel reveals the priority of *theosis* since it enables *missio*.

I have revisited a missiological theme, *missio Dei*, because it relies heavily on the Fourth Gospel. The theme first emerged as a counter-reaction to church-centred mission or, more precisely, to agency-centred mission in the 19th century and beyond. Karl Barth provided the Trinitarian basis for the missiological theme. However, scholars after Barth focused on the triune God merely as being a sending God, from which the theme of the sending of God or the mission of God developed. The critical problem in the discussions that have developed since then is that the theme has been distilled down to a matter of ownership and scope for mission. The Fourth Gospel does not support those claims. Instead, the Gospel reveals the relationship and oneness between the Father and the Son, then between the Son and the discipleship community, then the discipleship community and the people to come through their message and eventually the oneness of all of them. Therefore, the mission that the Fourth Gospel expresses is neither solely the mission of God nor the mission of the Church.

Based on the above observations, I have demonstrated the extent to which the Fourth Gospel contributes to a biblical understanding of mission. First, the Gospel focuses more on God [of mission] than on mission [of God], in other words, on the essence and attributes of the missional God rather than the activities of him. Secondly, the Gospel presents the relationship between the Father and the Son as the foundation of all activities in relation to the world and stresses the participation of the discipleship community in it. Thus, mission should be based on union with God. Thirdly, the Gospel confirms that the relationship is based on the premise that the sent one knows and obeys the will of the sending one. Considering those points, I concluded that mission characterized by the Gospel is 'co-mission'. By that term, I mean there exists a continuation from the mission of God and the mission of the discipleship community through Jesus in the Holy Spirit.

8. Conclusion

Introduction

In the previous chapter, I have demonstrated what I have found through a missional reading of the Gospel and its contribution to a biblical understanding of mission. The chapter functioned as a conclusion for reading the Gospel. In this final chapter, I will go back to the motivational questions I set forth in the Introduction of the study. I will examine the extent to which this missional reading has been able to respond to those questions. I will also revisit two aspects of a missional reading I have applied in this study to address the ways in which those aspects are valid for this reading. This includes the ways in which the text contributes to the adjustment of the missional hermeneutic. I will also address the limitation of the study and present some suggestions for the future study of missional reading.

The Response of the Gospel to the Motivational Questions

As I read the Fourth Gospel from a missional point of view, I was most vigilant about avoiding the tendency to find a particular topic of mission in the Gospel. The reason for this is that an attempt to find a particular theme of mission in the Gospel could reduce the research to the task of proving a mission I have already defined. Therefore, I have tried not to read the Gospel within a fixed framework. Nevertheless, a missional reading of the Gospel responded to the motivational questions raised during my missional journey. Those questions are: 1) What is the position of relationship in mission? (Task vs Relationship), 2) What is the missional identity of the church? (Delegation vs Engagement) and 3) How can local churches in mission fields improve their self-reflection? (Dependency vs Self-Initiative).

First, I found that *relationship* is crucial to mission. It provides the foundation, the process and the goal of mission. The divine relationship between the Father and the Son provides the foundation for the Father's sending of the Son. Likewise, Jesus' sending of his disciples is based on their relationship. It also relates to the process of mission. The Father always is with the Son in the Holy Spirit, and the Father and the Son are with the disciples in the Holy Spirit. The relationship is not merely an instrument for mission but the goal of mission. Sending (*missio*) itself is not the goal of the Father. The Father's sending of the Son and the Son's sending of the disciples aim for 'oneness' in their relationship. The interactions of Jesus with the disciples, including the gathering of them, accompanying them, an exclusive interaction with them prior to his passion and another interaction with them after his resurrection, encompass a notable amount of time and effort, thus emphasizing the significance of the relationship.

Secondly, I found that mission is the full engagement of the discipleship community, rather than merely delegated work to specific forces within the community. Despite the occasional interactions with individual disciples, Jesus' relationship with the disciples and his sending of them are communal. The Johannine discipleship is represented by 'the Twelve'. They are all chosen and sent into the world. Judas' betrayal demonstrates that not all who are called 'disciple' remain in him, but it does not signify that there is an exception to mission among the disciples.

Finally, the Fourth Gospel may not speak directly about the selfhood issue of the church, but the Gospel, as a whole, could be viewed as a product of the Evangelist's self-reflection. As seen throughout our reading of the Gospel, 'relationship' or 'intimacy' was a crucial theme, and we know that the Evangelist did not record what was abstract but what he understood through his intimate relationship with Jesus. I view the Fourth Gospel as an outcome of the Evangelist's cognitive process of reflection on the disciple's own experiences as a beloved disciple of Jesus, a Christ-centred understanding of the Hebrew Bible and an understanding of the identity of the discipleship community missionally. This example provides a guideline for a church, in any given context, to begin the selfhood and self-theologizing process.

The Fourth Gospel and a Missional Reading

I have demonstrated two dimensions of a missional reading that I applied to this study: a grand narrative view and an equipping dimension. I pointed out that a missional reading is a guideline and a set of questions for approaching a given text and not a fixed framework which might control the text. In this section, I will evaluate those dimensions to determine if they were valid for the reading of the Fourth Gospel.

One of the two dimensions of a missional reading in this study is the grand narrative view. This view provided a broad picture within which the Fourth Gospel could be read. Chris Wright (2009a, 38) proposes to read any passage in the Bible 'not only within its immediate literary and historical context, but also within its canonical context in the flow of the Bible'. This view was very appropriate for the reading of the Fourth Gospel. The view contributed to reading the whole Gospel as a creation process of a new community. It also helped to look at Jesus' encounters with the Jews and his interactions with individuals in relation to the grand narrative, rather than reading them as an immediate reflection of the contemporary community, as suggested by Martyn's (2003) 'two-level drama'. From that point of view, I was able to see how the Jews in the Gospel were devoid of the essence of the missional community, and I could read that Jesus' 'signs' and following discourses, when encountering them, were an indication of such an essence.

One of the relevant contributions of this grand narrative dimension is a Christ-centred understanding of the grand narrative. Chris Wright (2006, 41) suggests that a missional hermeneutic is a Christ-centred reading of Scripture: '*Jesus himself* provided the hermeneutical coherence within which all disciples must read these texts, that is, in the light of the story that leads *up to* Christ (messianic reading) and the story that leads *on from* Christ (missional reading)'. As Thatcher (2006, 27) points out, the Fourth Gospel includes 'a messianic reading of a passage from the Hebrew Bible'. In other words, the Evangelist illuminated the Hebrew Bible with Christ and Christ with the Hebrew Bible. In that sense, the Fourth Gospel is an outcome of the Evangelist's own missional reading of both the Bible and Christ. Of course, the Fourth Gospel is not a summary of the grand narrative. The grand narrative of the Bible provides the context in which the Gospel can be read as opposed to constructing a solid framework into which the Gospel should be interposed. For instance, the Johannine creation story begins with the pre-creation story that the Word was with God and also contains the return of Jesus back to the place from which he came. The grand narrative needs to be widened and adjusted according to the reading of the text rather than controlling the text.

The second dimension of a missional reading in this study is the equipping purpose of the writings. As Goheen (2006, 7) states, the New Testament was written for forming and equipping people in the early church 'for their missional calling in the world'. I will address the extent to which this dimension relates to the reading of the Gospel.

First, this dimension provides a whole narrative approach to understanding the purpose of the Gospel. The argument for the purpose of writing the Gospel is often based on the tense of the verb 'to believe' (πιστεύω) in 20:31 (see 6.3.1). However, this equipping dimension helps readers to leave that debate and see the text from a broader perspective. Flemming (2011, 8) asserts:

> Biblical texts, then, do not have to focus on evangelizing non-Christians (such as we might find in Acts) in order to reflect God's mission. Christian nurture and formation are profoundly missional, in that they equip Christian communities to engage in the loving, healing, reconciling mission of God.

Secondly, this equipping dimension does not specify any community, unless the text refers to a community to be equipped. In the case of the Epistles with clearly intended recipients, the text functions to shape and equip the recipients. Even in such cases, it should not be overlooked that the recipients are representative. In the case of the Fourth Gospel, without any specific recipients identified, there is a risk of distorting the meaning if a hypothetical community is created and the text is interpreted as shaping and equipping that community. The Gospel conducts the equipping function through the whole process as Jesus shapes and equips the discipleship community.

Those two dimensions of a missional hermeneutic illumined our reading of the Gospel. However, the Gospel also provides a perspective on how to look at the two dimensions. Even though they are valid approaches through which to read the biblical text, they are proffered as two separate views. Flemming (2011, 6) observes that they relate to 'what Scripture is *about*' and 'what Scripture *does*' respectively. The Gospel, however, reveals that those two are interrelated. It is not just that Jesus provides one lens through which to view the two dimensions but also because the Gospel addresses the mission of God and the mission of the community as a progression. In that sense, a missional hermeneutic, those two dimensions of it in particular, should provide one perspective for reading the essence of the text rather than merely providing two separate methods for reading.

Limitations

I have read the Fourth Gospel as a whole to find out what the Gospel as a whole says about mission. The direction of the study presupposes reading the whole Gospel faithfully rather than extracting parts of it. The strength of this approach is that it enables a reader to see the big picture of the Gospel and to understand the purpose of the Gospel record from the holistic point of view. The weakness of this reading is that the depth of the research is not as exhaustive for the entire book as an analytical approach to a particular part or issue in the Gospel might be. One defence for the chosen approach is that the analytical approach to a particular topic would be in danger of developing beyond the scope of what the Gospel actually says. I already pointed out how the *missio Dei* concept, which has found support in the language of 'sending' in the Gospel, has been over-developed, regardless of what the Fourth Gospel essentially states. Nevertheless, I acknowledge that there remains a challenge to study in more detail the issues discovered, while recalling the overall picture illuminated by the missional reading.

Suggestions

Recent attempts to read the Bible missionally have developed because the former 'biblical basis for mission' has been reduced to finding evidence in verses for a pre-determined understanding of mission. The first thing to do with this new approach is to look at the entire Bible as one grand story. Scholars such as Chris Wright and Michael Goheen set the foundation for this direction.

Then, the next step is to read each book of the Bible in the context of the grand narrative, applying a missional hermeneutic to the reading. There have been a few attempts in this direction, but more effort needs to be made in the future. This study is one attempt in this regard.

There are a few directions that future research could go, based on this research both within the Fourth Gospel and in comparison with books related to the Gospel.

First, deeper research on the Old Testament themes in the Gospel could be explored in connection with the relationship God desires to have with humanity and with his chosen people, in particular. The research could contribute to a wider and deeper understanding of the shaping and equipping of the chosen disciples.

Secondly, further research on 'oneness' in the Gospel could clarify what commonalities and differences exist between the Son's relationship and the community's relationship with the Father. This could contribute to understanding the meaning of the participation of the church in the mission of God.

Thirdly, the Johannine letters could be explored with a missional hermeneutic based on the findings of this study. The letters could be examined more explicitly, exploring how the letters equip readers to participate in the mission of God in a Johannine way.

Finally, a missional reading of the Synoptic Gospels and a comparison of that with the current study could be a natural next step. Those studies would contribute to the formation of the holistic biblical mission as understood from the Gospels.

Bibliography

Aagaard, Johannes, 1965. 'Some Main Trends in Modern Protestant Missiology.' *Studia Theologica*, 19, 238-59.

Abbott, Edwin A., 1906. *Johannine Grammar*. London: Adam and Charles Black.

Adams, Michael. tr., 2005. 'Introduction to the Gospel According to John.' In: *The Navarre Bible: Saint John's Gospel*. Dublin: Four Courts Press, 11-34.

Anderson, Paul N., 2007. 'Why This Study is Needed, and Why It is Needed Now.' In: Paul N. Anderson, Felix Just & Tom Thatcher, eds. *John, Jesus, and History, Volume 1: Critical Appraisals of Critical Views*. Atlanta: Society of Biblical Literature, 13-70.

Agourides, S. C., 1968. 'The "High Priestly Prayer" of Jesus.' *Studia Evangelica*, 4, 137-145. Edited by F. L. Cross. Berlin: Akademie.

Appold, Mark L., 1976. *The Oneness Motif in the Fourth Gospel: Motif Analysis and Exegetical Probe into the Theology of John*. Tübingen: Mohr Siebeck.

Ashton, John, 1985. 'The Identity and Function of the Ἰουδαῖοι in the Fourth Gospel.' *Novum Testamentum*, 27 (1), 40-75.

_______. 1986. 'The Transformation of Wisdom: A Study of the Prologue of John's Gospel.' *New Testament Studies*, 32, 161-86.

_______. 2014. *The Gospel of John and Christian Origins*. Minneapolis, MN: Fortress Press.

Balz, H. and Schneider, G. eds., 1993. *Exegetical Dictionary of the New Testament*. 3 vols. Grand Rapids, MI: Eerdmans.

Barclay, William, 1975. *The Gospel of John: Vol 1 – Chapters 1 to 7*. Revised ed. Edinburgh: Saint Andrew Press.

Barram, Michael D., 2007. 'The Bible, Mission, and Social Location: Toward a Missional Hermeneutic.' *Interpretation, 61 (1)*, 42-58.

Barrett, C. K., 1947. 'The Old Testament in the Fourth Gospel.' *The Journal of Theological Studies, 191 (2),* 155-69.

_______. 1978. *The Gospel According to St John: An Introduction with Commentary and Notes on the Greek Text*. 2nd ed. London: SPCK.

Barrosse, Thomas, 1958. 'The Seven Days of the New Creation in St. John's Gospel.' *The Catholic Biblical Quarterly,* 21, 507-16.

Bartholomew, Craig G. & Goheen, Michael W., 2004a. 'Story and Biblical Theology.' In: Craig Bartholomew, Mary Healy, Karl Möller & Robin

Parry, eds. *Out of Egypt: Biblical Theology and Biblical Interpretation.* Exeter: Paternoster, 144-71.

_______. 2004b. *The Drama of Scripture: Finding Our Place in the Biblical Story*. Grand Rapids, MI: Baker Academic.

Barth, Karl, 1975. *Church Dogmatics*. Translated by Geoffrey W. Bromiley. Edinburgh: T & T Clark.

Barth, Karl & Thurneysen, Eduard, 1964. *Revolutionary Theology in the Making: Barth-Thurneysen Correspondence, 1914-1925*. Translated by James D. Smart. London: Epworth Press.

Bauckham, Richard, 2015. *Gospel of Glory: Major Themes in Johannine Theology*. Grand Rapids, MI: Baker Academic.

_______. 2016. 'Mission as Hermeneutic for Scriptural Interpretation.' In: Michael W. Goheen, ed. *Reading the Bible Missionally*. Grand Rapids, MI: Eerdmans, 28-44.

Bauckham, Richard & Mosser, Carl. eds., 2008. *The Gospel of John and Christian Theology.* Grand Rapids, MI: Eerdmans.

Bauer, W., 2000. *A Greek-English Lexicon of the New Testament and Other Early Christian Literature*. 3rd ed. Revised and edited by F. W. Danker. Translated by W. F. Arndt, F. W. Gingrich, and F. W. Danker. Chicago and London: University of Chicago Press.

Bavinck, J. H., 1960. *An Introduction to the Science of Missions*. Translated by David H. Freeman. Philadelphia, PA: Presbyterian and Reformed Publishing.

Beale, G. K., 2004. *The Temple and the Church's Mission: A Biblical Theology of the Dwelling Place of God.* Downers Grove, IL: InterVarsity Press.

Beasley-Murray, George R., 1992. 'The Mission of the Logos-Son.' In: F. van Segbroeck, C. M. Tuckett, G. van Belle & J. Verheyden, eds. *The Four Gospels 1992: Festschrift Frans Neirynck*. vol.3. Leuven: Leuven University Press, 1855-68.

_______. 1999. *John*. 2nd ed. Word Biblical Commentary, vol.36. Exeter: Paternoster.

Beeby, Harry Daniel, 2000. 'A Missional Approach to Renewed Interpretation.' In: Craig Bartholomew, Colin Greene & Karl Möller, eds. *Renewing Biblical Interpretation*. Exeter: Paternoster, 268-83.

Bennema, Cornelis, 2005. *Excavating John's Gospel: A Commentary for Today*. Delhi: ISPCK.

_______. 2009a. *Encountering Jesus: Character Studies in the Gospel of John.* Milton Keynes: Paternoster.

_______. 2009b. 'The Character of John in the Fourth Gospel.' *Journal of the Evangelical Theological Society,* 52 (2), 271-84.

_______. 2009c. 'The Identity and Composition of οἱ Ἰουδαῖοι in the Gospel of John.' *Tyndale Bulletin*, 60, 239-63.

_______. 2011. 'Spirit and Mission in the Bible: Toward a Dialogue between Biblical Studies and Missiology.' *Trinity Journal*, 32, 237-58.

_______. 2012. 'The Giving of the Spirit in John 19-20: Another Round.' In: I. Howard Marshall, Volker Rabens & Cornelis Bennema, eds. *The Spirit and Christ in the New Testament*. Grand Rapids, MI: Eerdmans, 86-104.

_______. 2014. 'Mimesis in John 13: Cloning or Creative Articulation?' *Novum Testamentum*, 56, 261-74.

Bernard, J. H., 1929. *A Critical and Exegetical Commentary on the Gospel According to St. John*. vol.1. Edited by A. H. McNeile. New York: Charles Scribner's Sons.

Bieringer, R., Pollefeyt, D. & Vandecasteele-Vanneuville, F., 2001. 'Wrestling with Johannine Anti-Judaism: A Hermeneutical Framework for the Analysis of the Current Debate.' In: R. Bieringer, D. Pollefeyt & F. Vandecasteele-Vanneuville, eds. *Anti-Judaism and the Fourth Gospel*. Louisville, KY: Westminster John Knox Press, 3-37.

Billington, Antony, 1995. 'The Paraclete and Mission in the Fourth Gospel.' In: Antony Billington, Tony Lane & Max Turner, eds. *Mission and Meaning: Essays Presented to Peter Cotterell*. Carlisle: Paternoster, 90-115.

Bosch, David J., 1978. 'Hermeneutical Principles in the Biblical Foundation for Mission.' *Evangelical Review of Theology,* 17 (4), 437-51.

_______. 1980. *Witness to the World: The Christian Mission in Theological Perspective*. Eugene, OR: Wipf & Stock.

_______. 1984. 'The scope of mission.' *International Review of Mission,* 73 (289), 17-32.

_______. 1986. 'Towards a Hermeneutic for "Biblical Studies and Mission".' *Mission Studies,* 3 (2), 65-79.

_______. 1991. *Transforming Mission: Paradigm Shifts in Theology of Mission.* Maryknoll, NY: Orbis Books.

Boyd, W. J. Peter, 1967. 'The Ascension according to St John: Chapters 14-17 not Pre-passion but Post-resurrection.' *Theology*, 70 (May), 207-11.

Brown, Raymond E., 1966. *The Anchor Bible: The Gospel According to John I-XII*. Garden City, NY: Doubleday.

_______. 1970. *The Anchor Bible: The Gospel According to John XIII-XXI.* Garden City, NY: Doubleday.

_______. 1979. *The Community of the Beloved Disciple: The Life, Loves, and Hates of an Individual Church in New Testament Times*. New York: Paulist Press.

_______. 1994a. *The Death of the Messiah: From Gethsemane to the Grave.* vol. 1. New York: Doubleday.

_______. 1994b. *The Death of the Messiah: From Gethsemane to the Grave.* vol. 2. New York: Doubleday.

Brownson, James V., 1994. 'Speaking the Truth in Love: Element of a Missional Hermeneutic.' *International Review of Mission,* 83 (330), 479-504.

Burge, Gary M., 1987. *The Anointed Community: The Holy Spirit in the Johannine Tradition*. Grand Rapids, MI: Eerdmans.

Busch, Eberhard, 1975. *Karl Barth: His Life from Letters and Autobiographical Texts*. Translated by John Bowden. London: SCM Press.

Byers, Andrew J., 2017. *Ecclesiology and Theosis in the Gospel of John*. Cambridge: Cambridge University Press.

Calvin, Jean, 1961. *The Gospel According to St. John 1-10*. Translated by Parker T. H. L. Grand Rapids, MI: Eerdmans.

Carson, D. A., 1991. *The Gospel According to John*. Nottingham: Apollos.

_______. 2005. 'Syntactical and Text-Critical Observations on John 20:30-31: One More Round on the Purpose of the Fourth Gospel.' *Journal of Biblical Literature,* 124 (4), 693-714.

Chan, M. L. Y., 2008. 'Hermeneutics.' In: William A. Dyrness & Veli-Matti Kärkkäinen, eds. *Global Dictionary of Theology*. Downers Grove IL: InterVarsity Press, 379-86.

Coloe, Mary L., 2001. *God Dwells with Us: Temple Symbolism in the Fourth Gospel*. Collegeville, MN: Liturgical Press.

_______. 2004. 'Welcome into the Household of God: The Foot Washing in John 13.' *The Catholic Biblical Quarterly,* 66 (3), 400-15.

Conn, Harvie M., 1984. *Eternal Word and Changing Worlds: Theology, Anthropology, and Mission in Trialogue*. Grand Rapids, MI: Zondervan.

Crane, William H., 1969. 'Dropping the S.' *International Review of Mission,* 58 (230), 141-44.

Cullmann, Oscar, 1962. *Peter: Disciple, Apostle, Martyr*. London: SCM Press.

Culpepper R. Alan, 1983. *Anatomy of the Fourth Gospel: A Study in Literary Design*. Philadelphia, PA: Fortress Press.

Daise, Michael A., 2007. *Feasts in John: Jewish Festivals and Jesus' 'Hour' in the Fourth Gospel*. Tübingen: Mohr Siebeck.

Dalcour, Edward L., 2005. *A Definitive Look at Oneness Theology: Defending the Tri-Unity of God*. Lanham, MD: University Press of America.

Daugherty, Kevin, 2007. 'Missio Dei: The Trinity and Christian Missions.' *Evangelical Review of Theology,* 31 (2), 151-68.

De Boer, Martinus C., 2001. 'The Depiction of "the Jews" in John's Gospel: Matters of Behavior and Identity.' In: R. Bieringer, D. Pollefeyt & F. Vandecasteele-Vanneuville, eds. *Anti-Judaism and the Fourth Gospel*. Louisville, KY: Westminster John Knox Press, 141-57.

De Jonge, Henk Jan, 2001. '"The Jews" in the Gospel of John.' In: R. Bieringer, D. Pollefeyt & F. Vandecasteele-Vanneuville, eds. *Anti-Judaism and the Fourth Gospel*. Louisville, KY: Westminster John Knox Press, 121-40.

Dodd, C. H., 1963a. *Historical Tradition in the Fourth Gospel*. Cambridge: Cambridge University Press.

_______. 1963b. *The Interpretation of the Fourth Gospel*. Cambridge: Cambridge University Press.

Dowsett, Rose, 2007. 'Combined Fuel.' *Connections: The Journal of the WEA Mission Commission*, 6 (2), 35-39.

Edwards, Ruth, 2003. *Discovering John*. London: SPCK.

Ellis, Peter F., 2003. 'Understanding the Concentric Structure of the Fourth Gospel.' *St Vladimir's Theological Quarterly,* 47 (2), 131-54.

Erdmann, Martin, 1998. 'Mission in John's Gospel and Letters.' In: William J. Larkin Jr. & Joel F. Williams, eds. *Mission in the New Testament: An Evangelical Approach*. Maryknoll, NY: Orbis Books, 207-26.

Ferguson, Duncan S., 1986. *Biblical Hermeneutics: An introduction.* London: SCM Press.

Flebbe, Jochen, 2009. 'Feasts in John.' In: Christopher Tuckett, ed. *Feasts and Festivals*. Leuven, Belgium: Peeters, 107-24.

Flemming, Dean, 2011. 'Exploring a Missional Reading of Scripture: Philippians as a Case Study.' *Evangelical Quarterly*, 83 (1), 3-18.

_______. 2013. 'A Mission of Sending Love: Being, Doing and Telling in John's Gospel.' In: Dean Flemming, *Recovering the Full Mission of God: A Biblical Perspective on Being, Doing, and Telling*. Downers Grove, IL: InterVarsity Press, 113-32.

_______. 2015. *Why Mission?* Nashville, TN: Abingdon.

_______. 2016. 'A Missional Reading of Colossians.' In: Michael W. Goheen, ed. *Reading the Bible Missionally*. Grand Rapids, MI: Eerdmans, 213-37.

Flett, John G., 2010. *The Witness of God: The Trinity, Missio Dei, Karl Barth, and the Nature of Christian Community*. Grand Rapids, MI: Eerdmans.

Franklin, Kirk J., 2017. *Towards Global Missional Leadership: A Journey Through Leadership Paradigm Shift in the Mission of God.* Oxford: Regnum.

Frey, Jörg, 2016. 'Between Torah and Stoa: How Could Readers Have Understood the Johannine Logos?' In: Jan G. van der Watt, R. Alan Culpepper & Udo Schnelle, eds. *The Prologue of the Gospel of John: Its Literary, Theological, and Philosophical Contexts*. Tübingen: Mohr Siebeck, 189-234.

Froehlich, Karlfried, 1985. 'Biblical Hermeneutics on the Move.' *Ex Auditu,* 1, 3-13.

Genette, Gérard, 1997. *Paratexts: Thresholds of Interpretation.* Translated by Jane E. Lewin. Cambridge: Cambridge University Press.

Goheen, Michael W., 2000. *"As the Father Has Sent Me, I Am Sending You": J. E. Lesslie Newbigin's Missionary Ecclesiology.* Zoetermeer: Boekencentrum.

_______. 2008. 'The Urgency of Reading the Bible as One Story.' *Theology Today,* 64 (4), 469-83.

_______. 2011. *A Light to the Nations: The Missional Church and the Biblical Story*. Grand Rapids, MI: Baker Academic

_______. 2016. 'A Missional Reading of Scripture and Preaching.' In: Michael W. Goheen, ed. *Reading the Bible Missionally*. Grand Rapids, MI: Eerdmans, 241-62.

Gorman, Michael J., 2009a. *Elements of Biblical Exegesis: A Basic Guide for Students and Ministers*. Peabody, MA: Hendrickson.

_______. 2009b. *Inhabiting the Cruciform God: Kenosis, Justification, and Theosis in Paul's Narrative Soteriology*. Grand Rapids, MI: Eerdmans.

_______. 2018. *Abide and Go: Missional Theosis in the Gospel of John.* Eugene, OR: Wipf & Stock.

Guder, Darrell L., 1999. *The Incarnation and the Church's Witness*. Eugene, OR: Wipf & Stock.

_______. 2000. *The Continuing Conversion of the Church*. Grand Rapids, MI: Eerdmans.

_______. 2007. 'Missional Hermeneutics: The Missional Authority of Scripture.' *Mission Focus: Annual Review*, 15, 106-21.

_______. 2015. *Called to Witness: Doing Missional Theology*. Grand Rapids, MI: Eerdmans.

Hallonsten, Gösta, 2007. '*Theosis* in Recent Research: A Renewal of Interest and a Need for Clarity.' In: Michael J. Christensen & Jeffery A. Wittung, eds. *Partakers of the Divine Nature: The History and Development of Deification in the Christian Traditions*. Grand Rapids, MI: Baker Academic, 281-93.

Harris, Elizabeth, 1994. *Prologue and Gospel: The Theology of the Fourth Evangelist*. London: T & T Clark.

Harris, R. Geoffrey, 2004. *Mission in the Gospels*. Eugene, OR: Wipf and Stock.

Hartin, P. J., 1990. 'The Role of Peter in the Fourth Gospel.' *Neotestamentica*, 24 (1), 49-61.

Harvey, A. E., 1976. *Jesus on Trial: A Study in the Fourth Gospel*. London: SPCK.

Hastings, Ross, 2012. *Missional God, Missional Church: Hope for Re-Evangelizing the West*. Downers Grove, IL: InterVarsity Press.

Hesselgrave, David J., 1993. 'A Missionary Hermeneutic: Understanding Scripture in the Light of World Mission.' *International Journal of Frontier Missiology*, 10 (1), 17-20.

Hoekendijk, J. C., 1964. *The Church Inside Out*. Translated by Issac C. Rottenberg. London: SCM Press.

Hunsberger, George R., 2016. 'Mapping the Missional Hermeneutics Conversation.' In: Michael W. Goheen, ed. *Reading the Bible Missionally*. Grand Rapids, MI: Eerdmans, 45-67.

Hunsberger, George R. & Van Gelder, Craig. eds., 1996. *The Church between Gospel and Culture: The Emerging Mission in North America*. Grand Rapids, MI: Eerdmans.

Jannaris, A. N., 1903. 'The Fourth Gospel and John the Apostle.' *British Periodicals*, 84-98.

Jenkins, Philip, 2002. *The Next Christendom: The Coming of Global Christianity*. Oxford: Oxford University Press.

_______. 2006. *The New Faces of Christianity: Believing the Bible in the Global South*. Oxford: Oxford University Press.

Jeremias Joachim, 1964. 'ἀμνός, ἀρήν, ἀρνίον.' In: Gerhard Kittel, ed. 1993 (reprinted). *Theological Dictionary of the New Testament, 1,* Translated by Geoffrey W. Bromiley. Grand Rapids, MI: Eerdmans, 338-41.

Johnson, Todd M., 2010. 'Globalization and Identity: Globalization, Christian Identity, and Frontier Missions.' *International Journal of Frontier Missiology,* 27 (4), 165-69.

Johnson, Darrell W., 2002. *Experiencing the Trinity.* Vancouver: Regent College.

Jung, Sungkook, 2010. *Paul's Missional Use of Scripture: A Redefined Approach with Special Reference to 2 Cor. 3.* Unpublished Dissertation (Ph.D.), Westminster Theological Seminary.

Kanagaraj, Jey J., 2005. *The Gospel of John.* Andhra Pradesh, India: OM Books.

Kanagaraj, Jey J. & Kemp, Ian S., 2002. *The Gospel According to John.* Asia Bible Commentary Series. Singapore: Asia Theological Association.

Kelly, Michael B., 2010. 'Biblical Theology and Missional Hermeneutics: A Match Made *for* Heaven… on Earth?' In: P. Enns, D. J. Green & M. B. Kelly, eds. *Eyes to See, Ears to Hear: Essays in Memory of J. Alan Groves.* Phillipsburg, NJ: P&R, 61-76.

Kerr, Alan R., 2002. *The Temple of Jesus' Body: The Temple Theme in the Gospel of John.* New York: Sheffield Academic Press.

Kierspel, Lars, 2006. *The Jews and the World in the Fourth Gospel: Parallelism, Function, and Context.* Tübingen: Mohr Siebeck.

Kinnamon, Michael & Cope, Brian E. eds., 1997. *The Ecumenical Movement: An Anthology of Key Texts and Voices.* Geneva: WCC Publications.

Kok, Kobus, 2010. 'As the Father Has Sent Me, I Send You: Towards a Missional-Incarnational Ethos in John 4.' In: Ruben Zimmermann, Jan G. van der Watt & Susanne Luther, eds. *Moral Language in the New Testament: The Interrelatedness of Language and Ethics in Early Christian Writings.* Tübingen: Mohr Siebeck, 168-93.

Köstenberger, Andreas J., 1998. *The Missions of Jesus and the Disciples according to the Fourth Gospel.* Grand Rapids, MI: Eerdmans.

_______. 1999. 'The Place of Mission in New Testament Theology: An Attempt to Determine the Significance of Mission within the Scope of the New Testament's Message as a Whole.' *Missiology: An International Review,* 27 (3), 347-62.

. 2004. *John.* Grand Rapids, MI: Baker Academic.

_______ 2009 *A Theology of John's Gospel and Letters.* Grand Rapids, MI: Zondervan.

_______. 2013. *Encountering John.* 2nd ed. Grand Rapids, MI: Baker Academic.

_______. 2014. 'Sensitivity to Outsiders in John's Gospel and Letters and its Implication for the Understanding of Early Christian Mission.' In: Jacobus (Kobus) Kok, Tobias Nicklas, Dieter T. Roth & Christopher M. Hays, eds. *Sensitivity towards Outsiders: Exploring the Dynamic Relationship between Mission and Ethics in the New Testament and Early Christianity.* Tübingen: Mohr Siebeck, 171-86.

Köstenberger, Andreas J. & O'Brien, Peter T., 2001. *Salvation to the Ends of the Earth: A Biblical Theology of Mission.* Downers Grove, IL: InterVarsity Press.

Köstenberger, Andreas J. & Swain, Scott R., 2008. *Father, Son and Spirit: The Trinity and John's Gospel.* Downers Grove, IL: InterVarsity Press.

Kysar, Robert, 2001. '"As You Sent Me": Identity and Mission in the Fourth Gospel.' *Word & World,* 21 (4), 370-76.

Lamarche, Paul, 1964. 'The Prologue of John.' In: John Ashton, ed. 1997. *The Interpretation of John.* 2nd ed. Edinburgh: T & T Clark, 47-65.

La Potterie, Ignace de, 1963. 'The Truth in Saint John.' In: John Ashton, ed. 1997. *The Interpretation of John.* 2nd ed. Edinburgh: T & T Clark, 67-82.

Lash, Nicholas, 1985. 'What Might Martyrdom Mean?' *Ex Auditu,* 1, 14-24.

Lewis, C. S., 1970. *The Magician's Nephew.* New York: Macmillan.

Lincoln, Andrew T., 1994. 'Trials, Plots and the Narrative of the Fourth Gospel.' *Journal for the Study of the New Testament,* 56, 3-30.

_______. 2000. *Truth on Trial: The Lawsuit Motif in the Fourth Gospel.* Peabody, MA: Hendrickson.

_______. 2002. 'The Beloved Disciple as Eyewitness and the Fourth Gospel as Witness.' *Journal for the Study of the New Testament,* 85, 3-26.

_______. 2005. *The Gospel according to St John.* London: Continuum.

Lindbeck, George A., 1984. *The Nature of Doctrine: Religion and Theology in a Postliberal Age.* Philadelphia, PA: Westminster Press.

Lozada, Francisco, Jr., 2011. 'Journey and the Fourth Gospel: A Latino/a Exploration.' *Interpretation,* 65 (3), 264-75.

Marshall, I. Howard, 2004. *New Testament Theology: Many Witnesses, One Gospel.* Downers Grove, IL: InterVarsity Press

Martyn, J. Louis, 2003. *History and Theology in the Fourth Gospel.* 3rd ed. Louisville, KY: Westminster John Knox Press.

Mason, Steve, 2007. 'Jews, Judaeans, Judaizing, Judaism: Problems of Categorization in Ancient History.' *Journal for the Study of Judaism,* 38, 457-512.

McGrath, Alister E., 1990. *The Genesis of Doctrine: A Study in the Foundation of Doctrinal Criticism.* Grand Rapids, MI: Eerdmans.

Metzger, Bruce M., 1994. *A Textual Commentary on the Greek New Testament.* 2nd ed. Stuttgart: Deutsche Bibelgesellschaft.

Michaels, J Ramsey, 2010. *The Gospel of John.* The New International Commentary on the New Testament. Grand Rapids, MI: Eerdmans.

Milne, Bruce, 1993. *The Message of John.* Nottingham: InterVarsity Press.

Minear, Paul S., 1983. 'The Original Functions of John 21.' *Journal of Biblical Literature,* 102 (1), 85-98.

Moessner, David P., 2005. 'Reading Luke's Gospel as Ancient Hellenistic Narrative.' In: Craig Bartholomew, Joel B. Green & Anthony C. Thiselton, eds. *Reading Luke: Interpretation, Reflection, Formation.* Exeter: Paternoster, 125-54.

Moloney, Francis J., 2002a. 'Revelation and Concealment of Christ. By Saeed Hamid-Khani.' *Journal of Theological Studies,* 53 (2), 643-49.

_______. 2002b. '"The Jews" in the Fourth Gospel: Another Perspective.' *Pacifica,* 15, 16-36.

Morris, Leon, 1989. *Jesus is the Christ: Studies in the Theology of John.* Grand Rapids, MI: Eerdmans.

Motyer, Stephen, 1997. *Your Father the Devil? A New Approach to John and 'the Jews'*. Carlisle: Paternoster.

Myers, Alicia D., 2015. 'A Voice in the Wilderness: Classical Rhetoric and the Testimony of John (the Baptist) in John 1:19-34.' In: Alicia D. Myers & Bruce G. Schuchard, eds. *Abiding Words: The Use of Scriptures in the Gospel of John.* Atlanta: SBL, 119-39.

Nations, Archie L., 1985. 'Historical Criticism and the Current Methodological Crisis.' *Ex Auditu,* 1, 125-32.

Newbigin, Lesslie, 1982. *The Light Has Come: An Exposition of the Fourth Gospel.* Grand Rapids, MI: Eerdmans.

Newman, Barclay M. & Nida, Eugene A., 1980. *A Translator's Handbook on the Gospel of John.* New York: United Bible Societies.

Okure, Teresa, 1988. *The Johannine Approach to Mission: A Contextual Study of John 4:1-42.* Tübingen: Mohr Siebeck.

Olson Birger, 1999. '*Deus semper maior*? On God in the Johannine Writings.' In: Johannes Nissen & Sigfred Pedersen, eds. *New Readings in John: Literary and Theological Perspectives.* Sheffield: Sheffield Academic Press, 143-71.

Ott, Bernhard, 2001. *Beyond Fragmentation: Integrating Mission and Theological Education.* Oxford: Regnum Books International.

Phillips, Peter M., 2006. *The Prologue of the John's Gospel: A Sequential Reading.* London: T & T Clark.

_______. 2013. 'The Woman Caught in Adultery: Nameless, Partnerless, Defenceless.' In: Steven A. Hunt, D. Francois Tolmie & Ruben Zimmermann, eds. *Character Studies in the Fourth Gospel: Narrative Approaches to Seventy Figures in John.* WUNT 314. Tübingen: Mohr Siebeck, 407-21.

Porter, Stanley E., 2015. *John, His Gospel, and Jesus: In Pursuit of the Johannine Voice.* Grand Rapids, MI: Eerdmans.

Powell, Mark A., 1990. *What is Narrative Criticism?* Minneapolis, MN: Fortress Press.

Prickett, Stephen & Barnes, Robert, 1991. *The Bible.* Cambridge: Cambridge University Press.

Pryor, John W., 1990. 'Jesus and Israel in the Fourth Gospel – John 1:11.' *Novum Testamentum,* 32 (3), 201-18.

Reinhartz, Adele, 2001. *Befriending the Beloved Disciple: A Jewish Reading of the Gospel of John.* London: Continuum.

Rengstorf, Karl Heinrich, 1964. 'ἀποστέλλω, et al.' In: Gerhard Kittel, ed. *Theological Dictionary of the New Testament, 1,* Translated by Geoffrey W. Bromiley. Grand Rapids, MI: Eerdmans, 398-447.

Roxburgh, Alan J. & Boren, M. Scott, 2009. *Introducing the Missional Church: What It Is, Why It Matters, How to Become One.* Grand Rapids, MI: Baker Books.

Ruhulessin, John, 2015. 'Eight Decades of Planting, Watering, and Growing Historic Socio-Theological Reflection of GPM.' Paper presented to the 80th Anniversary Mission Conference, Ambon, Indonesia, 6 September.

Salier, Willis H., 2004. *The Rhetorical Impact of the Semeia in the Gospel of John*. Tübingen: Mohr Siebeck.

Santram, P. B., 1975. 'The Purpose of St John's Gospel: The Spread of the Good News.' In: Christopher Duraisingh & Cecil Hargreaves, eds. *India's Search for Reality and the Relevance of the Gospel of John*, Delhi: ISPCK, 104-21.

Schirrmacher, Thomas, 1996. 'Biblical Foundations for Missions: Seven Clear Lessons.' *International Journal of Frontier Missions,* 13 (1), 33-9.

Schnackenburg, Rudolf, 1980a. *The Gospel According to St John: Volume One Introduction and Commentary on Chapters 1-4*. Translated by Kevin Smith. London: Burns & Oates.

_______. 1980b. *The Gospel According to St John: Volume Two Commentary on Chapters 5-12*. Translated by Cecily Hastings, et. al. London: Burns & Oates.

_______. 1982. *The Gospel According to St John: Volume Three Commentary on Chapters 13-21*. Translated by David Smith and G. A. Kon. London: Burns & Oates.

Schneiders, Sandra M., 2003. *Written that You May Believe: Encountering Jesus in the Fourth Gospel*. Revised and expanded ed. New York: Crossroad.

Schuchard, Bruce G., 2015. 'Form Versus Function: Citation Technique and Authorial Intention in the Gospel of John.' In: Alicia D. Myers & Bruce G. Schuchard, eds. *Abiding Words: The Use of Scriptures in the Gospel of John*. Atlanta, GA: SBL, 23-45.

Scott, Ernest F., 1908. *The Fourth Gospel: Its Purpose and Theology*. Edinburgh: T & T Clark.

Segovia, Fernando F., 1991. 'The Journey(s) of the Word of God: A Reading of the Plot of the Fourth Gospel.' *Semeia* 53, 23-54.

Shenk, Wilbert R., 1981. 'Rufus Anderson and Henry Venn: A Special Relationship?' *International Bulletin of Missionary Research*, 5 (4), 168-72.

Skinner, Christopher W. ed., 2013. *Characters and Characterization in the Gospel of John*. London: Bloomsbury.

Smalley, Stephen S., 1978. *John: Evangelist and Interpreter*. Exeter: Paternoster.

So, Damon, 2006a. *Jesus' Revelation of His Father: A narrative-Conceptual Study of the Trinity with Special Reference to Karl Barth*. Milton Keynes: Paternoster.

_______. 2006b. 'The Missionary Journey of the Son of God into the Far Country: A paradigm of the holistic gospel developed from the theology of Karl Barth.' *Transformation,* 23 (3), 130-42.

Stanton, Graham N., 1985. 'Interpreting the New Testament today.' *Ex Auditu,* 1, 63-73.

Stibbe, Mark W. G., 1992. *John as Storyteller: Narrative Criticism and the Fourth Gospel*. Cambridge: Cambridge University Press.

Stroup, George W., 1981. *The Promise of Narrative Theology: Recovering the Gospel in the Church*. Atlanta, GA: John Knox Press.

Thatcher, Tom, 2006. *Why John Wrote a Gospel: Jesus–Memory–History*. Louisville, KY: Westminster John Knox Press.

_______. 2007. 'John's Memory Theater: The Fourth Gospel and Ancient Mnemo-Rhetoric.' *The Catholic Biblical Quarterly,* 69 (3), 487-505.

Thomas, John C., 2014. *Footwashing in John 13 and the Johannine Community*. 2nd ed. Cleveland, TN: CPT Press.

Tomson, Peter J., 2001. '"Jews" in the Gospel of John as Compared with the Palestinian Talmud, the Synoptics, and Some New Testament Apocrypha.' In: R. Bieringer, D. Pollefeyt & F. Vandecasteele-Vanneuville, eds. *Anti-Judaism and the Fourth Gospel*. Louisville, KY: Westminster John Knox Press, 176-212.

Torrey, Charles Cutler, 1936. *Our Translated Gospels: Some of the Evidence*. New York: Harper.

Trocmé, Etienne, 1995. 'Light and Darkness in the Fourth Gospel.' *Didaskalia,* 6 (2), 3-13.

Tuner, Max, 1996. *The Holy Spirit and Spiritual Gifts: Then and Now*. Carlisle: Paternoster.

Vallianipuram, Thomas, 2004. 'John 17 as a Mission Prayer.' *Indian Theological Studies*, 41, 5-30.

Van Engen, Charles E., 1991. *God's Missionary People: Rethinking the Purpose of the Local Church*. Grand Rapids, MI: Baker Academic.

Van Gelder, Craig, 2000. *The Essence of the Church: A Community Created by the Spirit*. Grand Rapids, MI: Baker Books.

_______. 2007. *The Ministry of the Missional Church: A Community Led by the Spirit*. Grand Rapids, MI: Baker Books.

Verkuyl, J., 1978. *Contemporary Missiology: An Introduction*. Translated by Dale Cooper. Grand Rapids, MI: Eerdmans.

Vincent, Marvin R., 1889. *Word Studies in the New Testament*. vol. II. New York: Charles Scribner's Sons.

Volf, Miroslav, 1998. *After Our Likeness: The Church as the Image of the Trinity*. Grand Rapids, MI: Eerdmans.

Von Wahlde, Urban C., 1982. 'The Johannine "Jews": A Critical Survey.' *New Testament Studies*, 28, 33-60.

_______. 2000. '"The Jews" in the Gospel of John: Fifteen Years of Research (1983-1998).' *Ephemerides Theologicae Lovanienses*, 76, 30-55.

Wallace, Daniel B., 1996. *Greek Grammar: Beyond the Basics*. Grand Rapids, MI: Zondervan.

Walls, Andrew F., 1996. *The Missionary Movement in Christian History: Studies in the Transmission of Faith*. Maryknoll, NY: Orbis Books.

Walls, Andrew F. & Ross, Cathy. eds., 2008. *Mission in the Twenty-first Century: Exploring the Five Marks of Global Mission*. Maryknoll, NY: Orbis Books.

Westcott, B. F., 1908. *The Gospel According to St. John*. vol. I. London: John Murray.

Wheaton. Gerry, 2015. *The Role of Jewish Feasts in John's Gospel*. SNTS.MS 162. New York: Cambridge University Press.

Wiles, Maurice F., 1960. *The Spiritual Gospel: The Interpretation of the Fourth Gospel in the Early Church.* London: Cambridge University Press.

Wink, Walter, 1968. *John the Baptist in the Gospel Tradition.* New York: Cambridge University Press.

Winter, Ralph D., 1973. 'The Two Structures of God's Redemptive Mission.' In: Ralph D. Winter & Steven C. Hawthorne, eds. 1999. *Perspectives on the World Christian Movement: A Reader.* Pasadena, CA: William Carey Library, 220-30.

Wright, Charles James, 1950. *Jesus the Revelation of God: His Mission and Message According to St. John.* London: Hodder and Stoughton.

Wright, Christopher J. H., 2004. 'Mission as a Matrix for Hermeneutics and Biblical Theology.' In: Craig Bartholomew, Mary Healy, Karl Möller & Robin Parry, eds. *Out of Egypt: Biblical Theology and Biblical Interpretation.* Exeter: Paternoster, 102-43.

_______. 2006. *The Mission of God: Unlocking the Bible's Grand Narrative.* Nottingham: InterVarsity Press.

_______. 2010. *The Mission of God's People: A Biblical Theology of the Church's Mission.* Grand Rapids, MI: Zondervan.

Wright, Christopher J. H. & Lamb, Jonathan, 2009a. *Understanding and Using the Bible.* London: SPCK.

Wright, N. Thomas, 1992. *The New Testament and the People of God.* Minneapolis, MN: Fortress Press.

_______. 2002a. *John for Everyone: Part 1.* London: SPCK.

_______. 2002b. *John for Everyone: Part 2.* London: SPCK.

_______. 2013a. *Scripture and the Authority of God.* 2nd ed. London: SPCK.

_______. 2016. 'Reading the New Testament Missionally.' In: Michael W. Goheen, ed. *Reading the Bible Missionally.* Grand Rapids, MI: Eerdmans, 175-93.

Yee, Gala A., 1989. *Jewish Feasts and the Gospel of John.* Eugene, OR: Wipf & Stock.

Electronic Resources and Others

Barram, Michael D., 2006. '"Located" Questions for a Missional Hermeneutic.' Paper presented November 2006. https://gocn.org/library/95/ [8 April 2012].

Goheen, Michael W., 2006. *Notes Toward a Framework for a Missional Hermeneutic.* http://www.biblicaltheology.ca/blue_files/Notes%20Toward%20a%20Framework.pdf [30 December 2017].

Tan, Kang San, 2007. 'Chris Wright's The Mission of God: A Missiologist's Perspective.' *Encounters Mission Ezine*, [Online] June, Issue 29. http://www.redcliffe.org/uploads/documents/Prophet to the Nations – Missional Reflections on the Book of Jeremiah 29.pdf [14 June 2010].

Wright, Christopher J. H., 2003. *Whose world? Whose mission?* Paper

presented at the NEAC, Blackpool, 19-23 September.
http://www.neac.info/talks/211145cw.pdf [8 April 2012].

Wright, Christopher J. H., 2009b. 'Prophet to the Nations: Missional Reflections on the Book of Jeremiah.' *Encounters Mission Ezine*, [Online] June, Issue 29.
http://www.redcliffe.org/uploads/documents/Prophet to the Nations – Missional Reflections on the Book of Jeremiah 29.pdf [14 June 2010].

Wright, N.T., 2013b. *A Missional Reading of the New Testament.*
http://calvinseminary.edu/academics/continuing-education/missional-reading [30 September 2014].